Modern Korean Society

KOREA RESEARCH MONOGRAPH 30

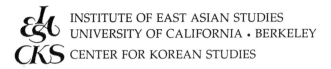 INSTITUTE OF EAST ASIAN STUDIES
UNIVERSITY OF CALIFORNIA · BERKELEY
CENTER FOR KOREAN STUDIES

Modern Korean Society
Its Development and Prospect

EDITED BY
Hyuk-Rae Kim and Bok Song

1

A publication of the Institute of East Asian Studies, University of California, Berkeley. Although the institute is responsible for the selection and acceptance of manuscripts in this series, responsibility for the opinions expressed and for the accuracy of statements rests with their authors.

The Korea Research Monograph series is one of several publications series sponsored by the Institute of East Asian Studies in conjunction with its constituent units. The others include the China Research Monograph series, the Japan Research Monograph series, and the Research Papers and Policy Studies series.

Send correspondence and manuscripts to

Ms. Joanne Sandstrom, Managing Editor
Institute of East Asian Studies
2223 Fulton St., 6th Fl.
Berkeley, California 94720-2318

Library of Congress Cataloging-in-Publication Data

Modern Korean Society : its development and prospect / edited by Hyuk-Rae Kim, Bok Song.
    p. cm. -- (Korea research monograph ; 30)
Includes bibliographical references and index.
ISBN 1-55729-086-5
1. Korea (South)--Social conditions. 2. Korea (South)--Politics and government--1988- 3. Korea (South)--Economic conditions--1960- I. Kim, Hyong-nae. II. Song, Pok.
HN730.5.A8M6 2006
306.095195'09045--dc22
                    2006047903

Contents

Acknowledgments

This book is the product of a six-year joint project by the Institute for Modern Korean Studies at the Graduate School of International Studies and the Institute for Social Development Studies at the Department of Sociology, Yonsei University. The two institutions agreed to launch the project to compile an introductory-level survey textbook on modern Korean society. The journey to the completion of this volume has been painstaking but also rewarding in that we have had the unique opportunity to bring together prominent scholars writing on Korean society from both Korea and the United States.

The past several years have witnessed the inception of several English-language Korean Studies curricula. There is still a need, however, for teaching materials on modern Korean society. The dearth of teaching materials that introduce and explicate Korea's modernization process, from its development thus far to its future prospects, had proven to be particularly burdensome to those who lecture at the university level. Although some insightful books related to Korean society exist, we feel that compilation of a comprehensive text is crucial for this field. The chapters in this book provide discussion on key issues of modern Korean Studies. Each chapter retains as common themes the impact of Korea's unique traditional elements on the modernization process and the prospects for the future.

For many years teaching students, we have resorted to a wide variety of chapters and academic articles. Not coincidentally at all, those oft-assigned authors are exactly the people whose work makes up this volume. In the future we will be able to lay our hands on essays covering the gamut of modern Korean society all conveniently bound into one volume.

In the process of compiling this volume we have been assisted by a good number of wonderful institutions and individuals. First of all, this project would never have gotten off the ground without the encouragement and initial financial support offered by the Institute for Modern Korean Studies and the Institute for Social Development Studies at Yonsei University. We are deeply grateful for their continuous support, encouragement, and valuable guidance over the past few years. Each of the contributors deserves our hearty thanks for their careful authorship and patience through a good number of e-mail messages, faxes, and letters back and forth. Colleagues Yong-Hak Kim and Dong-No Kim provided valuable comments on earlier drafts of chapters. They took the trouble to go through the manuscript while it was still quite rough. They comments they gave were of great help, but their encouragement and support were of even greater value. We would also like to note that earlier versions of some chapters were published elsewhere: chapter 5 in *Journal of Contemporary Asia* (2000) and chapter 10 in *Korea Observer* (2002).

Notwithstanding these efforts, the project would have come to naught without a whole cast of other wonderful individuals and institutions. First of all, we must thank Joanne Sandstrom, managing editor at the Institute of East Asian Studies, University of California, Berkeley, for her support and work in shepherding the publication from manuscript to bound book and the two anonymous reviewers who read the manuscript for IEAS for their comments and belief in this project. Michele Wright's copyediting work on several chapters is also greatly appreciated. Research assistants Aileen Cabigayan, Frank O'Brien, and Cedar Bough Saeji provided invaluable assistance during the manuscript stages. In particular, Cedar Bough Saeji did a fine job of seeing the manuscript through the copyediting and proofing stages. Finally, the Korea Foundation, an angel to all of us in Korean Studies, blessed this project with an important infusion of funding in the final stages.

Perhaps most important was the motivation provided by students who deserve a comprehensive survey textbook on Korean society. It is our fervent wish that the kindred spirits who are studying and teaching modern Korean society will find this volume useful.

ONE

The Contour of Modern Korean Society

HYUK-RAE KIM

The forced opening of Korea to the Western world in the latter half of the nineteenth century thrust it into a dynamic process of modernization. One brief century has wrought significant political, economic, and social change in Korea, largely through such dramatic events as an onerous period of repressive colonization and the Korean War. Soon after the end of Japanese colonialism, the destructive civil war that ensued divided Korea into two hostile states—the Democratic People's Republic of Korea (North Korea) and the Republic of Korea (South Korea). In 1953, when the armistice that called for cessation of hostilities was signed, the ravages of that war had turned the peninsula into an impoverished, pale shadow of its traditional agrarian form. A rapid series of reforms and measures in both North and South Korea have since profoundly affected their respective social infrastructures.

South Korea (hereafter, Korea) has significantly focused on three major national projects: economic development (H. R. Kim and Fields in this volume), political democratization (D. Kim and H. R. Kim in this volume), and national reunification (Cumings in this volume). At considerable social cost, seven consecutive five-year economic plans implemented from the early 1960s to 1997 under authoritarian regimes elevated Korea as a "model country" of the East Asian miracle or capitalist model (Fields in this volume; Kim et al. 2000). State intervention in economic governance was a crucial force in this advance, but that same intervention impeded the growth of civil society and democracy (Choi and Lim 1993; H. R. Kim 2003; S. Kim 2000; Lim and Choi 1997; Koo, ed. 1993; KSA and KPSA, eds. 1992). Successive authoritarian regimes until the 1987 Democratic Movement selectively co-opted capital interests to forge a developmental coalition and consistently repressed challenges to their ruling alliance from political democratization efforts.

As Dong-No Kim describes in his chapter, direct and intense confrontation between the state and grassroots activists ignited the "bottom-up" democratization movements that have since been an engine for dynamic social changes in modern Korean society. Particularly, during the rapid industrialization of the 1960s and 1970s, peasant and working-class social movements catalyzed social change and intensified confrontation with the state to realize class-based interests. These movements vehemently denied the legitimacy of governance based on the alliance of state elites' political interests with bourgeoisie economic concerns. In contrast to such class-based peasant and working-class social movements, student-led causes directly focused on political democratization and national reunification. However, as both D. Kim and H. R. Kim argue in their chapters, with the demise of the student-led causes in the 1990s, people from all walks of life assumed a central place in social movements (Choi and Lim 1993; H. R. Kim 2002, 2004; S. Kim 2000; Kim and McNeal 2005; Koo 2001; KSA, ed. 1990; Lim and Choi 1997). Although these groups share the traditional concern with political and economic issues, their more moderate movement strategies concentrate on improving citizens' everyday lives.

The recent democratic transition from a state-dominated to a citizen-driven society has deposed the state as sole guardian and provider of institutions in the sociopolitical domain. Civil society has become a salient political actor, an institutional hybrid that undertakes public functions through private initiatives (H. R. Kim 2000, 2003, 2004). It endeavors to provide and ensure protection and advancement of such public goods as the environment, human rights, social security, women's issues, and grassroots development. It also serves as policy entrepreneur, proposing and helping implement policies and forming organizations that pursue public interests by monitoring government and business activities (Kim and McNeal 2005). As H. R. Kim points out in his chapter, the civil society sector has flourished in scale and scope in a progressively decentralized and deregulated environment and continues to campaign for a variety of political and economic reforms in the ongoing transition toward democracy.

For the greater part of the accelerated modernization, Korea focused exclusively on economic development and political democratization. The third national project of national

reunification was systematically ignored and politically suppressed throughout the successive authoritarian regimes (see the
details in Cumings' chapter). However, the democratic regimes
have turned their focus on reunification. The two nations remain
divided along a heavily fortified demilitarized zone with no concrete agenda or clear course of action for either side apparent. But
the beginning of the new millennium showed the two nations
making clear progress in talks and taking meaningful steps toward
coexistence. The two Koreas began concerted overtures toward
each other when they revealed and took up several reunification
principles born of secret talks in July 1972. In December 1991,
their prime ministers signed an Agreement on Reconciliation,
Nonaggression, Cooperation, and Exchange calling for mutual
recognition of their respective political systems. At his February
1998 inauguration, President Kim Dae Jung announced a policy of
engagement for reconciliation and cooperation with North Korea
known now as the "sunshine policy," most dramatically expressed
by the June 2000 summit. However, national reunification remains
a distant possibility, as most Koreans view North Korea's leaders
as enemies. National consensus on the process and specifics of
cross-border talks needs to be built for future negotiation between
the two Koreas.

In pursuit of these national projects and agendas, Korea has
exhibited a dynamic of social change that sets it apart. Represen-
tationally, this dynamic comprises three forces—regional (Y. Kim
in this volume), occupational, and class (Koo in this volume; Kim
and Song in this volume)—rotating as a swirling mass, each
around a distinct axis. These forces for social mobility and change
have been rapidly spiraling upward, each along with its axis, but
all contained within a boundary that society itself sets. In a process of checks and balances, the three revolving axes stabilize the
social structure in a rapidly changing environment, propel it forward, and prevent implosion. At the same time, the pursuit of
self-interest via personal network extensions on the basis of blood,
school, and regional ties occupies the cavity at the mass's center.
This central force poses a sometimes paradoxical and regressive
threat to social development. Emphasis on personal network
extension has the potential to shatter the sense of community that
social unity requires. This regressive force, like the "eye of the
storm," ironically plays a counterforce that keeps the society from
developing in the right direction. Such coexistence of opposite
forces evident in the incessant demographic, social, economic, and

political flux along the three axes is a distinctive characteristic of modern Korea and has shaped the contour of modern Korean society.

Multiple Fronts of Social Change

Unprecedented change—social, economic, and political—has visited a modern Korea that lacks any foundational social organization. Socially, demographic change has dramatically raised the average age of the population and reduced fertility (see the details in Ahn's chapter). Average age rose from 23.6 in 1960 to 32.6 in 1999 and is projected to be 39.5 by 2020. A steep decline in the fertility rate is probably the most significant demographic change in four decades. On average each woman bore 6.2 children in 1960 but only 1.08 in 2005. Coupled with fewer births, increased longevity has swollen the ranks of the older population. Korea has fewer young people and more old than ever before. The population of 0–14-year-olds decreased to 19.1 percent of total population in 2005, from 41.2 percent in 1960; the elderly population increased to 9.1 percent from 3.3 percent. Projected figures for 2030 are 11.2 percent and 24.1 percent.

Increases in age and decreases in the economically active population have dramatically affected workforce dynamics, retirement age, and marriage. The imbalance threatens to generate intergenerational tension and increased pressure for social legislation of benefit to the old. It could also be argued that the economic miracle of the 1970s and 1980s was possible in part because the government could mobilize a population overwhelmingly of economically active age (Ahn in this volume). Gradual decline in the proportion of youth and active population in the foreseeable future threatens to deplete the labor force and reduce economic viability.

As Seung-Kyung Kim describes in her chapter, another sort of fluidity derives from radical changes in family structure in the latter half of the twentieth century. The traditional Korean family—patriarchal, patrilineal, and patrilocal—has been historically critical. Patrilineal inheritance favored the firstborn male, and daughters were disinherited and excluded from ancestor veneration (Kendall 1996)—worship that expressed the social significance of continuation of the family through sons. Patrilocality served to define the social boundaries of the life of individuals, maintain social class consciousness, and ensure kin loyalty. Such traditional institutional norms continue to influence gender relations and the broader social structure in various ways.

However, Japanese colonization disrupted traditional family norms. Japanese land ownership displaced the paternalistic gentry and broke the deep attachment farmers and peasants had to the land. Industrialization in the early 1960s brought further dramatic changes. Relations between parents and adult children have attenuated (Hong and Byun 1998). This is perhaps best indicated by a marked decline in arranged marriages. Thirty years ago 80 percent of Koreans thought parents' choice of a marriage partner outweighed that of their sons, but by 1990 that proportion gave sons' opinions priority (N. I. Kim et al. 1994). Young people increasingly choose not to marry. Age at first marriage has risen substantially, and a marked proportion of young people, especially women, hold quite liberal views on marriage (Choe 1998). Nuclear families are becoming the norm: with the drop in fertility rate, three-generation households have given way to two-generation households, as fewer Korean couples choose to live with their parents. As a result, more elderly live alone than ever before in Korean history. All of these demographic shifts have brought fundamental, broad-ranging change to modern Korean society.

Altered demographics and family structure have been accompanied by extremely accelerated economic development that propelled GDP per capita to match that of some European Union economies (see the details in Fields' chapter). In the early 1960s, agriculture, forestry, and fisheries comprised 47.3 percent of GDP, but in 1998, a mere 4.9 percent. Mining and manufacturing swelled from 9.0 percent in 1953 to 30.7 percent by 1998. Industrial development has radically modified sectoral distribution of the labor force (see also Koo's chapter, table 1). In 1963, 62.9 percent of labor worked in agriculture, 15.0 percent in industry. Three decades later, these numbers were reversed. Agriculture accounted for 10.9 percent by 2000, while manufacturing more than doubled to 31.9 percent in 1993 and then retreated to 20.2 percent by 2000. This change marked the leap of South Korea from an economically isolated agricultural nation into an export-based member of the global economy under the Park regime.

The Axis of Occupational Mobility

As Hagen Koo points out in his chapter, change in the sectoral distribution of labor usually entails significant shifts in occupational structure, particularly in composition. Farmers, who comprised 58.1 percent of the total workforce in 1966, made up 34.0 percent in 1980, 17.8 percent in 1990, and 10.2 percent in 2000 in an unprecedented shift out of agriculture into both industry and service (see also table 2 in Koo's chapter). During the rapid economic growth of the 1970s, the state drive toward heavy and chemical industrialization expanded the occupational category of wage workers. Wage workers in production, transportation, and construction swelled from 16.7 percent of the labor force in 1966 to 29 percent in 1980, and then tapered off to 34.8 percent in 1990 and 33.8 percent in 2000.

No less significant was the change in the middle strata of the urban occupational structure. Increase in the category of professional, technical, and white-collar workers was particularly profound. In 1966, professional, managerial, and technical workers comprised only 3.1 percent of the total workforce, but in 1993, 10.2 percent. As Koo points out, the new occupational classification system adopted in 1993 separated these workers into two categories: managerial and high-ranking bureaucrats declined from 2.7 percent of labor in 1993 to 2.3 in 2000; professional and technical workers increased from 12.3 percent to 16.1 during the same period.

White-collar workers more than tripled from 4.7 percent of the labor force in 1966 to 15.0 percent in 1993. According to the new occupational classification system, they numbered 12.5 percent in 1993 and 11.4 in 2000. Service workers increased significantly from 5.6 percent in 1966 to 12.3 in 1993 and 12.7 in 2000. Sales workers expanded moderately from 11.8 percent in 1966 to 15.5 percent in 1985, but declined slightly from to 15.9 percent in 1993 to 13.4 percent in 2000. Together, sales and service workers grew from 17.4 percent of the labor force in 1966 to 26.3 percent in 1985 then to 27.1 percent in 2000. All of these shifts in occupational composition indicate high mobility along the occupational axis.

The Axis of Class Formation

Profound shifts also occurred in the class system in the short period of modernization, from one relatively simple and rigid to one more complex and fluid. Almost complete destruction of the old class system came with the end of Japanese colonialism. The

Chosŏn traditional status system was legally and morally sanctioned, with clear, fairly impenetrable strata boundaries. Its integrity began to wane in the latter half of the nineteenth century, and the dominant *yangban* (Confucian literati) social class lost legal recognition around the end of colonialism and the Korean War. Industrialization introduced great social mobility and social leveling toward a fluid, egalitarian society. Class reform occurred much faster than in other newly industrialized countries, and the country now stands on the brink of crystallization of a new social order.

Korean modernization as a whole has been markedly dynamic. It fostered an egalitarian ethic and drive for social mobility that created high mobility between classes. One of the most significant shifts associated with export-oriented industrialization was rapid formation of the industrial working class (see Koo 2001). Factory workers alone increased from 1.3 million in 1970 to 4.8 million in 1990—a working-class expansion almost unprecedented internationally. Wage workers in general numbered little more than two million when export-oriented industrialization took off in the early 1960s; by the mid-1980s, they had quadrupled to eight million. Production workers in manufacturing increased even faster, from 417,000 to 3.1 million. Koo argues in his chapter that such expanded numbers and rigorous labor union and labor group activism have ensconced a socially identifiable working class with a relatively strong class consciousness and sense of worker solidarity.

In contrast, the capitalist class lagged in achieving social distinction. Business group owners, political elites, intellectuals, and the rising professional and managerial class are only now coalescing as a class. Before the beginning of the new millennium, the capitalist class enjoyed little ideological and moral social prowess, notwithstanding enormous economic clout and increasing political influence (see the details in Kim and Song's chapter). The International Monetary Fund (IMF) economic crisis, however, thrust it toward hegemony and increased its influence on society's major institutions and value system as well as on state economic policies. Soon it can be expected to occupy a distinct niche in the status hierarchy, with signature capitalist-class marriage patterns, values, and lifestyles.

Rapid economic development brought on by export-oriented industrialization over the past four decades also swelled middle-class ranks. Various social surveys before the 1997 IMF crisis

commonly found that 60–70 percent of respondents considered
themselves middle class, an identification that dropped to 40 percent thereafter. Democratization before the 1987 June Uprising
was initially taken up by people's groups (*minjung*), not capitalists
or laborers. However, as it progressed in the late 1980s, middle-
class citizens mounted a massive, but fragile, resistance (Koo in
this volume; KSA 1990; KSA and KPSA 1992). Ironically, the capitalist class most adamantly opposed democratization, but with the
ruling authoritarian elite, gained the most from it. Middle-class
citizens and laborers were politically trounced. Lack of criteria
that draw clear boundaries between the middle class and lower
and upper classes may encourage middle-class overidentification.
According to Lett (1998), growth of the middle class is analogous
to erstwhile "yangbanization" of Korean society. This insecure
identity and ambiguous class boundaries tend to prompt people
into conspicuous consumption.

The Axis of Regionalism

Regionalism arises when institutions encourage persons to
favor those within their region. As Yong-Hak Kim argues in his
chapter, regionalism has been a key axis for extending personal
networks and forming social organizations for the last few
decades in modern Korean society. Specifically, *yŏnjul* developed
as a self-help system in the absence of state concern for social welfare. Each *yŏnjul* provided its members with reliable resource
mobilization and deployment. *Yŏnjul* practiced a double standard
that created different rules for "us" and "them." Regionalism and
its networking device, *yŏnjul*, provided flexibility, mutual understanding, and trust within the "in group" to its benefit. "Out-
group" members experienced discrimination and mistrust (Fukuyama 1995).

Flexibility within the *yŏnjul* undermines predictability, as it
overrides institutional rules and universal codes of conduct. Lack
of predictability drives people to rely on *yŏnjul* more heavily in an
effort to overcome uncertainty, driving a vicious cycle. Favoritism
and cronyism in traditional *yŏnjul* impair social efficiency and
jeopardize the legitimacy of society beyond their boundaries. Pursuit of self-gain through extensions of personal networks within
yŏnjul boundaries creates and supports a cavity within the broader
society. Ironically, the self-help system focus on self-interest and
group boundaries thwarts any sense of broader community,

mitigating the strength of the society that provides the groups' self-interested freedom.

Block voting has been one significant manifestation of regionalism and *yŏnjul*. Presidential and parliamentary elections in recent years have commonly reflected regional voting that betrays both in-group solidarity and out-group animosity (H. R. Kim 2004; Y. Kim in this volume). Regional networks have also figured in high-ranking appointments and recruiting. As Yong-Hak Kim analyzes in this volume, elite offices typically have been region-based prizes: Yongnam provided three times as many presidential appointments of ministers and vice-ministers as any other region from the Third to the Seventh Republic. The principle of regionalism in recruitment is also apparent in occupational and class mobility.

Institutional uncertainty and out-group mistrust due to regionalism promote heavy investment in personal connections and consolidate personal networks. Regionalist networks become the main channel of resource allocation and collective identity, fostering regionally bounded friendship and business relations. This counterforce poses a sometimes paradoxical and regressive threat to the development of society. Emphasis on personal network extension has the potential to shatter the sense of community that bonds the society together, but it continues to be figured in high-ranking political appointments and recruiting.

In sum, Korea has pursued the three mentioned national projects and agendas (H. R. Kim, Fields, D. Kim, and Cumings in this volume) and showed a great deal of vitality and fluidity along the three axes of occupation, class, and regionalism (Y. Kim, Koo, Kim and Song, S. Kim, and Ahn in this volume). Through these vital dynamics, modern Korean society has taken a distinct evolutionary path toward modernization, characterized by initial strengthening and subsequent liberalization of authoritarian repression, revival of civil society, and democratization (Choi and Lim 1993; H. R. Kim 2002, 2003; Lim and Choi 1997).

In its efforts to give more earnest heed to the rise of globalization, Korea should also show competitiveness in its drive for academic excellence. Like any other scholars in the world, Korean scholars should actively respond to the growing challenges and enormous questions presented to Korean society. This volume is part of this endeavor to put together the pieces of the Korean "puzzle" and to advance our understanding of modern Korean society. The Institute for Modern Korean Studies at the Graduate

School of International Studies and the Institute of Social Development Studies at the Department of Sociology at Yonsei University have taken the initiative of providing funds to undertake the project to jointly publish this book on modern Korean society, which can be used widely in classrooms.

Chapter Summaries

As the authors in this volume respond to the growing challenges and enormous research questions presented to modern Korean society, they examine not only the three aforementioned national projects and agendas—economic development, political democratization, and national reunification—but also analyze the vitality and fluidity of social change over the past half century. The eleven chapters here deal with regionalism, class formation, gender politics, economic development and governance, population changes and urbanization, social movements and democratization, civil society and nongovernmental organizations (NGOs), and reunification.

Yong-Hak Kim in chapter 2 outlines the often discussed term "regionalism" by describing the historical and political processes that shaped this crucial aspect of information and resource exchange in Korean society. He stresses that the persistence of regionalism has been fundamental in Korea's modern social connections. As a network pattern, regional ties were historically helpful, but they have evolved through modern political machinations to reduce institutional predictability. Kim concludes by summarizing regionalism's economic impact and stressing the influence the information age is having on Korea's regionalist network pattern. In chapter 3, Hagen Koo examines a critical social outcome of modern Korean history: destruction of the old class system and its ruling class during the Chosŏn dynasty and formation of a modern industrial class system. He provides a detailed overview of the traditional class system, followed by the historical factors that forced its demise. The historical survey emphasizes how the early processes of Korean modernization helped instill a lasting egalitarian ethic and desire for social mobility and outlines how rapid industrialization transformed the traditional class structure into a more elaborate, modern incarnation. A final analysis helps the reader gauge how Korea's class structure historically has been shaped and reshaped into a fully class-divided structure with diminishing social mobility. The chapter illuminates two important aspects of Korea's altered class structure: the degree of ambiguity in social identity and the rapidity with which change in class structure occurred.

Wang-Bae Kim and Bok Song in chapter 4 attempt to explore class reproduction in everyday life. While most previous works about class have focused on the position and roles in production relations, Kim and Song emphasize how classes are reproduced through various practices in social relations. In other words, they approach class in terms of culture. Class is not determined simply by economic relations as Marxists insisted. Instead, classes are formed by complicated social relations reproduced by the various lifestyles and practices of their constituents. Class boundaries— which are not static or firmly demarcated—are defined by various forms of capital such as social and cultural capital as well as economic capital. Class reproduction is thus not only the process of creating the physical conditions for the class members and economic production relations, but also the process of retaining and enlarging their overall forms of life. Such a process of reproduction is constituted of various consuming behaviors or familial and social relations such as education, politics, and organizations in everyday life.

Hyuk-Rae Kim's chapter 5 moves the discussion into the business sphere to explore the source of Korea's current economic structure. It traces the historical and political elements that have forged Korea's capitalist framework by outlining business changes and the "bias toward bigness" that state intervention required, thereby providing a historical and developmental context to understand Korea's *chaebol* (business conglomerates) system on the basis of interrelated dimensions of economic governance— organizational vitality, size dispersion, managerial hierarchy, and market integrity. By scrutinizing the unique structure of Korean economic governance, Kim provides the grounds for assessing whether it can be reformed or must collapse to make way for some other form.

In chapter 6 Karl Fields traces Korea's industrialization and economic development using a modern historical framework. He then groups and compares various viewpoints used to explain it in three broad categories—market, statist, and cultural approaches. However, Fields warns against adopting monocausal explanations for Korea's development and suggests a more ecumenical approach that explores Korea's institutional aspects. This approach conveys how traditional Korean elements, market forces, and state influence have all helped shape the modern Korean developmental experience. It suggests how political institutions have interacted with both the historical and cultural legacies of Korea, and it outlines Korea's relation to the Asian miracle and Asian meltdown. More important, Fields's discussion helps the reader assess how the institutions have both benefited and hindered Korea's economic development.

Seung-Kyung Kim in chapter 7 discusses changes in Korean views of family and gender occasioned by modernization. More specifically, she details traditional gender roles in Korea and their shift over time. By defining the family unit in terms of gender relationships, Kim also traces changing notions of family. She first discusses how families have combined certain core elements of cultural tradition (particularly, Confucian ideology) with new social elements associated with modernization. The chapter then follows gender roles through the historical contexts of the Chosŏn dynasty, colonization, and industrialization and shows how changes interacted with broader social movements in Korea's modernization. It ends by evaluating the importance of these shifts within the family and society and suggesting future prospects for family and gender roles.

In chapter 8, Kye-Choon Ahn details demographic shifts in Korea since the 1920s in terms of age, gender, religion, urbanization, industry, and occupation. Ahn places the empirical data in the context of historical and technological changes relevant to alterations in Korea's makeup over time. Data comparisons show how shifts in certain areas directly or indirectly influenced shifts elsewhere. Ahn's outline of transitional demographics based on historical circumstances so conveys Korea's unique and rapid demographic changes as to suggest where it may be headed in terms of future change.

Dong-No Kim in chapter 9 analyzes the evolving forms of popular protest against a consistently oppressive state apparatus historically allied with the economic ruling class. He detects four historical stages of resistance, each led by a particular sector of the populace—peasants, laborers, students, and citizens. The reader learns the major grounds of protest in each stage, their aims, and their impact then and now. The complexity within each broad category is clear, but a degree of continuity in the protests is apparent and suggests the importance of current civil movements. Such movements undeniably have been fundamental to social reform throughout modern Korean history.

Hyuk-Rae Kim's chapter 10 explores the form of civil society peculiar to Korea and its historical genesis. This chapter analyzes the relationship between the state and civil society over three historical periods in modern Korea. The three distinct but intricately interrelated historical periods have characterized the development of civil society in Korea. The first, from liberation to the end of the Park regime, was characterized by successive authoritarian state-centric governance, which practiced state corporatism and repressed civil society to achieve modernization through rapid economic growth. The second period lasted to the beginning of the 1987 Democratic Movement and abounded in academic discourse on the state and its critical role in economic development. Discussion of civil society as an alternative mechanism of governance emerged during this period. The third stage is the transitional period toward democracy, during which Korea is experiencing actual growth in civil society and interest-group politics. This chapter then evaluates the current state of civil society and proposes new visions in transition to democracy in Korea.

Bruce Cumings's chapter 11 clarifies the historical background for one of the most fundamental features of modern Korean society: division into North and South Korea. It explores the recent flux in relations and suggests prospects for reunification. Cumings first relates events involved in the beginning division of Korea, and then examines the political developments that led to the outbreak of the Korean War. Finally, he bridges the recent past with current events and shows how the reunification process and policies have been improving. The chapter's comprehensive historical and political perspective indicates the complexities that surround continued division and the reunification struggle.

References

Choe, Minja Kim. 1998. "Changing Marriage Patterns in South Korea." In Karen O. Mason, Noriko O. Tsuya, and Minja Kim Choe, eds., *The Changing Family in Comparative Perspectives: Asia and United States*, 43–62. Honolulu: East-West Center.

Choi, Jang-Jip, and Hyun-Jin Lim. 1993. *Simin sahoe ŭi tochŏn* (Challenges of civil society). Seoul: Nanam.

Fukuyama, Francis. 1995. *Trust: The Social Virtues and the Creation of Prosperity*. New York: Free Press.

Hong, Moon-Sik, and Yong-Chan Byun. 1998. "Intergenerational Relations in South Korea." In Karen O. Mason, Noriko O.

Tsuya, and Minja Kim Choe, eds., *The Changing Family in Comparative Perspectives: Asia and United States*, 175–191. Honolulu: East-West Center.

Kendall, Laurel. 1996. *Getting Married in Korea: Of Gender, Morality, and Modernity*. Berkeley: University of California Press.

Kim, Hyuk-Rae. 2000. "The State and Civil Society in Transition: The Role of NGOs in South Korea." *Pacific Review* 13:595–613.

———. 2002. "NGOs in Pursuit of 'the Public Good' in South Korea." In Sally Sargeson, ed., *Collective Goods, Collective Futures in Asia*, 58–74. London: Routledge.

———. 2003. "Unraveling Civil Society in South Korea: Old Discourses and New Visions." In David Schak and Wayne Hudson, eds., *Civil Society in Asia*, 192–208. London: Ashgate.

———. 2004. "Dilemmas in the Making of Civil Society in Korean Political Reform." *Journal of Contemporary Asia* 34.1:55–69.

Kim, Hyuk-Rae, and David K. McNeal. 2005. "From State-centric to Negotiated Governance: NGOs as Policy Entrepreneurs in South Korea." In Robert P. Weller, ed., *Civil Life, Globalization, and Political Change in Asia: Organizing between Family and State*, 95–109. London: Routledge.

Kim, Hyuk-Rae, et al. 2000. *Politics and Markets in the Wake of the Asian Crisis*. London: Routledge.

Kim, Nam-Il; Soon Choi; and Insook Han Park. 1994. "Rural Family and Community Life in South Korea: Changes in Family Attitudes and Living Arrangements of the Elderly." In Lee-Jay Cho and Moto Yada, eds., *Tradition and Change in the Asian Family*, 273–317. Honolulu: East-West Center.

Kim, Sunhyuk. 2000. *The Politics of Democratization in Korea: The Role of Civil Society*. Pittsburgh, Penn.: University of Pittsburgh Press.

Koo, Hagen, ed. 1993. *State and Society in Contemporary Korea*. Ithaca, N.Y.: Cornell University Press.

———. 2001. *Korean Workers: The Culture and Politics of Class Formation*. Ithaca, N.Y.: Cornell University Press.

Korean Sociological Association (KSA), ed. 1990. *Han'guk sahoe ŭi pipanchŏk insik* (Critical recognition of the Korean society). Seoul: Nanam.

KSA and Korean Political Science Association (KPSA), eds. 1992. *Han'guk ŭi kukkawa simin sahoe* (The Korean state and civil society). Seoul: Hanul.

Lett, Denise P. 1998. *In Pursuit of Status: The Making of South Korea's New Urban Middle Class.* Cambridge: Harvard University Asia Center.

Lim, Hyun-Jin, and Jang-Jip Choi. 1997. *Han'guk sahoe wa minju juŭi* (Korean society and democracy). Seoul: Nanam.

TWO

Regionalism and National Networks

YONG-HAK KIM

A man newly retired from the military completed numerous job application forms, invariably leaving blank the entry line for listing family members of social influence or serving as managers in the company. He repeatedly failed to secure a job and thought that his lack of social connection might be the reason. One day, while waiting for an elevator at a company he planned to apply to, he encountered an employee identified by a name tag as Mr. Kim B. S., director of general affairs. He subsequently identified Mr. Kim on his application as his cousin. He secured an interview, only to find himself facing an astonished Mr. Kim among his interviewers. When Mr. Kim inquired, "Do you know me?" the man deftly replied, "I have respected you as my cousin." Mr. Kim smiled and asked a few questions, and a week later the man received an acceptance letter. Mr. Kim took him aside on his first day of work and confided that he had used the same ruse to obtain employment, commencing and sealing a unique sort of kinship.

Introduction

MBC Radio's recent broadcast of the above story vividly depicts the importance of social networks in the modern Korean labor market. Firms routinely ask job applicants to list names of socially influential persons in their families because they use personal connections to conduct business. Firms in legal trouble, for instance, benefit from connections with prosecutors; those seeking government permits use connections with bureaucrats to get results.

Connections are important in every society, including advanced industrial nations. Whether a *guanxi* (Yang 1994), an old boys' network, an F-connection, an alumni network, or a cozy triangle, personal networks loom large in business and politics. But the ways in which networks are structured and the types of goods they exchange vary across societies. First, Korean social networks involve not only dyadic but also generalized exchanges (Ekeh 1974). Dyadic exchange involves two transaction partners who reciprocate favors. Generalized exchange features multiple actors: A gives valuable resources to B, B passes the favor to C, C to D, and so on. A's favor may or may not be returned in the unspecified future by other network members. Second, the personal nature of Korean ties promotes not only information exchange but also control exchange. Control exchange occurs when network members exchange among themselves institutional resources, rights, or power they own or control. High political loyalty, for instance, may be given a network member of higher party position irrespective of his or her competence in exchange for party favors; bureaucratic control over permits for entering a certain industry may be exchanged for the petitioner's donation, gift, or bribe.

Control exchange through personal ties continues to condition the Korean economy, society, and politics despite the rapid advance of industrialization and democratization. Against the contention of modernization theories that industrialization and capitalism breed universalism (Tönnies 1971: 76–98; Durkheim 1933: 203–4; Lerner 1958: 183–89; Parsons and Shils 1951) and that meritocracy eventually erodes traditional social arrangements, particularistic ties have not attenuated in modern Korea (Chang 1991). On the contrary, most people invest in social networks as a rational decision because they have personally experienced their value as resource distribution channels and sources of collective identity. The old boys' network undeniably played a decisive role during Korea's rapid economic development, facilitating information flow among bureaucrats and capitalists (Amsden 1989). State-led industrialization succeeded by drawing on state–business networks based on particularistic ties (Evans 1995).

Three *yŏnjul*—regional, school, and kin ties—are the most important networks in Korea. For instance, when a new political party assumes power, senior state bureaucratic positions fall to persons who share the party leader's regional origin. Family members of a *chaebol* owner head its subsidiary companies as CEOs and managers. A recent study reports that 63 percent of *chaebol* founders' sons, 37 percent of founders' siblings, and 20 percent of siblings' sons occupy the respective *chaebol*s' top managerial positions. Market transactions also occur frequently and regularly through alumni connections. A national survey confirms Koreans' conscious, extensive reliance on these three relations (KSA 1990). Fifty-eight percent of respondents reported using kin relations, 46 percent regional relations, and 29 percent school ties in their everyday lives. Reliance on school ties was lowest because of the expense of acquiring that sort of social capital.

This chapter analyzes how Korean social networks operate and proposes a theory as to why particularistic social networks, or *yŏnjul,* have become major sources of resource allocation and collective identity. It focuses specifically on regional networks because regionalism and regional conflict have become major social problems in recent years, and empirical studies on this issue accordingly abound. Based on the analysis of regional networks, the chapter concludes with the generalization that low institutional accountability and transparency have facilitated the development of *yŏnjul* and with an exploration of whether *yŏnjul* will prevail in the information age as in the industrial age.

Regional Network Structure

Regional network consolidation and regionalism are two sides of the same coin. Regionalism can be defined as a set of ideologies (or prejudices) and institutions that encourage people to favor others within their region above those outside. Recruitment of economic and political elites almost exclusively through regional networks derives from the regionalism of power holders and from institutional factors that promote in-region favoritism.

The structure of regionalism is best clarified through considering the seven basic regional units in South Korea, based on administrative provinces: Seoul, Kyŏnggi, Ch'ungch'ŏng, Honam, Yŏngnam, Kangwon, and Cheju (figure 2.1). The precise administrative boundaries of these regions were set by the Japanese colonial regime, but borders had existed since the Chosŏn dynasty, founded in 1392. The social distance among these regions is a good indicator of the significance and structure of regionalism.

Figure 2.1. Map of South Korea

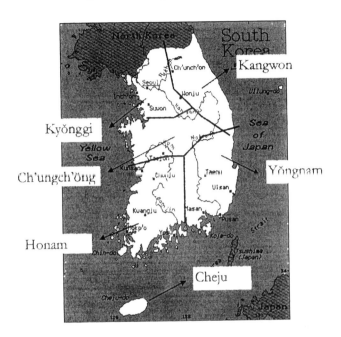

Subjective Social Distances

The social distance scale developed by Borgardus (1958) and his students shows the extent to which people refrain from interacting with others from certain regions.[1] Figure 2.2 is a simplified depiction of subjective regional distance, where arrow thickness represents magnitude of social distance. First, all regions express strong anti-Honam sentiment. Indeed, anti-Honamism among Koreans appears stronger than anti-Semitism among Americans. A large proportion of people eschew a Honam person as a business partner (32 percent), spouse (28 percent), friend (24 percent), or neighbor (20 percent). Because trust in

---

[1] The social distance scale used in a 1989 national survey measured four indicators: respondents' willingness to accept individuals from each region as a spouse, business partner, close friend, or neighbor.

Figure 2.2. Structure of regional attitude

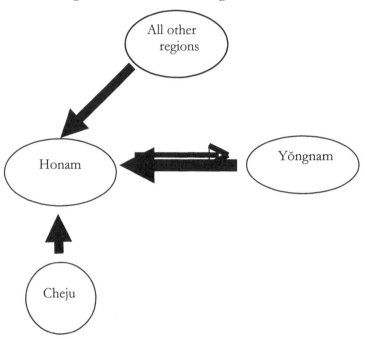

business relations is essential—particularly in a rapidly growing economy—the strong disdain for people from Honam as business partners may derive from their stereotype as being opportunistic. Second, the greatest anti-Honam attitude is in Cheju and Yŏngnam, where almost 50 percent refuse to accept Honam business partners. Third, Yŏngnam is also rejected, but only by Honam. In short, Honam is the center of negative social distance, with no other region so uniformly cast out (Cho 1987; M. Kim 1987).

Regionalism and Politics

Regional cleavage is most apparent in presidential elections. The election of Kim Dae Jung as president in 1997 represented the first regime change since foundation of the republic in 1948. The power base of his political party was Honam; presidents since 1963 had came from Yŏngnam. Table 2.1 shows that more than 90 percent of Honam residents voted for Kim Dae Jung in the 1997 election, while only 11–15 percent of Yŏngnam supported him.

Table 2.1. Changing patterns of presidential voting by region

Region	1963 Park vs. Yoon	1967 Park vs. Yoon	1971 Park vs. D.J. Kim	1987* Ro vs. D.J. Kim	1997 D. J. Kim vs. Lee
Seoul	32; 68	47; 53	40; 60	28; 28	45; 41
Kyŏnggi	37; 63	44; 56	50; 50	44; 20	39; 34
Kangwon	45; 55	55; 45	61; 39	70; 2	24; 42
Ch'ungch'ŏng	45; 55	50; 50	56; 44	35; 4	41; 26
Honam					
North	54; 46	46; 56	37; 63	14; 82	91; 8
South	62; 38	49; 51	35; 65	5; 94	93; 5
Yŏngnam					
North	61; 39	71; 29	76; 24	65(89)**; 2	14; 62
South	67; 33	75; 25	74; 26	37(88)**; 3	11; 54
Pusan	50; 50	67; 33	56; 44		15; 53
Total	51; 49	55; 45	54; 46	37; 22	

Notes: Park was from Yŏngnam South, Yoon and Lee were from Seoul, Kim was from Honam South.

* %s do not sum to 100 because of third candidate, Y. S. Kim.

** Numbers in parentheses calculated by adding votes received by Y. S. Kim from Yŏngnam South.

Such bloc voting was new in Korean political history; presidential elections between 1963 and 1971 revealed no such pattern. Former president Park, who originated from Yŏngnam, for instance, received roughly half of Honam's votes in the 1963 and 1967 elections, no lower a percentage than the national average. In 1987,[2] however, in both Honam and Yŏngnam, about 90 percent of voters favored candidates from their own region.[3] Furthermore, only in Honam could a man's regional origin predict his wife's vote (Y. Kim 1997). Region thus served as a strong predictor of probable vote choice.

However, bloc voting reflects not only in-group solidarity, but also out-group animosity (Bae 1990). During the 1987 election campaign, for instance, several riots broke out. When Kim Dae Jung visited Yŏngnam for a campaign speech, residents cast stones and beat campaign crews. Kim Young Sam from Yŏngnam received similar treatment when his campaign visited Honam. Why have regional bloc voting and out-group animosity in these two areas intensified in recent years? Are there historical roots to regionalism? The next section examines these questions.

Causes of Regionalism

Two theories purport to explain Korean regionalism. One, which I identify as Theory H, traces the origin of regionalism far back into history to the tenth-century Koryŏ dynasty (J. Kim 1998: 237). It focuses on the subjective aspects of regionalism, such as social prejudice. This view contends that regional inequality and conflict are consequences of historically rooted prejudice (Song 1990).

The earliest written historical document supporting Theory H is King Wang-gun's ten commandments, promulgated in 943 C.E. The king warns, "Do not promote Honam people to higher government positions, for their minds resemble the rugged mountains surrounding them." Three additional materials from the Chosŏn dynasty that characterize Honam people as opportunistic are often cited.[4] The importance of these historical documents,

---

[2] No popular vote for president took place during the sixteen-year dictatorship.

[3] This regional voting was even more remarkable considering that candidates were not leaders in local politics. The Korean state is highly centralized, without local governments or parties.

[4] Lee Chung Whan's *T'aekrijee*, Ahn Jong Bok's *P'aldop'yung*, and *Chŏgkamrok* (author unknown).

however, remains obscure because we have no way of knowing whether they reflect the prejudice of a few power holders or the broader population. Extensive historical analysis of elite recruitment during the Koryŏ dynasty, for instance, reveals no regional discrimination.

The second perspective, Theory P, focuses on political processes set in motion by the assumption of state power in 1961 by General Park Chung Hee (from Yŏngnam) through a coup d'etat. It views regional inequality as a cause, not consequence, of anti-Honam prejudice. Honam backwardness stems from the fact that policy decisions belonged to military and political leaders mainly from Yŏngnam (Cho 1987; J. Kim 1988; M. Kim 1987: 76, 1991; Moon 1990; Na 1990). Theory P accordingly views economic and political inequalities among regions (e.g., based on leaders' origins) as the prime cause of regionalism. Theory P analyses of political elite recruitment show that higher political positions were essentially the province of people from Yŏngnam from the Third Republic to the Seventh. Figure 2.3 clearly betrays heavy reliance on regional networks for recruiting elites. The cumulative numbers of ministers and vice-ministers appointed by presidents serving military juntas shows Yŏngnam overrepresentation: Yŏngnam provided 160 ministers, three times as many as any other region.[5] Inequality rose exponentially after General Chun

Figure 2.3. Cumulative distribution of ministers and vice-ministers by region

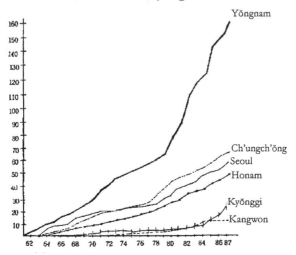

---

[5] I end data with 1987 because when Kim Young Sam assumed the presidency that year, he deliberately sought to reduce regional inequality based on the power of political elites.

Doo Hwan from Yŏngnam took power by coup in 1980. The same pattern described regional distribution of CEOs in government-run companies, generals in the military, and congressmen in government-appointed positions (Y. Kim 1990). The conspiracy theory, a variant of Theory P, argues that the dictatorial military regime created and exploited regional conflict as a divide-and-conquer strategy to weaken political resistance to the regime (Choi 1991).

Differences between the two theories in terms of causal sequences can be summarized as follows: In Theory H, long-standing historical views lead to regional prejudice, which leads to regional inequality and regionalism. In Theory P, political processes since 1960s lead to regional inequality and conflict, which lead to regional prejudice (figure 2.4).

Regional newspapers reflect these differences in revealing ways. *Kwangju Daily* (Honam) adopts Theory P, while *Taegu Daily* (Yŏngnam) follows Theory H. Theory H would imply that policies seeking to reduce regional conflict should adopt a long-term perspective because regional sentiments have deep roots in historical experiences (J. Kim 1988). Theory P, conversely, would encourage immediate attention to reducing current structural aspects of regional inequality to resolve conflict.

Integrating variables the various theories consider, we can describe the main causal sequence suggested by figure 2.2.

1. During the Chosŏn dynasty (1392–1910) a higher proportion of peasants from Honam than from elsewhere moved to other regions to escape exploitation by landlords. Perhaps, as unwelcome poor immigrants, they had negative interactions with natives. Such interactions perhaps fostered unfavorable stereotypes of Honam (Song 1990). The authoritarian government's reliance on regional networks within Yŏngnam to recruit power elites created economic and political inequalities as elites advanced industrialization by investing almost exclusively in Yŏngnam.

2. Honam's backwardness had two outcomes. First, it exacerbated the clustering of lower-class people from Honam in urban areas when in urban cities of other regions.[6] Second, it

---

[6] People from Honam currently comprise one-quarter of Seoul's population, making them the largest group in the city—even larger than the group of Seoul natives. Their income levels fall in the lowest bracket.

Figure 2.4. Causal network among variables explaining regionalism

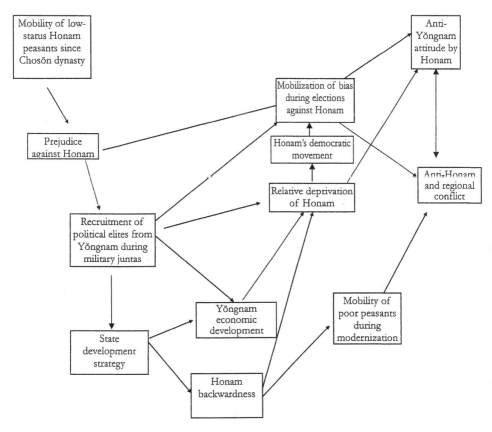

reinforced the relative deprivation of people from Honam, who are already victims of social prejudice.[7]

3. Under the leadership of Kim Dae Jong (elected president in 1997), Honam challenged Yŏngnam's monopoly of economic and political resources. The dictatorial regime countered by mobilizing anti-Honam bias (Na 1990; M. Kim 1987; Bae 1990).[8]

4. Because such mobilization of bias resorted to prejudice, anti-Honamism was widely accepted and escalated. In reaction, Honam developed negative attitudes toward Yŏngnam, which monopolized resources.

In sum, the development of regionalism made the regional network a primary channel of information and resource flows. In-group solidarity and out-group animosity regionally bounded friendship and business relations in a process that alienated Honam from all regions.

Low Institutional Trust Consolidates Personal Networks

We need, then, to determine why political elites of the military regimes so extensively relied on regional networks and, in so doing, to explain why Koreans in general rely on particularistic ties in their business and everyday lives. From this I will elaborate a general theory, not specific to Korea, a theory of unintended consequences of individual actions to cope with institutional uncertainty. Specifically, when institutional predictability and accountability are low, individuals rely on personal networks to reduce uncertainty.

The literature on organizations gives special attention to the issue of leader succession. Numerous studies indicate that problems surrounding leader succession within state bureaucracies, public organizations, and private firms encourage consolidation of particularistic personal networks (Meyer 1975; Helmich and Brown 1972; Meyer and Brown 1977; Grusky 1964: 96–98, 1961: 261–69, 1960: 114; Kriesberg 1962). For instance, in Gouldner's (1954) case

---

[7] A survey shows that half of the people from Honam thought that government economic development policy was the most important source of regionalism (KSA 1990).

[8] One illustration of their manipulation of mass media occurred during the 1980 Kwangju massacre: all newspaper dailies—all subject to tight junta censorship—featured an article falsely alleging that "Honam rioters set cars with Yŏngnam license plates on fire" (S. Moon 1990).

study of succession within a gypsum factory, a newly appointed factory leader who lacked general support replaced current managers with individuals with whom he had personal ties. In other words, the new leader strategically attempted to reduce the disruptive effect of succession—to control uncertainty—by mobilizing particularistic ties.

Similarly, political elites from Yŏngnam since the 1960s sought to reduce political uncertainty concerning loyalty by recruiting cronies from their own region for responsible positions. Because the dictatorial military regime lacked legitimacy and faced a possible countercoup, it "internalized externalities" to reduce its vulnerability (Williamson 1975, 1981). As Downs argues (1967: 70–71), when a power holder can distribute resources freely, it behooves him or her to channel such resources to personal contacts in exchange for loyalty. Thus, overrepresentation of a certain region among political elites was not an intended but an unintended consequence, as illegitimate power holders sought to secure their positions.

The above discussions can be generalized to nonpolitical settings. When the behavior or circumstances of public institutions are unpredictable, individuals create and rely on personal networks to circumvent uncertainty. For example, when the judicial process lacks transparency or accountability, court judgments are unpredictable. Because this situation leaves individuals without legitimate means to approach the court, to reduce unpredictability they may turn to unorthodox strategies, such as using personal connections with people with court influence (e.g., judges and other officials). A recent study reports that 90 percent of university students in Korea doubt the fairness of the judicial system (Y. Kim 1996).

Low institutional accountability has long characterized the traditional patrimonial state. According to Weber, power holders in such states "privately own the means of administration"; this situation creates irrationalities in the administration of law and taxes that defy all calculation (Weber 1968: 240). Comparing Roman with Chinese law, Weber argues that

> the [Roman] formalist law is, however, calculable. In China it may happen that a man who sells a house to another may later come to him and ask to be taken in because in the meantime he has become impoverished. If the purchaser refuses to heed the ancient Chinese command to help a brother, the spirits will be disturbed; hence the impoverished seller comes into the house as a renter who pays no rent. Capitalism cannot operate on the basis of law

so constituted. What it requires is law which can be counted upon, like a machine. Ritualistic-religious and magical considerations must be excluded. (Weber 1981: 342)

Weber's insights help illuminate the modern era in Korea as well. Though the Korean legal system and bureaucracy are imported from the West and therefore formally represent universalism, in their actual workings they are unpredictable and incalculable. Content analysis of news articles in the national newspapers indicates the degree to which institutional distrust became a greater social issue following the 1997 economic crisis (table 2.2).

I searched all the newspaper articles carrying the key words "trust" or "distrust" during the 1997–99 period and found 8,100 articles. Frequency increased dramatically over the period as Korea attempted to reform the economic and government sectors to overcome the economic crisis (i.e., the 1997 IMF bailout). Among these articles I sampled roughly 10 percent to identify the context in which the word appeared.[9] Some trust issues concerned the information society (e.g., whether a cyber shopping mall is trustworthy), but most related to trust of government institutions, including the congress, politicians, and legal and economic institutions.

More recently, the state took no action to prevent Daewoo conglomerates from going out of business, but is subsidizing the insolvent Hyundai with a few billion won. Why the difference? Hyundai supported the state's unification policy by investing in North Korea, losing vast funds but securing government loyalty. The process tied survival of private firms to political decisions. Such activity encourages interpersonal networking between influential individuals in business and government. Predictability and accountably diminish, and networking grows ever more crucial.

Extensive reliance on kin networks within *chaebol* management occurs in the same manner. When a firm's audit system is not regulated, its owner recruits individuals he most trusts as managers, most often family members (Fukuyama 1995). Again, institutional uncertainty fosters heavy reliance on personal connections. Merit and performance may be outweighed by other factors more important to providing predictability.

---

[9] I used the database at http://www.kinds.or.kr.

Table 2.2. Content analysis of national newspaper articles

Subject — Key word	Trust/Distrust 97	98	99
Government and institutions	4	3	35
Government authorities	0	3	19
Prosecutor and legal system	10	7	46
Government policies and services	5	12	28
Financial system and its reform	0	9	6
Market and economic institutions	0	8	0
Education system	4	6	17
Foreign policy	4	22	20
Relations with North Korea	4	5	24
Credibility of the nation	35	26	18
Politicians and congress	36	28	101
Firms and CEOs	17	22	34
Media	3	4	11
NGOs	0	2	1
Interpersonal relations	0	2	14
Labor relations	5	7	3
Morality and social trust	8	3	13
Technology and risk management	0	1	11
Internet shopping	0	1	14
Information and data	1	5	6
Public opinion research	26	22	36
Total sample/	158/	214/	468/
population	1,973	1,836	4,691

Implications for the Network Society

Western scholars have described East Asian capitalism as network capitalism, alliance capitalism, relational capitalism, Confucian capitalism, and crony capitalism (Biggart 1991; Biggart and Hamilton 1992; Orru, Biggart, and Hamilton 1991; Dore 1986; Gerlach 1992). Despite the various appellations, all emphasize that East Asian capitalism relies on particularistic ties in market transactions, state–business interactions, and state policy implementation (Moon and Prasad 1994; Amsden 1989). How, then, will East Asian nations, particularly Korea, proceed into the information age? A "network society" emerges as information technology develops through increases in interpersonal, organizational, and production networks (Castells 1996). It differs from a *yŏnjul* society in being driven by information technology and globalization and, therefore, being open and universalistic. What lies ahead for Korea?

Historically, Koreans developed *yŏnjul* as a self-help system to redress public-sector neglect of social welfare. Within the boundaries of each *yŏnjul*, members could rely on processes of resource mobilization and deployment. The system developed a double standard, such that rules for "us" differed from those for "them." *Yŏnjul* provided flexibility, tolerance, self-help, mutual understanding, and trust among the in-group. The out-group, beyond each particular *yŏnjul*, were "non-persons," subject to mistrust, discrimination, and hostility (Fukuyama 1995).

Flexibility within a *yŏnjul*, no matter how locally efficient, undermines broader institutional predictability. It subverts institutional and universal codes of conduct. When institutions fail to provide certainty, persons turn still more to *yŏnjul* (Hamilton 1985), creating a vicious cycle. A society that attempts to use traditional *yŏnjul* will suffer from favoritism and cronyism, jeopardizing the openness that a network society requires. Instances abound in Korean modern politics in which special favors (e.g., market monopoly rights, bank loans, subsides) were unjustifiably given to *yŏnjul* members.

Yŏnjul harm social efficiency because they exclude competent persons beyond their borders. The intense market competition of the global age requires open membership that encourages all competent actors to operate as an inclusive network. For instance, for start-up companies to develop strategic alliances, their CEOs cannot limit alliances to the firms whose CEOs share the same regional origin. No society that hopes to succeed in the information age can operate through *yŏnjul*. It must become a network society, with inclusive openness and the reliability openness requires.

Let me elaborate on why *yŏnjul* lower efficiency in the information age. Imagine a matrix whose columns and rows represent regions and whose cells denote frequencies of strategic alliance between firms classified by CEOs' regional origin. The matrix then shows a pattern of cross-regional alliances among startup companies. If strategic alliances occur only when CEOs share a regional origin stemming from in-group favoritism, then nonzero numbers will appear only in the diagonal cells because cross-region networks occur in off-diagonal cells. In the early phase of Korean capitalistic development, there was no need to facilitate the off-diagonal interactions because higher trust existed in the diagonal cells. The rise of the network society, however, means that off-diagonal interactions must increase beyond the *yŏnjul* boundary. A simple calculation proves the point. In a (n by n) matrix, there are only n diagonal cells and (n^2-n) off-diagonal cells; that is, off-diagonal cells outweigh diagonal cells. Refraining from making alliances with a certain firm simply because it is outside the *yŏnjul* boundary undermines competitiveness, especially when competent firms are likely to arise outside *yŏnjul*. For this reason, the *yŏnjul* society is maladaptive to the network society and suffers from low social efficiency. What needs to be done is to promote cross-border networks, and that can be achieved only by higher institutional accountability.

Conclusion

This chapter reviews how personal connections, or *yŏnjul*, operate in Korean politics, business, labor markets, and everyday life. In particular, it shows how regional networks and regionalism became major channels for resource allocation and collective identity in a political process begun in 1961 with industrialization. Extensive reliance on regional networks to recruit elites developed as power holders sought to cope with the political uncertainty created by their lack of popular legitimacy. Political elites from Yŏngnam promoted economic development of their own region to build a regional power base they could rely upon. Political parties accordingly became little more than regional parties assured election by bloc votes from their own region, and there was no party loyalty from other regions. Differences in policy or vision among candidates mattered far less than regional origin. The logic that institutional uncertainty strengthens regional networks applies similarly to other types of *yŏnjul*, such as school and kin ties. All serve to cope with institutional unpredictability.

Advocates of Confucian capitalism and "Asian values" argue that *yŏnjul* have been efficient and should be encouraged. I disagree on two grounds. First, *yŏnjul* resist productive and competent innovations that develop outside their boundaries, reducing economic efficiency. They are therefore dysfunctional in the network society of the information age, which requires open membership that allows free exchange of ideas, services, and products. Second, *yŏnjul* favoritism and cronyism jeopardize the legitimacy of ties within the broader society beyond *yŏnjul* boundaries. Universal norms and rules that normally integrate an entire nation attenuate and worsen regional isolation and contention. The free information flow essential to the network society creates institutional transparency, which, if allowed to thrive, will slowly erode the role and viability of *yŏnjul*.

References

Amsden, A. 1989. *Asia's Next Giant: South Korea and Late Industrialization*. Oxford: Oxford University Press.

Bae, K. 1990. "Sonko kwachong kwa chiyŏk kamchŏng" (Processes of election and emergence of regionalism). In Korean Sociological Association, ed., *Han'guk ŭi chiyŏk jŭi wa chiyŏk kaldung* (Regionalism and regional conflict in Korea). Seoul: Sung Won Sa.

Biggart, Nicole. 1991. "Explaining Asian Economic Organization: Toward a Weberian Institutional Perspective." *Theory and Society* 20:199–232.

Biggart, Nicole, and Gary Hamilton. 1992. "On the Limits of a Firm-Based Theory to Explain Business Networks: The Western Bias of Neoclassical Economics." In Nitin Nohria and R. Eccles, eds., *Networks and Organizations: Structure, Form, and Action*. Boston: Harvard Business School Press.

Borgardus, E. S. 1958. "Racial Distance Changes in the United States during the Past Thirty Years." *Sociology and Social Research* 43:127–35.

Castells, Manuel. 1996. *The Rise of the Network Society*. Oxford: Blackwell.

Chang, Yun-Shik. 1991. "The Personalistic Ethic and the Market in Korea." *Comparative Studies in Society and History* 33:106–29.

Cho, Kyung-Keun. 1987. "Yŏnghonam chiyŏk kamchong yŏnku: Kwangju mit Taegu taehaksaengdŭl e taehan sŏlmunchosarul chungsim ŭro" (A study of regionalism in Yŏngnam and Honam: A survey analysis of Kwangju and Taegu students). *Wolgan chosŏn* (Chosŏn monthly) 9:196–211.

Choi, Jang-Jip. 1991. "Chiyŏk kamchŏng ŭi chipae ideolrokichŏk kinŭng" (The ideological function of regionalism). In *Chiyŏk kamchŏng yŏnku* (Studies of regionalism). Seoul: Hak Min Sa.

Dore, R. 1986. *Flexible Rigidities*. Stanford, Calif.: Stanford University Press.

Downs, Anthony. 1967. *Inside Bureaucracy*. Boston: Little, Brown.

Durkheim, Emile. 1933. *The Division of Labor in Society*. New York: Free Press.

Ekeh, P. 1974. *Social Theory: The Two Traditions*. Cambridge: Harvard University Press.

Evans, P. 1995. *Embedded Autonomy: States and Industrial Transformation*. Princeton, N.J.: Princeton University Press.

Fukuyama, Francis. 1995. *Trust: The Social Virtues and the Creation of Prosperity*. New York: Free Press.

Gerlach, Michael. 1992. *Alliance Capitalism*. Berkeley: University of California Press.

Gouldner, Alvin W. 1954. *Patterns of Industrial Bureaucracy*. Glencoe, Ill.: Free Press.

Grusky, Oscar. 1960. "Administrative Succession in Formal Organizations." *Social Forces* 39:5–15.

———. 1961. "Corporate Size, Bureaucratization, and Managerial Succession." *American Journal of Sociology* 67:261–69.

———. "The Effects of Succession: A Comparative Study of Military and Business Organization." In Morris Janowitz, ed., *The New Military*, 83–109. New York: John Wiley and Sons.

Hamilton, G. 1985. "Why No Capitalism in China? Negative Questions in Historical Comparative Research." *Journal of Asian Perspectives* 2:187–211.

Helmich, Donald, and Warren Brown. 1972. "Successor Type and Organizational Change in the Corporate Enterprise." *Administrative Science Quarterly* 39:475–591.

Kim, J. 1988. "Chiyŏk kamchŏng ŭi silsangkwa kŭ haeso pangan" (The nature of regionalism and means to abolish it). In Han'guk simrihakhyŏphoe (Korean Psychological Association), ed., *Simrihak esŏ pon chiyŏk kamchŏng* (Regionalism seen from psychological perspectives). Seoul: Sung Won Sa.

Kim, Man-Heum. 1987. "Han'guk sahoe ŭi chiyŏk kamchŏng yŏnku: yŏngnam honam ŭl chŭngsim ŭro" (A study of regional conflicts in Korean society focusing on the conflict between Yŏngnam and Honam). Mimeograph. Hyundai Social Research Center.

Kim, Yong-Hak. 1990. "Elritŭ ch'ungwŏne itŏsŏ ŭi chiyŭk kyŏk'cha: misichŏk tongki wa kŏsichok kyŏl'kwa" (Regional difference in elite recruitment: Micro motivation and macro result). In Han'guk sahoehakhoe (Korean Sociological Association), ed., *Han'guk chiyŏk juŭi wa chiyŏk kaldŭng* (Regionalism and regional conflict in Korea). Seoul: Sung Won Sa.

―――. 1996. *Sahoe kuchowa haengwi* (Social structure and action in social theory). Nanam.

―――. 1997. "Regionalism and Regional Networks in Korea." In Ho-Youn Kwon, ed., *Contemporary Korea: Democracy, Economic Development, Social Change, and the Re-Unification Process*, 263–86. Chicago: Center for Korean Studies, North Park College and Theological Seminary.

Korean Sociological Association (KSA). 1990. *Han'guk chiyŏk juŭi wa chiyŏk kaldŭng* (Regionalism and regional conflict in Korea). Seoul: Sung Won Sa.

Kriesberg, Louis. 1962. "Careers, Organization Size, and Succession." *American Journal of Sociology* 68:355–59.

Lerner, Daniel. 1958. *The Passing of Traditional Society: Modernizing the Middle East*. New York: Free Press.

Meyer, John, and Brian Brown. 1997. "Institutionalized Organizations: Formal Structure as Myth and Ceremony." *American Journal of Sociology* 83:340–63.

Meyer, Marshall W. 1975. "Leadership and Organizational Structure." *American Journal of Sociology* 81:514–42.

Moon, Chung-In, and R. Prasad. 1994. "Beyond the Developmental State: Networks, Politics, and Institutions." *Governance: An International Journal of Policy and Administration* 7:360–86.

Moon, S. N. 1990. "Chiyŏk kyŏkcha ŭi yŏksachŏk paekyŏng: haepangŭroput'o 1960 nyŏntae kkachirŭl chungshimŭro" (The historical background of regionalism: From 1945 to 1960). In Han'guk sahoehakhoe (Korean Sociological Association), ed., *Han'guk chiyŏk juŭi wa chiyŏk kaldŭng* (Regionalism and regional conflict in Korea). Seoul: Sung Won Sa.

Na, G. 1990. "Chiyŏkkan ŭi sahoechŏk kŏrikam" (Social distances among regions). In Han'guk sahoehakhoe (Korean Sociological Association), ed., *Han'guk chiyŏk juŭi wa chiyŏk kaldŭng* (Regionalism and regional conflict in Korea), 360–86. Seoul: Sung Won Sa.

Orru, M.; N. Biggart; and G. Hamilton. 1991. "Organizational Isomorphism in East Asia." In Walter W. Powell and Paul DiMaggio, eds., *The New Institutionalism in Organizational Analysis*, 361–89. Chicago: University of Chicago Press.

Parsons, Talcott, and Edward Shils. 1951. *Toward a General Theory of Action*. New York: Harper and Row.

Schelling, Thomas. 1978. *Micromotives and Macrobehavior*. New York: Norton and Company.

Song, B. 1990. "Chiyŏk kaldŭng ŭi yŏksachŏk sŏlmyŏng" (Historical explanations of regional conflict). In Han'guk sahoehakhoe (Korean Sociological Association), ed., *Han'guk chiyŏk juŭi wa chiyŏk kaldŭng* (Regionalism and regional conflict in Korea). Seoul: Sung Won Sa.

Tönnies, F. 1971. *On Sociology: Pure, Applied, and Empirical*. Chicago: University of Chicago Press.

Weber, Max. 1968. *Economy and Society*. Berkeley: University of California Press.

———. 1981. *General Economic History*. New Jersey: Transaction Books.

Williamson, Oliver. 1975. *Markets and Hierarchies: Analysis and Antitrust Implications*. New York: Free Press.

———. 1981. "The Economics of Organization: The Transaction Cost Approach." *American Journal of Sociology* 87:548–79.

Yang, Mayfair M. 1994. *Gifts, Favors, and Banquets: The Art of Social Relationships in China*. Ithaca, N.Y.: Cornell University Press.

THREE

The Korean Stratification System: Continuity and Change

HAGEN KOO

Koreans frequently give the impression to foreigners that they are very status-conscious people. Indeed, Koreans seem to pay extra attention to their clothes and seem to be very concerned about how they appear in public. They all seem anxious to send their children to prestigious schools, and they are willing to devote an incredible amount of time and money to give extra edge to their children. They pay much attention to others' family backgrounds, especially when it comes to selecting marriage partners for their children. Foreign visitors to Seoul these days are often impressed by the rows of fashionable boutique shops, high-class department stores and hotels, and fancy restaurants and bars, and by the many well-dressed and good-looking people, all exuding the image of an affluent, middle-class society. What a remarkable change for a country that was one of the world's poorest countries in the world only one generation ago!

One of the most remarkable changes resulting from rapid industrial development in South Korea over the past four decades is a profound change in Korea's stratification system, from a relatively simple and fluid stratification system to a fully class-divided structure with diminishing social mobility. A significant change in the stratification system is usually accompanied by a concomitant change in the individuals' desires, aspirations, anxieties, and social relations. It is this large-scale social change in Korea's status system that is at the base of the intense status competition and status-conscious behavior patterns that seem to strike many foreign visitors. How has the Korean stratification system changed over time, and what is the nature of the newly emerged class structure in contemporary South Korean society? What are the dominant social characteristics of the major social classes in today's South Korea, and what are their social implications for the individuals and for the society at large? These are the main questions this chapter tries to answer. Despite a large volume of writings on South Korea's economic development, there are few systematic accounts of the changing stratification system in Korea. This chapter is to fill this void by providing an overall analysis of the major changes in Korea's class system and the nature of the contemporary class structure in South Korea.

The Breakdown of the Old Status System

Class structure or stratification system in most societies enjoys extraordinary historical continuity and resilience. Some natural calamities or revolutionary upheavals may bring a rupture to an existing class system, but human history has shown repeatedly that the old system of social inequality is capable of reviving after the dust of the turmoil has settled down. The old ruling class, which seemed to have been defeated by a revolution, often found its way back to power and privilege in postrevolutionary societies, though in a different guise.

The Korean experience with modernization seems unusual in this regard. Korea began a painful process of modernization toward the end of the nineteenth century, going through a series of dramatic events: the forced opening to the Western world, Japanese colonial rule, the end of World War II and a sudden liberation from colonialism, political turmoil during the postliberation period, division of the nation into two hostile states, and the Korean War. One of the most important social consequences of these historical events was the almost complete destruction of the old class system and its ruling class.

Korea's old stratification system during the Chosŏn or Yi-dynasty period (1392–1910) was a mainly hereditary and legally ordered system of status based on Confucian philosophy. The status system was divided into four strata: *yangban* (nobility), *chung'in* (the middle stratum), *sang'in* or *yang'in* (commoners), and *ch'onmin* (the base or mean people). Most important in understanding the nature of this stratification system is to understand its dominant class, the *yangban*, the Korean aristocracy. *Yangban* was a stratum in which scholars, government officials, and landlords were fused together; often scholar-officials and landlords were one and the same persons. Unlike in capitalist societies, this traditional Korean upper class was not simply made up of families

of wealth. *Yangban* was a landed class, but it was not just the possession of land that conferred high status on its members but also
the demonstration of their scholarly and moral qualifications
through the state-run examination system. To maintain *yangban*
status, *yangban* families had to continuously produce heirs who
passed the exam; those who passed the exam were given official
posts and titles to land.

Yangban was a cultured class. In addition to proving their
scholarly and intellectual merits, *yangban* families had to follow an
elaborate code of ethics derived from Confucian principles and
exhibit morally respectable behavior patterns. They had to follow
closely all the elaborate rituals concerning ancestor worship, marriage, birthday celebrations, and funeral rites. They had to exhibit
generosity and care toward those in the lower orders of the status
hierarchy. Reciprocity was a critical social norm. *Yangban* had to
provide protection and moral leadership to the lower-class people
in return for their respect and submission.

The lower orders of Chosŏn society were primarily made up of
peasants who constituted the majority of the commoner class.
Also included in this category were artisans and merchants, who
were very small in numbers until the end of the nineteenth century. *Sang'in* were the main producers of the society and carriers
of heavy burdens of high rents (to their landlords), state taxes,
military duty, and other civic responsibilities.

Apart from this main lower social stratum, there were two
minor strata. The *ch'ungin* constituted a very small group that
existed between the dominant *yangban* class and the large commoner class. It was made up of government clerks and functionaries as well as those who performed the role of specialists
such as astronomers, accountants, translators or interpreters, medical doctors, or statute law clerks. Today, they would be regarded
as professionals and would command high status and income, but
in traditional Korea their status was far inferior and insecure and
drew a disproportionate number of *yangban* illegitimate sons, born
of *yangban* fathers and concubine mothers and thereby denied the
right to sit the imperial exam.

At the bottom of society were *ch'onmin*, the mean or base people, made up of house slaves, servants and maids, and those, such
as butchers, leather tanners, executioners, or shamans, engaged in
dirty and impure occupations. In some ways, they were comparable (though not identical) to the untouchables in India's caste system or *eta* or *burakumin* in the Japanese feudal system.

The status system in Chosŏn Korea was thus not a class system in which one's class position was determined by market relations and possession of market resources. Rather, it was a legally and morally sanctioned status system with clear and relatively impenetrable boundaries between the strata. As Deuchler describes, "Membership in all these status groups was ascribed by birth rather than acquired by achievement, and the law as well as social custom guarded against infringement of social boundaries" (Deuchler 1992: 13).

The yangban-dominated status system of Chosŏn Korea began to lose its integrity in the latter half of the nineteenth century. Historians observed several abnormal developments that under-mined the yangban hierarchy during this period, including a sharp increase in the number of families that claimed yangban status, an increased frequency of state-run exams and consequently an increased number of exam passers, a growing number of impover-ished yangban families, the illegal purchases of yangban titles by rich merchants, and an increasing number of forgeries of family lineage.[1] All these irregularities occurred as a symptom of the gen-eral decay of the Yi dynasty. The peasant economy declined con-tinuously while the landlords became more exploitative and parasitic and the state bureaucracy more corrupt. The inability of the ruling class to defend the nation against the onset of imperial intrusion at end of the nineteenth century also deprived the yang-ban class of its political and social legitimacy.

With Korea's annexation to imperial Japan in 1910, the yangban ceased to be a legally recognized class. So did other status categories such as chung'in, sang'in, and ch'ŏnmin. The colonial government, however, decided to keep the landlord system in order to secure Korean landlords' cooperation in controlling the Korean people. This meant that the material base of the Korean upper class did not change substantially, although many yangban families lost their fortunes gradually and along with it their social status in their communities as well. Social change during the colonial period, however, brought a significant modification to the Korean class system. The Japanese increased agricultural produc-tion in Korea with improved irrigation and seed varieties in order to increase their surplus extraction from Korean farming. They also promoted industrialization from the 1920s, primarily in

---

[1] See Lee 1984 and Eckert et al. 1990 for informative description of the yangban status system and its breakdown in the nineteenth century.

chemical and war-related industries, in order to assist Japan's military expansion into Manchuria. Rapid urbanization and a large volume of population movement also stimulated the rapid growth of commercial activities. These structural changes were bound to introduce significant changes into Korea's stratification system.

Especially important was the change in the position of Korea's traditional upper class. Although many *yangban* families were able to retain their landholdings, their political and social status diminished significantly. Politically, they were no longer the ruling class but were subordinate to the Japanese, and to maintain their privileges as landlords they had to collaborate with colonial rulers. Their power and status in the local communities were no longer based on their cultural and moral superiority but primarily on material possession and legal right supported by the hated colonial government. In the eyes of the masses, therefore, the old upper class degenerated into exploiters, parasites, and hated collaborators with the colonialists. Peasant protests against landlords increased continuously during the colonial period and came to shape postcolonial political dynamics.[2]

The landlord system, however, survived until the end of the colonial rule. What brought it down completely was the land reform during the postliberation period. It occurred first in North Korea, immediately after the Korean Communist Party took power in 1946. In the south, a more moderate land reform was carried out between 1948 and 1950. The landlord class and its representatives in the South Korean congress had tried to block it, but the peasants' demand for land reform was so strong and intense that the American military government and the South Korean political leaders realized that it would be impossible to maintain social and political stability without solving the explosive land problems. Although the government had adopted a land reform bill in 1948, the landlord class had delayed the full implementation of the reform until the outbreak of the Korean War in 1950. Much of the land was redistributed in 1950 under the direction of the invading North Korean army. In any event, this land reform had a far-reaching consequence in creating an egalitarian agrarian structure in South Korea.[3] After the land reform, the government imposed a

---

[2] See Shin 1996 for more information on peasant protests during and after Japanese colonialism.

[3] Many Korean scholars argue that this land reform was not particularly successful, certainly not as successful as the reforms implemented in North Korea or Japan. In South Korea, land was not freely distributed to poor peasants but sold to them, though at a bargain price in installments, and the long delay in implement-

limit on paddy holding of three *chŏngbo* (equivalent to about one hectare). This land reform shrank the landlord class considerably, and Korea became a society of small, independent farmers, mostly poor yet fairly equal in their landholdings as well as in their economic and social statuses.

The landlord system could have reemerged in South Korea after the initial shock was over, as it has done in many societies. The war that broke out in 1950, however, denied such a historic possibility. The Korean War had a more leveling effect on Korean society than any other historical event had. It destroyed almost all industrial and commercial properties, and it turned the government bonds that previous landlord families had received as a nominal price for their dispossessed land into junk paper. Many families that had been proud of their *yangban* lineage became impoverished, while others from humble social origins were able to amass a fortune in the war economy. Therefore, one decade from the end of the colonialism through the post–Korean War period was an era of great social mobility and social leveling in both Koreas. By the end of the 1950s, South Korean society had become a highly egalitarian society with a fluid and highly mobile social structure and with no upper class that could claim inborn superiority and privilege. It is this unique historical experience, painful as it was to those affected, that created a society with an exceptional degree of egalitarian ethic and intense desire for social mobility.

Transformation of the Class Structure

The class structure we see in South Korea today is the making of a relatively short time. By and large, it is the product of rapid industrialization over the past four decades. Before the export-oriented industrialization that began in the early 1960s, South Korea was predominantly an agrarian society with the majority of its population living and working on the farm and its industrial structure relatively simple and underdeveloped. Rapid industrialization, however, has brought about a radical change in the structure of its economy and in the ways people work and make a living.

---

ing the land reform gave time for many landlords to sell their land or hide it under false names. For a representative work in such a critical interpretation of the South Korean land reform, see Kang 1988.

First of all, industrial development has entailed a dramatic change in the sectoral distribution of its labor force. As shown in table 3.1, four-fifths of the total Korean labor force in the late 1950s was composed of agricultural workers, most of whom were small owner-cultivators. By 1980, the agricultural labor force was reduced to one-third of the total labor force, and by the late 1990s, only one out of ten working people remained on the farm. Thus, after only three decades of industrial advance, a nation of small cultivators became a nation of urban wage workers. The magnitude of industrial transformation that South Korea has undergone during the past three decades of export-oriented industrialization is equivalent to what took a century in early European industrialization.[4]

This large-scale sectoral mobility from agriculture to secondary and tertiary industries necessarily involved a significant change in the occupational structure. More and more people who had worked as independent producers became wage and salaried workers. The occupational structure accordingly became more industrial and urban with a more differentiated status hierarchy. Let us first examine the major trends in the occupational structure and then investigate the nature of the new class structure.

The most noticeable change in South Korea's occupational structure, as mentioned above, was a precipitous decline of agricultural workers. Statistics on occupational distribution, presented in table 3.2, indicate that the proportion of farmers declined continuously from 58.4 percent in 1965 to 34 percent in 1980, and to 10.5 percent in 1997. This change resulted from the massive exodus of farmers and their sons and daughters from rural areas. During the first three decades of economic growth, from 1957 to 1986, an estimated 14 million people migrated from rural to urban areas. The majority of them found jobs in the rapidly growing industrial sector as factory workers. The category of wage workers engaged in production, transportation, and construction increased sharply from 16.3 percent in 1965 to 33.6 percent in 1992. The number of factory workers alone increased from 1.3 million in 1970 to 4.8 million in 1990 (D. C. Kim 1995: 151). Thus, one of the most significant changes associated with export-oriented industrialization in South Korea was the rapid formation of the industrial working class.

---

[4] For a more detailed analysis of the growth of the Korean industrial workers, see Koo 1990.

Table 3.1. Sectoral distribution of the labor force by industry, 1958–1995 (in percentage)

Industry	1958	1965	1970	1975	1930	1985	1990	1995
Agriculture and fishery	81.6	58.6	50.4	45.9	34.0	24.9	17.9	12.5
Manufacturing and mining	4.6	10.3	14.3	19.1	22.6	24.5	27.6	23.6
Commerce and services	13.8	31.0	35.2	35.0	43.4	50.6	54.5	64.0
Total (in thousands)	6,262	8,206	9,745	11,830	13,706	14,935	18,085	20,377

Source: Economic Planning Board, *Annual Report on the Economically Active Population, 1972 and 1985;* National Statistical Office, *Social Indicators in Korea, 1998.*

Table 3.2. Occupational distribution of employed persons, 1965–1997 (in percentage)

Year	Professional, managerial	Clerical, white-collar	Sales workers	Service workers	Agricultural, fisheries, etc.	Production, transportation operatives
1965	2.9	4.1	12.0	6.4	58.4	16.3
1970	4.8	6.0	12.4	6.4	50.2	20.2
1975	3.6	6.4	13.0	7.1	45.8	24.1
1980	5.3	9.3	14.5	7.9	34.0	29.0
1985	7.3	11.5	15.5	10.8	24.6	30.3
1990	8.7	13.0	14.5	11.1	18.1	34.6
1992	10.0	14.4	14.9	11.5	15.6	33.6

Year	Top managerial	Professional, semi-professional	Clerical workers	Service and sales workers	Agricultural, fisheries	Craft, operators	Simple laborers
1993	2.7	12.3	12.5	20.9	13.2	27.3	11.0
1997	2.5	15.1	12.2	23.1	10.5	25.3	11.2

Source: Korean Statistical Association, *Social Indicators in Korea, 1990, 1995, 1998.*

No less significant was change in the middle strata of the urban occupational structure. In particular, the increase of professional, technical, and white-collar workers has been remarkable. In 1965, the category of professional, managerial, and technical workers comprised only 2.9 percent of the total workforce, but in 1992 it grew to 10 percent. White-collar workers more than tripled from 4.1 percent to 14.4 percent during the same period. All together, what might be broadly categorized as the "new middle class" occupations increased from 7 percent to 24.4 percent between the mid-1960s and the early 1990s. According to the new occupational classification system adopted in 1993, the proportion of this new middle-class category reached about 30 percent in 1997.[5]

Table 3.2 also shows a significant increase of service workers and a moderate increase of sales workers. Put together, the category of sales and service workers increased from 18.4 percent to 26.4 percent between 1965 and 1992. This category of sales and service workers represents a highly heterogeneous category in terms of social class position: some of these middle-class workers may represent what sociologists call the "old middle class" or the petty bourgeoisie; another part belongs to the "urban marginal class" or the urban poor. The former represents small-property owners, such as shopkeepers, wholesalers, restaurant or bar owners, and the like, while the latter includes diverse category of sales and service workers whose jobs are basically unstable, low income, and low prestige (such as street vendors, hawkers, shoe shiners, and domestic maids).

It must be noted that occupational structure is not synonymous with class structure: people in the same occupation may belong to different social classes.[6] The census category of professional and managerial occupations, for example, includes those who are part of the new middle class and those who belong to the capitalist class (such as top corporate executives). Similarly, the production and transportation category includes those who are members of

---

[5] The census category of professional, technical, and managerial workers includes business owners and top-level political elite, who are not part of the new middle class but belong to the old middle class or the capitalist class. But their numbers are relatively small and would not seriously affect our gross estimation of class structural change in South Korea.

[6] Korean sociologists have developed several different models of the South Korean class structure. For the most convenient review of this literature, see Hong and Koo 1993: 196–203.

the working class and those who can be regarded as the petty bourgeoisie, depending on their employment or self-employment status. In the absence of all the necessary information, however, occupational distribution serves as the best proxy measure of the class structure in a given society.

What is clear from the above analysis is that the South Korean class structure has quickly transformed from a relatively simple, preindustrial system of stratification to a modern industrial class system, resembling those in the advanced industrial societies. As in the latter, the Korean class structure is roughly divided into three social class categories: (1) the capitalist class, composed of large-business owners and top corporate executives; (2) the middle classes, which are subdivided into two groups, the "new middle class," composed of professional, technical, and white-collar workers, and the "old middle class," composed of small-business people; and (3) the working class, composed of industrial wage workers. Other strata, notably farmers and the urban poor, exist alongside this class hierarchy, but the dominant class relations and class dynamics in Korean society today are more or less determined by the relationships among these three principal classes of capitalist society.

This is not to say that the contemporary South Korean class structure has become almost identical with the structures in other advanced industrial societies. Even though the formal structure of South Korean class relations came to resemble the structures in the latter, the substance of the Korean class system—that is, the social character of each class and the nature of relationships among these classes—differs significantly from those of other advanced industrial societies because class structure and class relations in a given society are the products of history, shaped by the interplay of economy, politics, and culture in the course of the historical evolution of that society. In what follows, I describe some important features of the newly emerged social classes in South Korea and discuss their roles in shaping the social and political dynamics in Korean society.

The Capitalist Class

It is an interesting question to ask whether there is an established upper class in contemporary South Korean society. The upper class in a sociological sense refers to a class of individuals or families who possess large wealth and social resources and who also enjoy social distinction from the rest of the society in terms of their lifestyle, subculture, and social exclusiveness. The upper class usually means what Max Weber calls a status group with a clear group identity and cohesiveness among its members and a relatively clear boundary separating this privileged class from lower orders of society. In this sense, it can be argued that an upper class does not exist in today's Korean society. The class system in contemporary South Korea represents a transitional system in which the old system had been abolished but a new system has yet to crystallize in its place.

There are, however, several groups in contemporary South Korea that strive to appropriate the old prestige and social distinction enjoyed by the *yangban* class, including the large capitalists, the political elite, the intellectuals, and the rising professional and managerial class. Of them, the most serious contender and the most likely heir of the old upper class is the large capitalist class made of *chaebol* families. *Chaebol* refers to some thirty to fifty conglomerate firms owned and controlled by families. Although a few *chaebol*s had existed in the 1950s, they began to emerge as powerful economic actors only after the initiation of export-oriented industrialization in the 1960s and particularly after the Korean economy marched into the phase of heavy and chemical industrialization in the mid-1970s.[7] The Park Chung Hee government's development strategy was to rely on the large, proven players in the economy in order to increase exports and achieve accelerated economic growth. *Chaebol* groups with their business experiences and organizational resources met Park's criteria, although Park had initially attempted to prosecute most *chaebol* owners for engaging in "illicit capital accumulation" before his coming to power.

After achieving an economic takeoff by promoting labor-intensive, export-oriented industrialization in the 1960s, South

---

[7] The history of the capitalist class in Korea is very short, tracing back to the colonial period, when a few indigenous capitalists emerged by venturing into textile and food-processing industries. A few Korean capitalists who emerged during this period were from the landlord class and were well-educated men. In the 1950s, after the end of the Korean War, a new crop of capitalists appeared. They had obtained the Japanese-owned properties and business facilities at bargain prices and also had privileged access to American aid materials. Needless to say, they were closely connected to the political elites who were in charge of distributing these means of easy capital accumulation. In this sense, they were "political capitalists," produced not by their innovative entrepreneurship but by political power in the transitional economy.

Korea moved into a stage of industrial upgrading in the 1970s by aggressively promoting such industries as steel, petrochemical, shipbuilding, machinery, and electronics. To facilitate this heavy and chemical industrialization plan, the state allocated the chunk of subsidized policy loans and government-regulated foreign capital to *chaebol* firms that participated in state-designated strategic industries. The government also created the general trading companies, through which large *chaebol* groups were able to establish a monopolistic position in export and import businesses. The ten largest *chaebol* groups grew to become world-class business organizations during this period.

Notwithstanding its impressive growth in economic power, the Korean capitalist class has been, at least until recently, unable to obtain a commensurate level of political power. It has remained as a sort of dependent bourgeoisie, dependent upon the state for its primary sources of capital accumulation and for ensuring tight labor control. However, as their economic power grew continuously, *chaebol* became increasingly dissatisfied with their lack of political power. After the democratic transition in 1987, Korean capitalists became increasing vocal in the policy arena and openly opposed the huge political donations they had been forced to make each year. In 1987, Chung Ju Young, the founder of the Hyundai conglomerate, made history with his bold bid for the presidency. He created a new political party and ran for president. His adventure predictably failed and invited retaliation from the newly elected Kim Young Sam government. Nonetheless, this incident suggests an important change in the relationships between capital and political power; increasingly, capitalists do not need or welcome state interference in the economy and do not want to remain subordinate to political power.

The most interesting anomaly about the Korean capitalist class is that it enjoys little ideological and moral dominance over society, notwithstanding its enormous economic power and increasing political influence. The majority of Korean people seem to hold a very negative attitude toward the *chaebol* groups. The prevailing opinion about *chaebol* is that they have accumulated their wealth not from their entrepreneurial skills or hard work but from government's excessive subsidies to them. The majority of Korean people seem to believe that *chaebol* owners enjoy undeserving wealth and that they use it largely for private vanity rather than for the public good.

In short, the Korean capitalist class has failed to establish hegemony over society. Hegemony is an important concept that Italian Marxist Antonio Gramsci introduced into social science thinking. It refers to the fact that the dominant class enjoys not only economic and political power but also ideological and moral dominance over the subordinate classes. It also means that the ideologies and the worldview of the dominant class have been widely accepted by the subordinate classes. There are several reasons for this lack of hegemony on the part of the Korean capitalist class.[8] One is the way in which large capitalists in Korea have accumulated their wealth. The majority of Koreans seem to believe that *chaebol* were able to amass so much wealth in such a short time mainly because of their intimate connections with political leaders and the excessive favoritism they received from policy makers. They also believe that *chaebol* were able to make quick fortunes not simply from their industrial investments but from speculative real-estate investments. The general public's critical attitude toward the *chaebol* class was demonstrated clearly in one survey of middle-class citizens conducted in 1987 (Han, Kwon, and Hong 1987). More than two-thirds of the respondents to this survey endorsed the statement "The government must discontinue its policies of favoritism toward big business." More surprisingly, an absolute majority (88 percent) of the respondents agreed with the statement "Those who possess a large amount of property must return their property to society." Given that private property is a sacred institution of the capitalist society, this is indeed a startling response from the middle classes, but it demonstrates the depth of their dissatisfaction with the ways in which the rich amassed wealth in Korea in the past.

Another source of public disaffection with the *chaebol* was the very poor record of big-business owners in sharing their wealth with workers and with society at large. While *chaebol* businesses have grown at an impressive rate, the working conditions and wage levels of their workers have improved very slowly. Until quite recently, the state had suppressed workers' collective efforts to improve their conditions, and capitalists have employed every means to block union formation in their enterprises. *Chaebol* families and the rich in general were also criticized for their conspicuous consumption, which often involved such behavior as building

---

[8] See Eckert 1993 for an interesting historical analysis of the lack of hegemony among the Korean capitalist class.

extravagant houses, driving expensive imported cars, owning resort villas, going on shopping sprees in foreign countries, and the like.

Still another factor that hindered the *chaebol* class in establishing broad social respect is their relatively humble social origins. Except for a few, most of the founders of the top thirty or so *chaebol* groups came from undistinguished family backgrounds. Although some Western observers like to see *chaebol* families as a direct heir to the traditional *yangban* class,[9] the relationship between the two is more tenuous than that.

One empirical study, for example, shows that as of 1985 about 38 percent of the top fifty *chaebol* owners came from poor farm families or small-merchant families and only one-quarter originated from the landlord or big-business families (Suh 1991; Jones and Sakong 1980: 210–257). Thus, in the eyes of common people, *chaebol* are not a special group of people in terms of their social origins. In the 1970s and 1980s, many Koreans seemed to have felt that "they and I are the same folks," except that they were luckier or shrewder.

A noticeable change began to occur, however, in the class character of *chaebol* in the latter part of the 1980s. Gradually, both economic and social conditions led the top thirty *chaebol* to consolidate themselves as South Korea's upper class. Family fortunes aged, and ownership was slowly passed down to the second generation. As the South Korean economy became more liberalized under growing international pressure, the state's role in the economy began to wane, and business became less dependent on state support. From the 1980s, *chaebol* groups began to make a conscientious effort to translate their economic power into political and social power as well as to create social distinction between their group and the larger middle classes.

First to notice is that *chaebol* became better organized through such employers' organizations as the Federation of Korean Industries, the Korea Employers' Federation, and the Chamber of Commerce and became more vocal and effective in influencing state policy making. Some *chaebol* family members decided to enter politics themselves, as in the failed case of Chung Ju Young. To influence public opinion, *chaebol* groups increased their control

---

[9] Such an argument is more likely to be found in journalistic accounts, but some scholars also suggest status inheritance or status continuity from *yangban* to today's upper class. See, for example, Lett 1998.

over mass media. In 1989, eleven daily newspapers and twenty-five popular magazines were owned by some of the top thirty *chaebol* families (Hong 1993). Also, the large-capitalist class has greatly increased its involvement in educational institutions; in 1989 as many as thirty-three colleges and ten research *chaebol* groups owned institutes. The top ten *chaebol* groups also donated large amounts of money to several academic and cultural foundations. All these organizational activities can be interpreted as a collective attempt at hegemony building in Korean society. In the new millennium the Korean capitalist class could indeed emerge as a hegemonic class and exert powerful influence on society's major institutions and its value system as well as the state's economic policies.

Along with such a hegemony-building project, the large-capitalist class in Korea sought to establish its social distinction in the status hierarchy in Korea. Members of this class adopted lifestyles afforded by their wealth, and they also sought to marry their children to children of political elites or other *chaebol* families. The marriage pattern among *chaebol* families in the 1980s and 1990s became increasingly endogamous, favoring marriages among members of the same class position. Marriages between *chaebol* families and political families have become particularly noticeable since the mid-1980s (Kong 1989; Suh 1991; Hong 1993). If this trend continues, it is feasible to see the making of a new Korean upper class in the near future, one possessing its distinct lifestyle, family pattern, and value orientation.

The Middle Classes

One of the most significant social consequences of rapid economic development in South Korea is the rise of the middle classes. As we have seen earlier, industrialization in South Korea was accompanied by the rapid growth in the numbers of professional, managerial, and white-collar workers. At the same time, we have also noted that the stratum of small-business owners has also expanded. In short, both the new middle class and the old middle class have grown significantly during the export-oriented industrialization of the past four decades.

Apart from these actual changes in South Korea's occupational structure, another interesting phenomenon is that a large proportion of Koreans tend to see themselves as belonging to the middle classes in Korean. Before the arrival of the financial crisis in 1997, as many as 60 to 70 percent of the respondents to several surveys identified themselves as belonging to the middle strata (*chungsanch'ung*). Surveys conducted one or two years after the economic crisis revealed that the proportion of middle-class identifiers dropped to the 40 percent level, but such a drop may prove to be temporary.[10] Sociologists recognize the difference between objective class position and subjective class identification. What these data indicate is that Korean people's subjective identification with the middle class has grown even faster than their objective class position. Such a discrepancy between objective and subjective class standings is not unique to Korea, but the gap certainly seems to be large.

The middle class is a notoriously elusive and ambiguous category in most societies. In South Korea, it is particularly so because of the ambiguity of the emerging class system and because of people's strong desire for upward social mobility. Now that the old bases of class distinction have disappeared, Koreans are relatively free to identify themselves with any social class as long as they possess adequate material resources and can display some of the accoutrements appropriate to the class with which they want to identify. The term referring to the middle class in South Korea, *chungsanch'ŭng*, implies people with middle-level property ownership, or those who are not rich but not poor. One survey defined *chungsanch'ŭng* as "those who are not necessarily rich but economically comfortable enough to send their children to college, maintain social relationships with others at a socially respectable standard, be able to take family summer vacation trips, and enjoy a certain level of cultural life" (Han, Kwon, and Hong 1987). In other words, the middle class in popular conception is defined basically in terms of consumption style and economic resources that support it. As Hart (1993: 45) argues, "Material possession and the need for consumption have created and defined Korea's middle class, rendering it a group that would not exist and cannot identify itself vis-à-vis other groups without the products of mass production."

The significance of the middle class is that it serves as a major frame of reference in comparing one's social standing and social achievement and as a major destination of upward social mobility. Becoming part of the middle class is an important criterion of

---

[10] For information about the effect of the economic crisis on middle-class identification among Koreans, see Kim 1999: 245–265; Shin and Chang 2000.

social success for most ordinary people. In the self-assessment of one's status, Koreans seem to compare themselves not only with others, but also with their own situations in the past. It is this retrospective comparison that seems to boost middle-class identification significantly. Since the material conditions of the majority of Koreans have improved so remarkably, especially in consumption areas, there is ample room to consider themselves as having climbed to middle-class status. What used to be the status symbols of the middle class in the 1960s—such as the ownership of refrigerators, black-and-white television sets, telephones, or stereo sets—are long gone as middle-class symbols; the majority of working-class and farm families now own these things. In the 1980s, the new middle-class status symbols included automobiles, video systems, health club memberships, and a certain leisure style such as taking summer family vacations, going on ski trips, playing golf, having family dinners at nice restaurants, and the like. The rise of the middle class in South Korea has been intimately connected to this remarkable improvement in living standards and consumption style. Now that the outward symbols of middleness have spread widely, it is easy for many people to identify themselves with this new reference group. Included in this category are not only white-collar workers and shopkeepers but also a number of petty traders, taxi drivers, and factory workers.

Having appeared in a relatively short time in the context of fluid social conditions, today's Korean middle class represents basically the first-generation middle class. As such, its social identity and its differentiation from other classes remain ambiguous.[11] There are no clear boundaries separating the middle classes from the lower or upper classes, and there are no well-agreed-upon criteria to draw those boundaries. It is this insecurity of identity or ambiguity of class boundaries that prompts people into conspicuous consumption. Continuous efforts to acquire and display what are implicitly understood as middle-class status symbols seems to be an essential requirement to consider oneself, and to be considered by others, as belonging to the middle class in Korea. Conspicuous consumption is, therefore, a sine qua non of the Korean middle class.

---

[11] In this regard, the Korean middle class shares the essential similarities with the new middle classes in other East Asian newly industrialized countries. See Hsiao 1999.

Two major sources influence the Korean middle-class lifestyle. A primary source is the lifestyles and consumption patterns of the Western middle classes, especially those of the American middle class. As far as material aspects are concerned, the Korean middle-class lifestyle is but an imitation of the American middle-class lifestyle that has been disseminated through movies, television, magazines, or other media. In recent years, frequent visits by middle-class Koreans to the United States or Europe further facilitated the appropriation of the lifestyle of their more affluent counterparts. Imitating the lifestyle of the Western middle class—dining out with the family, often at a Western-style hotel, enjoying gourmet coffees, hosting outdoor barbecue parties, going on summer vacation trips to beaches or mountains, or taking foreign trips—is an essential part of and qualification for membership in the Korean middle class. The Western middle class is thus a primary reference group for the Korean middle class, with which they compare themselves and whose lifestyles they continue to emulate.

More recently, however, the Korean middle class has gradually turned inward to search for indigenous symbols of status distinction. From the 1980s, as the living standards of the majority of the population improved significantly and as middle-class status symbols became widely adopted across social strata, the upper strata of the Korean middle class began to search for other forms of status distinction to separate themselves from the rest of the middle classes. As prominent French sociologist Pierre Bourdieu (1984) argues, social and cultural distinction is the essential source of class differentiation in all societies. In their search for status distinction, Korea's upper middle class have realized that Western material culture is insufficient to assert their status above others because it is relatively easy for other classes to imitate that lifestyle. After all, it is hard to find any Seoulite today who does not wear brand-name clothes or shoes, be they genuine or fake, and very few who do not carry cellular phones.

In this shifting context of status competition, the once forgotten *yangban* culture reappeared as a new source of cultural distinction. But old culture never revives in purity; it usually reappears in a modified form tailored to the needs and circumstances of the present. Thus, only certain aspects of *yangban* culture have been reappropriated, such as a new attention to family lineage, landscaping ancestors' graveyards, having a traditional-style wedding, decorating rooms with traditional antique furniture, enjoying traditional Korean wine or tea, teaching traditional musical instruments to children, and so forth. As American anthropologist Denise Lett (1998: 212) argues, "Essentially, the growth of South Korea's middle class can be characterized as the *yangban*ization of Korean society in the modern context." I think that she overstresses the continuity between traditional *yangban* culture and contemporary middle-class culture, but she is right in pointing out a new tendency among upper-middle-class families—though not among all middle-class families—to usurp *yangban* culture in an effort to assert their high status.

So far my discussion has focused on the social meaning of the middle class and its lifestyles. But there are other important questions to be asked about the Korean middle class. What social and political attitudes do the middle class hold, and what role do those attitudes play in the political development in Korean society? The important role of the middle classes in the social and political development in a given society has been widely recognized by social scientists. Unfortunately, space limitation does not allow me to examine this issue adequately in this chapter. So let me just summarize what I have presented in my previous work (Koo 1991).

Because of its structural position between the dominant and subordinate classes, between haves and have-nots, and between oppressors and the oppressed, the middle class in any society is an inherently ambiguous, unstable, and internally contradictory class. There are two opposing theoretical views on the political role of the middle class. One is that the middle class is a democratic force. In this view, the members of the middle class are strongly committed to democratic values of freedom of expression, social participation, openness and rationality of institutional practices, and merit-based allocation of positions and social rewards. In times of political transition, this view predicts, the middle classes are assumed to act as a neutral force and help to prevent any radical drift to either revolutionary or reactionary social change and thereby help stabilize the political system along a parliamentary democratic system. The opposite view holds that the middle class is basically a conservative force because its members are beneficiaries of the present social order. They are assumed to fear any major social disruptions that might jeopardize their relatively privileged position. It is acknowledged that they tend to have a progressive view toward social change and often desire democratic change in the political system, but what they really desire tends to be moderate reform within the existing system rather than any radical change in the political and economic system. When an opportunity for radical change looms large, the middle class is believed to retreat from its progressive ideal and turn itself into a force defending the status quo.

To a great extent, this duality or contradictory nature of the middle class also holds true with the Korean middle classes. By and large, the Korean middle classes, especially the new middle class, represent a relatively progressive social force. Many social surveys conducted in the 1980s demonstrated that the Korean middle class held a strong democratic value orientation: they were critical of authoritarian rule, dissatisfied with the skewed distribution of income, especially with the enormous capital concentration in the hands of a few *chaebol*, had strong sympathy toward factory workers and poor farmers who worked hardest but received the least benefits from Korea's economic development, and showed strong support for the students who fought tenaciously for democracy. In 1987, a large number of white-collar workers joined the students' street demonstrations and took part in forcing the Chun Doo Hwan regime to surrender to the "people's power." The Korean new middle class had also shown their democratic aspiration in several occasions prior to 1987, as in the student-led April Revolution of 1960 and in the so-called Seoul Spring in 1980 after the assassination of Park Chung Hee, as well as in several general elections held during the 1970s and 1980s.

As soon as the political transition to democracy began to unfold, however, the dominant political attitude of the Korean middle class shifted and became increasingly conservative and stability oriented. Middle-class support for labor strikes and continuous student demonstrations dropped quickly; instead, the dominant mood favored moderate reform rather than any substantive and radical changes in the economic and political system. What the mainstream middle class seemed to have wanted was a "procedural" rather than a "substantive" democracy. The middle class gave only lukewarm support to workers' demands for expanded labor rights and became critical of the escalating labor strikes. Such a shift in middle-class attitudes toward labor unrest had a dampening effect on the labor movement in the 1990s.

In short, the role of the middle class in South Korea has been, and will be, complex and ambivalent. There is little question that this class is leading changes in values, social attitudes, and lifestyles. It provides the most active participants for many social movements, such as the environment movement, consumer movement, feminist movement, and movement for economic justice. And it will be the mainstay of the newly evolving civil society in South Korea. Exactly in what direction and with what ideologies the newly emerged middle-class will lead Korean society, however, is uncertain and will be determined in the continuing flux of economic, social, and political changes in this society.

The Working Class

No less significant than the rise of the middle class in South Korea was the rapid expansion of the working class. As previously discussed, the pace with which the industrial working class has come into being in South Korea is almost unprecedented in the world. At the inception of export-oriented industrialization in the early 1960s, there were a little more than 2 million wage workers in South Korea, but by the mid-1980s, the number had quadrupled to 8 million. Wage workers constituted 31.5 percent of the total labor force in 1963 but increased to 54.2 percent in 1985. The growth of production workers in manufacturing increased even faster, from only 417,000 to 3.1 million during the same period. The majority of semiskilled workers in export manufacturing were recruited from rural areas, and a large proportion of them (40–50 percent over the years) were female workers.

As is well known, Korean factory workers endured the world's longest workweek and suffered from extremely poor working conditions and despotic managerial control. In pursuing an export-oriented industrialization strategy, South Korea's main source of comparative advantage in the world market had been its disciplined, hardworking, and cheap labor force. To maintain this vital condition of growth, the government had maintained tight control over labor activities. Severe restriction on union organization and collective action had been applied by laws and presidential emergency decrees and by repressive police actions. Wage differentials between white-collar and blue-collar workers in Korea were much larger than in Japan and Taiwan. And neither companies nor the state provided adequate compensation for job-related injuries, layoffs, or medical expenses. In short, Korean workers had been one of the most severely exploited and oppressed industrial forces in the world.[12]

---

[12] For good references on the conditions of the Korean working class in the 1970s and the 1980s, see Ogle 1990; Bello and Rosenfeld 1990; Kim 1997; Koo 2001.

In addition to their poor material condition, Korea's industrial workers suffered as much in status. Societal attitude toward factory workers was contemptuous, scornful, and highly hypocritical; while praising them as "industrial warriors" who were essential in producing South Korea's economic miracle, middle-class people generally saw them as unworthy of social respect. This disdainful social attitude toward factory workers was expressed in the pejorative labels, *kongsuni* and *kongdoli*, popularly used to describe factory workers in the 1960s through the early 1980s. *Kongsuni* refers to female factory workers, while *kongdoli* refers to male workers. Both terms insinuate the image of housemaids or servants, only working in the factory setting. Workers' diaries and personal essays written in the 1970s amply demonstrate how much psychological pain many young workers suffered; the most affected were the young female workers who entered the factory with high aspirations for social mobility. The workers were deeply resentful toward the managers, the white-collar workers, and the whole society that treated them with contempt.

How did the first generation of Korean factory workers react to their dreadful situation? A well-known social scientist, Albert Hirschman, suggests that there are three alternatives available to a subordinate group: loyalty, exit, and voice (Hirschman 1971). His conceptualization is useful in considering Korean workers' reactions during the 1970s and 1980s. The first option was to submit oneself completely to managerial authority and work diligently as a loyal worker. Not many Korean workers seemed to have done that. They worked hard and were submissive to managerial authority, but they were far from being loyal or sincerely committed to company goals. The second alternative was to quit the job and search for better opportunities elsewhere. This was the most practical choice among disgruntled Korean workers. That is why the job turnover rate in the Korean manufacturing industry was extremely high, substantially higher than in other East Asian industrialized countries. But exiting industrial employment completely was not a real option for most workers because there were few good jobs they could realistically obtain outside the industry; they just moved from one factory job to another, looking for a slight improvement in wages.

The realization of the structural limit to which they could improve their situation eventually led many workers to resort to the third alternative, that is, to making their voices heard in defense of their collective interest. It began in the 1970s in the form of grassroots union movement. A growing number of workers came to realize that individual struggle for upward mobility was futile and that they could improve their situation only by a collective struggle. Union consciousness began to creep into the minds of many workers. Despite state and company oppression, many courageous workers participated in the union movement from the latter part of the 1970s. Workers' struggles for decent wages and "humane treatment" at work intensified in the 1980s. Gradually, working-class solidarity and identity spread across industrial areas. Their "exit" orientation gradually gave way to voice, and to stronger and positive group identity. This change in workers' class identity and consciousness was accompanied by workers' effort to create their own social and cultural milieu. Unlike their counterparts in early European or American industrialization, Korean workers were all literate and educationally motivated, and they produced a large volume of personal essays, diaries, poems, play scripts, and novels. Unions and labor groups published workers' newspapers and magazines, and they organized many cultural activities to promote class solidarity and cultural identity among workers. All these significant developments occurred under the harsh authoritarian rule of Chun Doo Hwan, openly defying his repression.

Resistance to the Chun regime—by students, workers, and citizens—climaxed in June 1987 when Chun attempted to renege on his promise of direct presidential election and to turn over his power to his military academy classmate, Roh Tae Woo. Huge demonstrations by students, joined by many white-collar workers and other citizens, succeeded in forcing Chun to accept the popular demand for a direct presidential election. Immediately after the victory of "people's power," an unprecedented level of labor conflicts occurred across the country. More than three thousand labor disputes occurred during the three-month period between July and September 1987, and about one thousand new unions were formed during this period. The "great worker struggle" was thus a watershed in the development of the Korean working-class movement.

Much has changed since this watershed event. Workers have become better organized; not only has the number of unions increased, but unions have become more representative of workers' interest, unlike many "company unions" in the old days. The center of union activism has shifted from women-dominated light-manufacturing industry to male-dominant heavy and chemical industries. Militant unions were formed at several large *chaebol* firms, where no union had been allowed before 1987. Furthermore, workers successfully agitated for hefty wage increases between 1987 and 1989. The balance of power between labor and management on the shop floor also shifted noticeably, and management no longer felt free to exercise patriarchal and despotic control over workers. As a consequence of all these changes, workers' self-identity as "workers" (*nodongja*) became more firmly established in the minds of workers, and they were no longer ashamed of being factory workers. Thus, by the early 1990s, Korea's working class had become a socially identifiable group with a relatively strong class identity and consciousness and with a relatively strong sense of solidarity among workers (Koo 2001).

Conclusion

Korea entered the postcolonial era with an almost complete breakdown of the old class system. The extensive land reform and the impact of the Korean War created a society with a pervasive egalitarian ethic and strong aspiration for upward social mobility. The stratification system that resulted from these tremendous social changes was a highly flexible, ambiguous, and fluid system. In many ways, it is this relatively open and mobile stratification system that has provided a crucial structural base for the remarkable economic development in South Korea by removing the landlord class, the most serious obstacle to industrialization in any society, and by making Koreans highly flexible and adaptive to social change. The absence of rigid class boundaries and obstacles for social mobility encouraged Koreans to aspire to upward mobility, to work hard, and to be alert for new opportunities in a rapidly changing economy.

Four decades of industrial development, however, gradually transformed the South Korean stratification system from a relatively open and flexible system to an increasingly structured and rigid system. New classes have emerged, and class boundaries have become sharper and less permeable. The new class structure resembles that found in other advanced industrial societies: the capitalists, the middle classes, and the working class. South Korea's social classes have been described as involving a great deal of ambiguity in their social identities and class dispositions. The dominant change observed is a continuous process of class crystallization in terms of class boundaries, internal solidarity, and distinct class culture and lifestyles. Class formation has occurred in South Korea much faster than in other newly industrialized countries in East Asia. At the dawn of a new millennium, I would argue, South Korea has become a class society, in which class represents a dominant principle of social organization and in which dynamic relations among social classes have a determining effect on the contour of politics, civil society, and culture.

References

Bello, Walden, and Stephanie Rosenfeld. 1990. *Dragons in Distress: Asia's Miracle Economies in Crisis.* San Francisco: Institute for Food and Development Policy.

Bourdieu, Pierre. 1984. *Distinction: A Social Critique of the Judgement of Taste.* Cambridge: Harvard University Press.

Deuchler, Martina. 1992. *The Confucian Transformation of Korea: A Study of Society and Ideology.* Cambridge: Council on East Asian Studies, Harvard University.

Eckert, Carter. 1993. "The South Korean Bourgeoisie: A Class in Search of Hegemony." In Hagen Koo, ed., *State and Society in Contemporary Korea*, 95–130. Ithaca, N.Y.: Cornell University Press.

_____. Lee Ki-baik, Lew Young Ick, Michael Robinson, and Edward W. Wagner. 1990. *Korea Old and New: A History.* Seoul: Ilchokak.

Han, Wan-sang; Kwon Tae-Hwan; and Hong Doo-Seung. 1987. *Han'guk ŭi chungsanch'ŭng: Chŏnhwanki ŭi han'guk sahoe chosa charyochip II* (Korean middle classes: Research data book 2 on Korean society in transition). Seoul: Hankook Ilbo, 1987.

Hart, Dennis. 1993. "Class Formation and Industrialization of Culture: The Case of South Korea's Emerging Middle Class." *Korea Journal* 33:42–57.

Hirschman, Albert O. 1971. *Exit, Voice, and Loyalty.* Cambridge: Harvard University Press.

Hong, Doo-Seung, and Hagen Koo. 1993. *Sahoe kyech'ŭng, kyekŭpron* (Study of social stratification and social classes). Seoul: Dasan.

Hong, Duk-yul. 1993. "Han'guk taechabonka ŭi chojikwa kyekŭp silch'ŏn'e taehan yŏnku" (A study on the organization and class practices among the large Korean capitalists). Ph.D. dissertation, Seoul National University.

Hsiao, Hsin-Huang Michael, ed. 1999. *East Asian Middle Classes in Comparative Perspective.* Taipei: Academia Sinica.

Jones, Leroy, and Sakong Il. 1980. *Government, Business, and Entrepreneurship in Economic Development: The Korean Case.* Cambridge: Harvard University Press.

Kang, Jeong-Koo. 1988. "Rethinking South Korean Land Reform: Focusing on U.S. Occupation as a Struggle against History." Ph.D. dissertation, University of Wisconsin, Madison.

Kim, Dong-choon. 1995. *Han'guk sahoe nodongja yŏnku* (A study of the Korean working class). Seoul: Yŏksawa pipyŏng.

Kim, Ho Ki. 1999. *Han'guk ŭi hyŏndaesong kwa sahoe pyŏndong* (Modernity and social change in Korea). Seoul: Nanam.

Kim, Seung-kyung. 1997. *Class Struggle or Family Struggle?: The Lives of Women Factory Workers in South Korea.* Cambridge; New York: Cambridge University Press.

Kong, Jung-ja. 1989. "Han'guk taekiop kajŏk ŭi honmaek'e kwanhan yŏnku" (A study on the marriage pattern among big-business families in South Korea). Ph.D. dissertation, Ehwa Women's University.

Koo, Hagen. 1990. "From Farm to Factory: Proletarianization in Korea." *American Sociological Review* 55:669–181.

———. 1991. "Middle Classes, Democratization, and Class Formation: The Case of South Korea." *Theory and Society* 20: 485–509.

———. 2001. *Korean Workers: The Culture and Politics of Class Formation.* Ithaca, N.Y.: Cornell University Press.

Lee, Ki-baik. 1984. *A New History of Korea.* Trans. Edward Wagner and Edward Shultz. Cambridge: Harvard University Press.

Lett, Denise P. 1998. *In Pursuit of Status: The Making of South Korea's "New" Urban Middle Class.* Cambridge: Harvard Asia Center.

Ogle, George. 1990. *South Korea: Dissent within the Economic Miracle.* London: Zed Press.

Shin, Gi-Wook. 1996. *Peasant Protest and Social Change in Colonial Korea.* Seattle: University of Washington Press.

———, and Kyung-Sup Chang. 2000. "Social Crisis in Korea." In Kongdan Oh, ed., *Korea Briefing 1997–1999,* 75–99. Armonk, N.Y.: M. E. Sharpe.

Suh, Jae Jean. 1991. *Han'gukŭi chabonka kyekŭp* (The Korean capitalist class). Seoul: Nanam.

FOUR

Inequality and Class Reproduction in Everyday Life

WANG-BAE KIM and BOK SONG

Class structure in contemporary South Korea has diversified rapidly in the past several decades in tandem with the country's stunning growth and export-led industrialization. Given the high social mobility that was achieved during this period of rapid industrialization, many observers seem to have concluded that class boundaries in South Korean society are relatively porous and flexible. Some have even pointed out that class antagonisms based on class-conscious conflicts are relatively scarce in South Korean society. However, frequent Korean workers' strikes and movements have garnered worldwide attention for their uncompromising militancy and rebelliousness in spite of the decline of the power of the working class around the globe, and there has been a widening gap between classes. At first sight, class boundaries seem to be obscured by the workings of mass consumer society in the postindustrialized era, but class boundaries have become more rigid, deepening inequalities in life opportunities based on social resources such as power, prestige, and property.

Distinction in Lifestyle and Class Reproduction

Existing class studies have focused mainly on the position and roles in production relations. Yet how are those classes reproduced? Classes are not just empty concepts hypostatisized by production relations. They are formed by complicated social relations reproduced by the various lifestyles and practices of their constituents. As Bourdieu (2000) describes, class boundaries are constantly changing and ambiguous and are defined by social and cultural capital as well as economic capital.

Members of one class are distinguished from members of another by lifestyle, by unique life chances in everyday life, by the distribution of specific social resources, and by the order of various strategies that are retained and enlarged to protect and preserve their vested rights. Here, class formation and the reproduction process will be examined in terms of consumer lifestyles and the social and cultural capital of respective classes. Reproduction is not merely the behavior or the process that produces the simple material conditions for existence or a single economic production relation; instead, it is the entire process that creates the overall modes of life. Reproduction preserves social relations by means of population reproduction through marriages and the diverse praxis in family and everyday life. Marx (1981: 37) stated that

> this mode of production must not be considered simply as being the reproduction of the physical existence of the individuals. Rather it is a definite form of activity of these individuals, a definite form of expressing their life, a definite mode of life on their part. As individuals express their life, so they are. What they are, therefore, coincides with their production, both with what they produce and with how they produce.

Likewise, the reproduction of class is not only the process of creating the physical conditions for the class members and for economic production relations, but the process of retaining and enlarging their overall forms of life. And such a process of reproduction is constituted of various consuming behaviors or familial and social relations such as education, politics, and organizations in everyday life.

Consumption Lifestyles and Class

Consumer behavior is one of the most significant practices for class formation and reproduction. Consumption is not merely the by-product of production, but a positive social process in itself that constitutes class. Just as late capitalism has been termed as the age of consumption beyond the age of production, we assert that it would be more proper to focus on the consumption process rather than the production process to explain the identity and behavior of class constituents. Crompton (1996) even insists that as consumption has become more significant in our lives, production-based class analyses have lost their relevance and meaning.

The basic function of consumption is the reproduction of the labor force, that is, the reproduction of life, and the most fundamental means of reproduction in a capitalist society is the commodity. The consumption of commodities, as a behavior to satisfy personal intangible desires as well as physical needs, is a process of acquiring the social meanings contained within them, that is, the symbols (Marx 1981; Shields 1992). For instance, the trademarks placed on costly imported clothes, expensive cars, large household appliances, famous works of art, and so on are symbols that signify the authority, wealth, and dignity of the higher classes. Some studies on consumer behavior often explain how differences among classes are revealed and reproduced. According to Veblen (1975) and Bocock (1993), the upper class exhibits conspicuous consumption for display, while the aspiring middle class shows imitative consumption in order to attain the status of the upper class. Similar distinctions among classes can be found in the consumption of food and clothes. The closer that individuals are to being in the upper class, the more they display the commodities they enjoy; the closer they are to the lower class, the more they stress the consumption of necessities such as household appliances. Subscription to certain newspapers and magazines as well as the purchase of expensive imported goods, overseas travel, and tickets to classical concerts exclude other classes and conspicuously distinguish the dignity and authority of the upper class. Appearances as revealed to others become a significant measure of identification of one's social position (Corrigan 1997).

We argue in this chapter that South Korean society entered the age of consumption capitalism by the late 1980s. Rapid industrialization brought about an explosive expansion in the amount of material goods in South Korea; likewise, the domestic markets for commodity consumption experienced a huge upsurge. In the international system of labor division linked to the United States and Japan, South Korea had pursued an industrialization strategy focused on exports. Therefore, domestic capital was accumulated through a strategy that mobilized a cheap labor force and an efficient assembly process that produced parts into a complete whole for export abroad, as opposed to importing parts, necessary technologies, and capital. As a result, South Korea's industrialization is cited as a prime example of successful export-substitution industrialization. However, in export-oriented industrialization based on lower wages, the domestic consumer markets cannot help but be narrow because the realization of values depends on foreign markets. Above all, the low wages of the working classes, as producing and consuming actors, were not able to reach an adequate purchasing power.

Nevertheless, as with the accumulation of capital by rapid industrialization, the domestic markets gradually expanded as the urban middle classes increased with rising real wages during the industrialization period. Especially after the massive labor protests in the summer of 1987 boosted wages, manual workers were able to strengthen their purchasing power. Accordingly, the domestic markets enlarged considerably (see National Statistical Office 1999 and You 1992 for detailed data). Other factors that played into this enlargement include the decline of the "Goldilocks" economy (neither too hot nor too cold) in South Korea in the late 1980s and the conglomerates' target adjustment toward domestic markets after they began to be blocked by export barriers.

The prominent consumption of durable goods such as motors and electrical products was a clear sign that the domestic markets had enlarged rapidly in the late 1980s. Meanwhile, thanks to the boost in wages, manual workers who had previously been excluded from the consuming sectors were considered to be consuming actors for the first time. As evidenced in national statistics, the average monthly household income for urban workers in 1997 was about 2,290,000 won, with about 1,700,000 of that being spent on consumer goods, eight times the rate of the 1980s (National Statistical Office 1998a).

As for the detailed items of consumption, there was a shift from the consumption of goods to the consumption of services, and the modes of consumption were becoming increasingly complex. With transportation, medical care, dining out, entertainment, and other such activities expanding with the consumption of provisions, the patterns of consumption were becoming increasingly high class (Baeck 1994). For example, expenditures for provisions, which indicate Engel's Coefficient, accounted for 61.3 percent of total expenditures in 1963, decreasing to 37.7 percent in 1985 and to 28.7 percent in 1997; meanwhile, expenditures on transportation and telecommunication and on culture and entertainment increased from 6.5 percent and 3.4 percent in 1985 to 12.5 percent and 4.9 percent in 1996, respectively. Likewise, expenditure on education grew from 5.4 percent in 1985 to 9.8 percent in 1996. Travel expenditures have also increased since the late 1980s (National Statistical Office 1998b).

The various indices offer sufficient evidence to define South Korean society as a form of consumption capitalism. It goes without saying that mass consumption is likely to blur boundaries between classes. However, we argue that the dynamics of capital is a dual process that has a paradoxical effect in class relations. On one hand, class boundaries collapse with the emergence of consumption capitalism; on the other hand, distinctions between classes by means of consumption are intensified as well. A series of recent studies on the division of residential space shows the explicit differences in modes of consumption according to class. The upper classes in South Korea own large mansions with high walls and security equipment around the Song-Buk area of Seoul, while the new middle classes such as the professional and managerial classes are concentrated in the Gangnam and Pyungch'ang-tong area (i.e., the outskirts of Seoul), the main residential area (W. B. Kim 2000). Furthermore, differences in consumption lifestyles, such as clothes, food, movies, fashion, music, and so on, also exhibit class divisions. For example, the professional and managerial classes seek out high-quality restaurants and consider factors such as overall mood as well as taste, quantity, and quality of dishes served. Similar differences are revealed in the kinds of leisure and sports activities classes engage in. The higher the class, the greater the preference for sports that require special skills or expensive equipment.

Social Relation and Capital in Classes

Many controversies have arisen from the definition of social capital as a contrasting concept to human capital. Social capital includes not only public institutions and physical resources such as infrastructure, but also the social relations that empower individuals with the capacity to mobilize various other resources in private life. Regarding this latter point, social capital can broadly be defined as any and all types of social relations (e.g., alumni groups, regional connections, neighbor relationships, and marriage networks) that function to achieve specific goals. In other words, social capital refers to the total capacity to realize benefits by belonging to and identifying with a certain kind of group. It is thus the relational gain that results from establishing a social network that is the representation of social identity and social support.

Social network as a social capital has various social effects not only on capabilities to mobilize social resources but also in increasing social solidarity, stability, and social support. The social network of a particular group is the most crucial component in the formation of social capital. Even though the amount of social capital is allocated among different classes to varying degrees, we argue that all classes have some social capital in the sense that class members have their own social networks for mobilizing social resources.

In this process, informal social networks with weak ties play an important role in mobilizing social resources despite their low mobilization capacity, as compared to formal social networks including those based on a bureaucratic organization. Much information is potentially exchanged under such conditions of loosely tied informal social networks since they allow for flexibility in interactions among groups or individuals (Granovetter 1973). In a society where personal relationships (*yongojooui*) are dominant as a socially constructed principle, informal networks (support from friends, alumni networks, etc.) play a powerful role in allowing relational benefits to be gained. Social networks contribute not only toward sustaining or stabilizing a vested interest, but also toward expanding the total amount of resources available by increasing the ways in which additional social resources may be gained. While physical capital generally appears in the form of tangible materials such as money and human capital, social capital is embedded in social networks as one of the subcategories of social relationships.

Marriage networks are a typical example of social relations that constitute social capital. Class reproduction through marriage networks is a conspicuous phenomenon in the upper class. As a consequence, marriage networks in the upper class function to construct a "distinguished clan," which has obtained for itself an exclusive status socially removed from the mass populace. Not only do marriage networks ascertain social resources for their members, but they also serve as symbols of social capital through their influence on others.

In South Korea, three major types of marriage networks have been documented (Kong 1989): between *chaebol* (business conglomerate) families, between *chaebol* and high-ranking bureaucrats or politicians, and between *chaebol* families and non–upper class or nonelite families. The third type is generally a case where a wealthy capitalist family decides to accept the marriage despite the spouse's relatively low family background or social status because of the spouse's personal talent or capacity. But such cases are rare and do not indicate a relatively open class structure. In general, *chaebol* families tend to construct "their own field" of economic and political networks through strategically formed alliances by way of marriage (Seoul Economy Daily News 1991). Although relatively open when compared to those of countries such as Great Britain, marriage networks among the upper class are being formed through, and function as, social capital to reproduce class.

Even though the exclusive marriage networks of the upper class gradually open themselves to others, the tendency of the upper class to marry within its own class system will remain for years, as networks composed of upper-class youths still hold certain class-bound features. Despite the fact that the numbers of arranged marriages determined by the parents are declining, it should be noted that even love marriages are often established within the same class boundary or at least within peripheral upper classes. In other words, even "love marriages" in the upper class are restricted to certain confines.

Education and Class Reproduction

Education is the most significant "cultural capital" to constitute and reproduce social class in modern society. Education takes the complicated role of cultural capital to confer qualifications and skills, socialize diverse knowledge and values, and deliver systematic ideologies. Moreover, cultural capital enables one to perform a socially recognized role by elevating the values of one's labor through knowledge and skill training, and brings a proportionately high income and dignity in return. In that Weber suggested that qualifications and skills were the resources of income that enable one to share market opportunities, education in modern society might be considered the core area that supplies those very qualifications and skills.

As education functions toward enhancing the value of human capital and raising productive capacity, it is assumed that it opens up opportunities for upward social movement (Karabel and Halsey 1977). Through education, an upward transfer among generations occurs, and the expansion of the new middle class is considered to be the result of diffusion of education. Academic background, formally certifying the level of education and producing a change in the distribution of resources, is an important element segmenting the labor markets.

It is still controversial to suggest that the diffusion of education enables overall social transfer and class ascension, or, on the other hand, that it reproduces and intensifies class inequality. Contrary to functional perspectives that perceive education as acquiring skills and enhancing the value of human capital, others argue that although education might confer opportunities for upward social mobility, these opportunities are available in different ways according to class and therefore only contribute to the reproduction of unequal class structures. Bowles (1977) argues that the general education system in the United States produces workers who accept the existing system, thereby reproducing the existing division of labor. Therefore education is no more than a means to secure the interests of the dominant classes.

Such reproducing processes of inequality operate in the socializing function of education as well. Education reproduces the "class habitus" by socializing the personality and tendency of the constituents of each class. As education in the household plays a crucial role in the formation of children's intelligence, the concrete modes of socialization are the very reflection and forming process of class habitus. In fact, individual personality and personal disposition are a product of a socialization process that takes place over a long time.

Education is also likely to be used as a closure strategy for classes or groups that wish to retain their vested rights. That is, the qualifications to a membership of a class are endowed only to those with formal academic degrees that entail a significant and prohibitive investment in cost and time that prevents others from approaching certain market opportunities. For instance, medical doctors are required to have six years of course work and more than four years of internship. There are similar educational hurdles to overcome in other occupations.

Education in Korean Society

South Korean society has been called an "academic clique" society, where education is the most fundamental factor in the formation of class structure. The excessive stress on academic background indicates the social situation where a person depends on his or her academic background and academic clique (*hakbol*) or the social logic that emphasizes an individual's capacity in the process of acquiring and selecting social position. In other words, social connections by means of academic background, and "the cultural symbols" and "social indication" implied in academic backgrounds, have powerful influences in real social processes (Han 1994). South Korean society, with its obsessive reliance on academic background, has been pejoratively termed a society of "academic cliques" given that academic degrees and social connections dominate the distribution of social resources and the recruitment of human capital and are stressed over one's actual capacity (B. T. Kim 1995).

Education is recognized as the most significant pathway to a successful entrance into South Korean society. Various social and cultural contexts explain why Korea has historically been a society ruled by the literati class with bureaucratic officials selected through a national state examination. Because highly skilled, educated elites have constituted the ruling class through the national examination system, being a member of the ruling elite alone was no guarantee for substantial power and wealth. Still, in contemporary society, education remains the core means to success in South Korea. It is already well known that "education fever" (*kyoyuk'yol*) is pervasive in the country as shown in the highest rates of school attendance and college admissions in the world. After the colonial period from 1910 to 1945, the segment of the populace that came from a low-education background sought new opportunities for upward social mobility by investing in the education of their children, the next generation. Such an obsession with education in overall Korean culture has been combined with a familism that is unique to Korean society, one that places exaggerated stress on academic background (Park 1987; I. Kim 1991).

In the meantime, it is worth noting that during the period of rapid industrialization, a large labor pool was required to provide the vast amount of human capital needed for the industrializing technologies. A belief that a high-quality labor force could be attained through the enhancement of educational opportunities and training prevailed broadly among policy makers. In spite of criticism about technological functionalism, schools and academic institutions in fact played the significant role of supply base for the skills and knowledge needed for industrialization.

For a more intensive debate, it is helpful to look to the "effects of latecomers" as pointed out by Dore (1976). He hypothesizes that the characteristics of education in late industrialized states reveals specific features, such as academic backgrounds playing a crucial role in employment and promotion, while education gradually becomes concentrated on the examination. Dore's effects can be seen prominently in the case of South Korea, where the state played a leading role in expanding education. Unlike the British system of elite education, in South Korea the state diffused education and introduced a national examination system that focused on individual aptitude to mobilize mass human capital in a short time.

In sum, to understand education expansion and the special stress on academic cliques, we must first fully consider the traditional cultural emphasis on education in Korea and the context of Korea as a competitive society as a result of rapid industrialization. As stated above, familism supplied the fuel for stimulating individual goal attainment in a competitive society, while the fundamental means for social elevation was academic background. Education has become the most fundamental element that divides labor markets and differentiates employment, promotion, income, and labor conditions.

How equal are opportunities for academic attainment in South Korean society? Does academic attainment depend on the individual or on the class that the individual belongs to? It seems that educational opportunity in South Korean society is relatively open compared to opportunity in other modern industrialized countries. Moreover, South Korean middle and high schools are equalized across the population, and there are no elite secondary schools exclusively for the upper class. The tuition for Seoul National University, the school with the highest reputation in South Korea, is lower than that of private schools, and the student population is not restricted to the upper class.

The relatively egalitarian college admissions policy reflects class structure in South Korea as newly formed and much more fluid. Because the opportunity for education is relatively open and not restricted to the upper class alone, social mobility is more frequent than in the past. In addition, contrary to what Bourdieu has observed, education may have little relation to the socialization of the habitus of a certain class. In that the South Korean education system is bereft of its function of initiating the capacity to recognize and appreciate the codes of arts or philosophy, it would be premature to assume that the class habitus is firmly formed and segmented in South Korean society to the degree that Bourdieu (2000) suggested. Nevertheless, some recent research studies (G. Kang 1992; H. Kang 1988) note that inequality in educational opportunities and in different educational effects among

classes gradually intensifies. In other words, educational opportunities tend to be segmented along class boundaries.

Hee-Don Kang (1988) suggests that the higher the income, the
more schools of the first rank are preferred; the higher the occupational status of the head of the household, the more likely that the
children will enter university; and the higher the incomes earned
by the parents, the higher the level of education that can be
expected of the children. In fact, the opportunities for academic
attainment are differentiated according to social stratification
structured by elements such as parents' income level and occupational status, and the unequal distribution of academic attainment
skewed toward the upper classes is serious. According to a recent
survey based on the 2000 national entrance examination, students
whose parents were upper administrative and managerial officials
or professional office workers comprised almost 70 percent of the
freshman class; this statistic indicates a monopolizing tendency by
the upper and the new middle class.

Differences among children according to social class reveal
another distinction among classes. According to Gil-Bong Kang
(1992), the higher the class to which parents belong, the more they
are interested in their children's friends; the lower the class, the
less the interest and concern. He also shows that the lower classes
are more likely to prefer stable occupations for their children and
that the frequency of conversation between parents and children is
higher in the lower classes (although the detailed contents of those
conversations showed no difference among classes).

What is interesting is that there is no difference in educational
enthusiasm among classes. According to one research study
(Kwon 1992), the urban poor, in spite of their environment, show
no less enthusiastic attitudes for the children's education than
higher classes and try to enhance their social position through
education. However, practical restrictions limit their children's
successes and their access to the concrete alternatives for education that exist. And even though they have attained a higher level
than their parents' generation, they cannot go beyond their class
boundaries and can only return to their previous position (Cho
and Cho 1987; Kwon 1992).

It is true that the opportunities for education are relatively
equalized across all classes. However, diverse differences among
sex, region, and classes are still found. Private after-school institutes known as *hagwon* and private tutoring are more prominent in
private-education sectors than in public ones. Existing research

also shows that the higher the social and economic background of
the family, the more the expenditure on private academies, extra-
curricular activities, and so forth. In addition, the children in such
a family generally achieve higher grade levels and have more
opportunities for their education (S. J. Kim 1994).

One important distinction strategy in education is to study
abroad, especially in the United States or in European countries
such as France, Germany, and the U.K. For South Koreans, studying abroad is rare and valuable cultural capital that signifies one's
capacity, future prospects, and family background. With few
exceptions, children from the upper class usually go abroad. In
this way, the offspring of the upper classes combine their educational capital and social capital to reproduce their own class.[1]

Because studying abroad for many South Koreans is not considered to be a matter of actually gaining particular skills or
knowledge but is, rather, a superficial matter of conferring
influence and status, it has a powerful influence on class mobility
and class reproduction. For example, an MBA in business
administration is a basic formal condition for the position of a professional manager. The following are excerpts from interviews
with South Koreans who have studied abroad:

Interviewee A: Actually, I had little thought of studying abroad.
But I could not think of any other alternative in a situation where
I had to compete with other younger men with MBA certificates.
Well, I didn't think that they were more qualified or knew more
about Korean management than me, but if I didn't do anything, I
wouldn't be promoted to chief of the department. Though I studied for two and a half years and completed a management course
in the U.S., I know nothing more than I did before. At least I got
a line written in English added to my curriculum vitae.

Interviewee B: France? Just something for the sake of appearance.
In fact, I completed the design institute's curriculum in only three
months out of the six months I've spent in France. What could I
have learned in such a short time? Nevertheless, if I go back to

---

[1] Meanwhile, competitive university admission rates and a high degree of educational enthusiasm have brought about the expansion of university quotas as well
as academic degree inflation since the 1980s. Bourdieu (2000: 243–253) estimates
that the inflation of academic degrees began as the ruling and the middle classes
extended their investment into the educational system in order to retain and inten-
sify the existing conditions for their social reproduction.

Korea, it means a significant career. A very competitive career. It would raise my worth.

Although the opportunity for education is not limited to formally recognized organizations, in the private-education sector the differences among classes are striking. Private education is a long-term process beginning in infancy and progressing through high school and university and into various careers. Though private institutes have supplemented the quest for a high score on the national university entrance examination, the desire for a well-rounded education in the liberal arts such as languages, arts, and physical education still exists. In South Korean society in particular, studying the English language is the most important resource in determining one's future marketability. Those without access to such opportunities—which are generally available only to the upper classes—have limited possibility for upward mobility through education.

Conclusion

During the last period of South Korea's industrialization, the classes in South Korean society have shown diverse areas of division. The opening of Korea's ports and the disruptive effects of colonization had already altered the existing traditional class structure. Rapid industrialization beginning in the 1960s brought about "social transfers" in occupations in addition to regional transfers and class formation. As Song (1993) has pointed out, social mobility has been remarkably high given the rapid industrialization of South Korea, and therefore the time spent on class structuring is understandably short. Except for the antagonistic relationship between individual capitalists and workers that has been a regular occurrence since the 1980s, the class consciousness and class conflicts that occurred in traditional Western European capitalism were generally absent in South Korea's case.

Although social mobility is relatively high in South Korea, class distinctions are solidified through class reproduction. In a capitalist consumer context, differentiation and inequality in modes of life become clearer. Since the economic crisis in 1997, the gaps between the upper classes and lower classes in income and life standards have grown wider, and middle-class households are on the verge of falling into a lower class. Class polarization continues under the global capitalism banner of neoliberalism.

Many Western scholars have declared "the end of class," seeing the decline of the working class in a postmodern or global world society. Beck (1997) insists that inequality in terms of class has lost its significance and that only the inequality of the individual remains. However, social processes have revealed the contradictory movements of the social forces of class. Initially, class may seem to disappear, but in some sense, class reformulates itself and rebounds. Class structure in South Korean society has been reformulated and reproduced by various factors in the country's own specific socio-historical context.

References

Baeck, Wook-in. 1994. "Taejung sobisaenghwal kujowa pyunhwa" (Changes in the structures of mass consumption life). *Kyungje wa sahoe* 21:45–69.
Beck, Ulrich. 1997. *Risikogesellschaft*. Trans. Seongtae Hong as *Wiheomsahoi*. Seoul: Saemulkyul.
Bocock, R. 1993. *Consumption*. London: Routledge.
Bourdieu, P. 2000. *La distinction*. Trans. Jongcul Choi as *Kupyuljiki*. Seoul: Saemulkyul.
Bowles, R. 1977. "Unequal Education and the Reproduction of the Social Division of Labor." In J. Karabel and A. H. Halsey, eds., *Power and Ideology in Education*, 137–153. New York: Oxford University Press.
Cho, Eun, and Ok-Ra Cho. 1987. *Toshi binmin ŭi samkwa konggan* (Life and space of the urban poor). Seoul: Seoul National University.
Corrigan, P. 1997. *The Sociology of Consumption*. London: Sage.
Crompton, R. 1996. "Consumption and Class Analysis." In S. Edgell, K. Hetherington, and A. Warde, eds., *Consumption Matters*, 113–132. Oxford; Cambridge, Mass.: Blackwell.
Dore, R. 1976. *Diploma Disease*. Berkeley: University of California Press.
Granovetter, Mark. 1973. "The Strength of Weak Ties." *American Journal of Sociology* 78:1360–1380.
Han, Joon-Sang. 1994. *Han'guk kyoyuk kaehy ŏkron* (Reformation of Korean education). Seoul: Hak-Ji.
Kang, Gil-Bong. 1992. "Sahoekyech ŭng e ddar un pumo ui chany ŏkyoyukt'aedo e kwanhan yŏn'gu" (Research on parents' attitudes in educating children according to classes). Ph.D. thesis, Bu-San University.

Kang, Hee-Don. 1988. *Han'gukeso ŭi sahoe idongkwa hakkyogyoyuk ŭi hyogwa* (Effects of social mobility and academic education on Korean society). Master's thesis, Korea University.

Karabel, J., and A. H. Halsey., eds. 1977. *Power and Ideology in Education.* New York: Oxford University Press.

Kim, Boo-Tae. 1995. *Han'guk hakryŏksahoeron* (Korean academic cliquism). Seoul: Naeil ul yunun chaek.

Kim, Hyungki. 1988. *Han'guk ŭi Tŏkjomjabon kwa imnodong* (Monopoly capital and labor in South Korea). Seoul: Kkachi.

Kim, In-Hoe. 1991. "Han'gukin ŭi kyoyukyŏl, hŏwasil" (Korean educational enthusiasm, its truth and falsehood). *Taehak kyoyuk* 50:71–77.

Kim, Shin-Ju. 1994. "Sakyoyukbi chich'ul e taehan chungsanch'ŭng hakpumodŭl ŭi ŭishik kujo" (Structures of middle class parents' consciousness on expenditure on private education). M.A. dissertation, Kyeong-Buk University.

Kim, Wang-Bae. 2000. "Inequalities in Classes, Spaces, and Life World." In *Tosi, kongkan saenghwal sekye* (Urban space, life world), 224–268. Seoul: Han-ul.

———. 2001. *Sanŏpsahoe ŭi nodonggwa kyegŭpŭi chaesaengsan* (Reproduction of labor and class in industrial society). Seoul: Han-ul.

Kong, Jongja. 1989. "Taejabon'ga kajok ŭi ky olhonyuhy ŏng yŏngu" (Study on the marriage patterns of the big-capitalist family). Ph.D. dissertation, Ehwa University.

Kwon, Hyun-Su. 1992. *Pinkon'gŭkpokŭl wihan sahoekwankyemang-e kwanhan yŏngu* (Research on social networks for overcoming poverty). Daegu: Kyoung-Buk University.

Marx, Karl. 1981. *The German Ideology.* New York: International Publishers.

National Statistical Office. 1998a. *Toshigagyeyŏnpo* (Annual report on urban households).

———. 1998b. *Topyoro bonŭn t'onggye* (Statistics in graphs).

———. 1999. *Sanŏp saengsan tonghyang* (Industrial production trends).

Park, Young-Shin. 1987. "Sahoe byŏndong, kyoyuk, undong" (Social changes, education, and movement). In Korean Sociology Institute, ed., *Yuksawa sahoebyŏdong* (History and social change). Seoul: Min-Young.

Seoul Economy Daily News. 1991. *Chaebol kwa kajok* (Chaebol and family). Seoul: Jisiksanopsa.

Shields, R. 1992. *Lifestyle Shopping: The Subject of Consumption.* London: Routledge.

Song, Bok. 1993. "Han'gukŭi sangch'sŭng" (The upper class in Korea). In *Yangyonghoi haksulronmunchip* (Yangyounghoi report).

Veblen, T. 1983. *The Theory of the Leisure Class.* Trans. Suyong Chong as *Yuhan keygŭp ron.* Seoul: Donnyok.

You, Choel-Kyu. 1992. "Palsip nyŏndae hubanihu naesuh-wakjangui sŏngkyuk" (Characteristics of expansion in domestic consumption since the late 1980s). *Tonghwangkwa jŏnmang,* Winter, 189–218.

FIVE

Economic Governance: Its Historical Development and Future Prospects

HYUK-RAE KIM

For the past several decades, the Korean economy has evolved rapidly from a poor agrarian economy to an advanced industrial economy, tripling in size every decade since 1960. This record of growth and transformation has been regarded as one of the most noteworthy economic success stories in the history of capitalist development. Some attribute the phenomenon to pervasive state intervention through export-driven industrialization strategies (Amsden 1989; Haggard 1990; Wade 1990); others, to liberal industrial policies and the invisible hand of the market (Balassa 1988; World Bank 1993; Young 1994). Although interpretation of the roles of the state and market remains controversial, it is widely agreed that state intervention has been a crucial factor in economic development, but also that it has impeded full development of the financial and corporate sectors.

With the increasing role of global capital markets, the domestic financial sector has shown various signs of weakness. Significant numbers of nonperforming loans, excessive and poor lending practices, and increasingly high levels of risky investment left Korean financial institutions vulnerable to fluctuations in credit availability.[1] In the corporate sector, excess investment in a few

---

[1] According to Korea's Ministry of Finance and Economy (1998), combined nonperforming loans of the country's twenty-six commercial banks amounted to 55.93 trillion won at the end of 1997, or 14.9 percent of total credits. Bad debt problems were equally serious in other financial sectors. Nonperforming loans in banking, securities, insurance, merchant banking, and leasing amounted to 67.79 trillion won, or 13.2 percent of total credits. Some bank analysts warned that such loans at all financial institutions could swell to 100 trillion won, or 25 percent of GDP, by the end of 1998. Others projected a surge to 157 trillion won, as the bankruptcy ratio was expected to reach 1 percent on average.

industrial sectors and in short-term corporate borrowings has left
businesses so highly leveraged that unprecedented numbers have
moved into bankruptcy since mid-1997.[2] Furthermore, the Asian
currency crisis has spilled over into and developed further in
Korea. Asian economies began to stagger in July 1997, when a
currency crisis and economic trouble struck Thailand. The Thailand crisis immediately infected neighboring Southeast Asia and
eventually triggered serious turmoil in South Korea's currency and
financial markets.[3]

Successive blows to the Korean national economy have brought
successive downgrades in international credit ratings and sharp
reductions in the availability of foreign capital. More important,
market liberalization and movement of massive amounts of capital
across national borders have attenuated the state's capacity to
exercise economic governance.[4] It has responded to current problems simply by increasing liquidity by drawing on the nation's
foreign reserves and introducing measures to facilitate liquidity
flows. It has failed to enforce effective market discipline or establish monitoring mechanisms. As a result, Korea now relies on a
$57 billion International Monetary Fund (IMF) rescue package.

---

[2] According to Korea's Fair Trade Commission (1998), the average debt-to-equity
ratio of the thirty newly designated largest conglomerates was 518.9 percent by the
end of 1997, up from 386.5 percent in 1996. The Ministry of Finance and Economy
(1998) reported that total foreign debt in the private sector was $95.5 billion, almost
half of the national total foreign debt ($170 billion). Among private foreign debts,
$42.3 billion were owed to domestic financial institutions; $53.2 billion were in
short-term overseas borrowing. In Korea, the rolling over of private-sector short-
term foreign liabilities became a central issue. Bankruptcies, chiefly found among
large businesses in 1997, spread to small and medium businesses in domino
fashion. The Ministry of Finance and Economy (1998) reported that the bankruptcy
ratio was estimated at 0.72 percent on average in the first quarter of 1997, when
restructuring of troubled corporations and financial institutions had not yet begun.

[3] Asia's troubled economies share these features: (1) dependence on short-term,
indirect foreign capital such as bonds, as opposed to long-term, direct foreign capital; (2) preference for speculative investment; (3) tolerance of corporate strategies
featuring low profit margins, high debt loads, and reliance on government bailout;
(4) use of fixed exchange rates; and (5) weak oversight by financial authorities.

[4] The term "governance" derives from the Greek *kybernetes*, which is etymologi-
cally related to navigation and helmsmanship. In general, the concept has been
loosely understood to mean use of power and exercise of control in managing
resources for social and economic development (Dhonte and Kapur 1997; Frischtak
1994; H. R. Kim 1998b; World Bank 1992). This chapter defines economic governance as the totality of institutional arrangements that regulate transactions inside
and across the boundaries of an economic system (Coase 1937; Williamson 1996).

This economic crisis brought an end to the $10,000 per capita income level achieved in 1996. The nation's per capita GNP declined 9.78 percent to $9,511 in 1997, from $10,543 the year before (Bank of Korea 1998). More significantly, the nation's economic growth rate plunged to negative 6.7 percent in 1998 as the nation underwent drastic restructuring under austerity measures prescribed by IMF.[5] In the years after the IMF crisis, the national economy got back on track and showed steady growth. In this process, the Korean government faced compound challenges—to revitalize the financial sector, restructure the corporate sector under market principles, reform the labor market, and create a lean and efficient public sector.[6]

Before the Asian financial crisis, the Korean economy and its governance were championed as among the greatest achievements in capitalist economic history. Now they are targets of international criticism. The rapidly changing environment inherent in globalization left the structural organization of the Korean economy vulnerable to a host of problems. Korea's economic governance was not designed to mobilize the appropriate resources for effectively operating in today's global economy. For any form of economic governance to remain viable, it must be able either to adapt to or control changing environments.

This chapter explores several questions concerning the viability of Korea's distinctive development pattern and its economic governance as they have been shaped until very recently. Does the economic crisis signal the end of Korea's economic miracle? Does it in fact indicate the vulnerability of Korean economic

---

[5] The IMF prescribes budget deficit reduction through raising taxes and cutting government spending, as well as tighter monetary policy through higher interest rates and less credit availability. It proposes a set of reforms comprising three elements: a clear and firm exit policy, strong market and supervisory discipline, and increased competition. These suggest that the government must ban *chaebol* (large business conglomerates) from giving affiliates debt guarantees. Loss of cross-guarantees will seriously curtail *chaebol* ability to raise funds from the debt market, forcing a focus on core businesses. In addition, requirements for full disclosure to independent auditors as well as limitations on filing and disclosures of consolidated statements will minimize transfers of funds from healthier subsidiaries to weaker ones ("window-dressing" financial results). Other reforms are being designed, including a requirement for conglomerates to appoint outside directors to their boards.

[6] However, short-term macroeconomic policies in the face of temporary lack of liquidity rather than fundamental insolvency become controversial (Feldstein 1998). Regardless of the appropriateness of the IMF's role, its directives are apparently providing Korea an opportunity to restructure the national economy.

governance and the possible collapse of Korean capitalism? This chapter argues that the crisis reflects structural flaws in Korea's dominant institutions. These include pervasive state intervention in economic development, bureaucratic control over financial institutions, unsound lending practices, and vertical integration of corporate organization and management (Amsden 1989, 1997; Chung and Lee 1989; Jones and Sakong 1980; Kang 1996; E. M. Kim 1997; H. R. Kim 1994, 2000). The following historical examination of Korean economic governance illuminates the unique nature of Korean capitalism and the origins of the economic crisis.

Analytical Framework

The divergence rather than convergence of economic governance across nations implies that no single, dominant form of economic rationality or logic of efficiency inexorably leads to a single way of structuring national economies (Chandler, Amatori, and Hikino 1997; H. R. Kim 1994, 2000; Whitley 1992, 1994). Similarly, a single set of general contingencies cannot explain variations in organizational structures within all institutional contexts (Maurice, Sorge, and Warner 1980; Sorge and Warner 1986).

This inquiry assumes that various institutional environments generate highly distinctive organizational forms of national economy (DiMaggio and Powell 1983; Hollingsworth and Boyer 1997; H. R. Kim 1994, 2000; Whitley 1992). Among those institutional environments, the state and the financial institutions are the key to governance. They significantly affect how organizational environments are constituted, how economic organizations are structured, and how economic activities are coordinated.

Accordingly, this chapter focuses on the structural configuration of economic governance in order to illustrate its historical evolution. It examines the four interrelated dimensions of the economy's structural configuration. First, organizational vitality is analyzed by examining the age structure of organizations according to their years of operation. Age distribution indicates overall industrial vitality, a major element in organizational change. Age composition also provides distinctions in a manner analogous to social class, suggesting inequalities in resource allocation. Such resources comprise not only goods and services, but also such crucial intangibles as social approval and acceptance. Further, age structure reveals a dynamic element by recognizing that aging is a process of mobility. As each age cohort flows through time, its respective size and characteristics may alter resource allocation, which in turn changes the dynamics of a population of organizations as well as reflects the viability of economic governance.

Second, size dispersion is analyzed by examining the distribution of organizations according to size. A positively skewed distribution by numerical dominance of small-scale organizations often implies production system flexibility. Conversely, negative skewed distribution by dominance of large-scale operations suggests a monopolistic market structure. The preferred, bimodal distribution indicates a symbiotic presence of both small and large organizations. Thus, size dispersion analysis assists in understanding the adaptability of an economic governance structure to rapidly changing economic environments.

Third, managerial hierarchy is scrutinized to reveal the nature of the relationships among various economic organizations. This involves exploring the ways in which business groups and businesses are vertically structured and horizontally coordinated. The goal is not so much to understand the nature of each business as to discern the critical economic agents in a market economy. In Korea, *chaebol* have been viewed as having authoritarian managerial hierarchies that served as key agents in shaping Korea's unique economic governance. Thus, the managerial hierarchy of large business groups and the high degree of internalization of their market transactions will be used to indicate the structural rigidity of major players in Korean economic governance.

Fourth, market integrity is examined to understand the nature of market structure as well as interorganizational relationships— that is, how businesses interact with each other, whether through market transactions or through patterned, monopolistic protocols oblivious to market conditions. Market integrity can be analyzed by examining the pattern of market structure and the degree of subcontracting, which in turn show the structure of organizational interdependence within the national economy.

These four interrelated dimensions—organizational vitality, size dispersion, managerial hierarchy, and market integrity—raise the following questions: How vital are economic organizations as a whole in face of rapidly changing environments? How evenly are economic organizations distributed according to size? How are business groups or any significant clusters of economic organizations internally organized? How tightly is the market organized through informal networks among businesses and business groups?

Historical Development of Economic Governance

The embryonic origins of Korean economic governance can be traced as far back as the late Chosŏn dynasty. However, its roots proper lie in the colonial experience and the immediate postcolonial years of division, war, and reconstruction (Eckert 1991; Jacobs 1985; Kang 1996; E. M. Kim 1997; H. R. Kim 1998a; McNamara 1990).

The Colonial Roots of Korean Economic Governance

Although Korean economic governance took form during the period 1945–60, several businesses had already begun during the colonial period. During colonial occupation, indigenous large-scale entrepreneurial firms developed distinctive features—family control, heavy reliance on the colonial state, and concentration of capital and ownership.

The colonial state guided development along the lines of Meiji Japan, focusing on the construction of a financial, legal, and organizational framework that promoted capitalist enterprise while also affording the state determinative control over the economy. A so-called capitalist framework was created in three areas: law, finance, and economic organizations. The legal framework gave authority to direct the economy to state policy makers, who assured business compliance through incentives and restraints (e.g., the Banking Law of 1906; the Corporation Law of 1910; and the Land Survey Law of 1910; see McNamara 1990: 40). The financial framework and control system were established through the Bank of Choso"n and the Choso"n Industrial Bank, a government-supported central bank and a developmental bank, respectively. Finally, the colonial state controlled business formation by appointing Koreans to elite positions within government and business associations, according them the increased prestige and credibility of close government ties.

Overall, colonialism brought Korea a measure of corporate growth, although it was orchestrated by and for the Japanese. Japanese corporations monopolized the entire market in some key modern industries such as metal, machinery, chemicals, and textiles (H. R. Kim 1998a). In contrast, Korean business primarily took the form of small commercial and agricultural enterprises.

According to Grajdanzev (1944), household production accounted for 40.1 percent of all Korean output in 1933. Even in 1938, the figure was 24.7 percent, indicating that Korean business was by and large insignificant and small—generally too small to compete for heavy investment projects and reap the associated profits. This profile of Korean business constraints with respect to capital resources in the colonial period reveals an economy distinctively dualistic in nationality and size (Grajdanzev 1944; H. R. Kim 1998a).

Despite the few material benefits that Koreans gained during colonialism, the course was set for future Korean economic governance. The years exposed Korean enterprise to industrial development justified by ideology (benign capitalism), supported by infrastructure (strong state), and driven by capital (Japanese private investment). Accordingly, the chief characteristics of Japanese prewar economic organizations—ownership and capital concentration, close business-state ties, and groups of companies in diverse fields—are evident in postcolonial Korean business (H. R. Kim 1998a; McNamara 1990). In particular, colonial state approval was the single most important factor for later development of Korean economic governance because it accustomed indigenous firms to a dependent relationship with the state for credit financing and subsidies.

Postcolonial Development of Economic Governance

After liberation from Japanese colonialism, the most significant factor affecting Korea's future economic environment was the three-year Korean War, which destroyed much of the industrial-plant and transportation networks in the south. The colonial and war legacies provided particular environmental characteristics that helped determine postwar development—state intervention in economic governance, bureaucratic control over financial institutions, and hierarchical coordination between state and business.

Postwar Korean economic development began with an extremely underdeveloped base facing severe constraints: low national income and savings levels, underdeveloped social and economic infrastructure, vast information asymmetry, anemic managerial capacity, poor natural resource endowments, and general lack of government administrative experience. These environmental perils forced the Rhee regime to focus not on growth, but on the short-term objectives of reconstruction and maintenance of minimum living standards. To that end it emphasized aid to the

neglect of investment and production. This inward focus promoted import-substituting industries, primarily in the manufac-
ture of consumer goods such as food and textiles, to maintain living standards. In addition, general social and political instability
drew the regime's attention toward politics before economics.
Economic decisions were determined by political goals, leading to
politicization of economic resource and opportunity allocations.

It was during this period that the *chaebol* sector arose. The primary mechanism of *chaebol* growth was resource and opportunity
transfer by the state in a usually noncompetitive process. The
greatest growth occurred in the three "white industries"—sugar
and flour, textiles, and cement—although *chaebol* in these industries remained much smaller than those to emerge during the next
decades in other sectors, such as heavy and chemical industries.
A few firms were able to grow, setting the stage for today's *chaebol*. Of the top ten *chaebol* in 1960, three began operating during
the colonial period and seven during the Rhee administration
(table 5.1). Of the thirty largest *chaebol* in 1988, six had started
before liberation, the majority (16) under Rhee, and the remaining
(8) under Park (H. R. Kim 1998b).

Significantly, while only two *chaebol* from the 1960s managed to
maintain their positions through 1975, no significant changes
occurred thereafter. The major groups had solidified their positions by 1975 and demonstrated their holding power over the next
decades. The largest *chaebol* have continued to expand their dominance of the Korean economy. As a result, relatively inexperi-
enced Korean firms have been able to effectively compete in the
global economy during postcolonial years.

As a result of rapid *chaebol* expansion, the average number of
subsidiaries of the thirty largest increased from 4.2 in 1970 to 11.2
in 1977, 20.8 in 1995, and 26.8 in 1998 (table 5.2). The increase in
the 1970s derived mainly from establishment of new businesses.
The number of new firms (54.5 percent) far exceeded the number
of acquisitions (36.4 percent) (H. R. Kim 1998b, table 3): *chaebol*
reaped greater advantages from establishing than taking over an
operation because they could start with new technology, man-
power, and financial resources. During that decade new markets
and government incentives also encouraged the establishment of
new firms targeted at *chaebol*.

However, when worldwide recession during the late 1970s
brought government rationalization of industry, the share of
acquisitions increased dramatically. *Chaebol* acquired failing firms

Table 5.1. Top ten *chaebol* in Korea at five points in history (founding years)

1960	1975	1985	1995	1998 (April 15)
Samsung (1938)	Samsung	Lucky-Goldstar	Samsung	Hyundai
Samho (1950)	Lucky	Hyundai	Hyundai	Samsung
Kaepoong (1949)	Hyundai (1947)	Samsung	LG	Daewoo
Taehan (1946)	Hanjin (1945)	Sunkyung (1953)	Daewoo	LG
Lucky (1931)	Hyosung (1957)	Daewoo	Sunkyung	SK (Sunkyung)
Tongyang (1956)	Ssangyong (1939)	Ssangyong	Ssangyong	Hanjin
Keukdong (1947)	Daewoo (1967)	Hanjin	Hanjin	Ssangyong
Korea Glass (1954)	Doosan (1896)	Korea Explosives (1952)	Kia (1944)	Hanwha
Dongrip (1949)	Dong-A (1930)	Daelim (1939)	Hanwha	Kumho
Taechang (1916)	Shin Dong-A (1940)	Hyosung	Lotte (1967)	Dong-ah

Sources: Kang 1996: table 2-2; H. R. Kim 1998b: table 1; Fair Trade Commission 1998.

Table 5.2. The thirty largest *chaebol:* average
number of affiliated companies and industries

Year	Average number of affiliated companies	Average number of industries
1960	5.1	
1970	4.2	
1977	11.2	
1987	16.4	
1992	19.7	16.0
1994	20.5	19.1
1995	20.8	18.5
1998	26.8	

Source: H. R. Kim 1998b; Fair Trade Commission
1998.
Note: The average number for 1960 is for the
fourteen largest business groups. The number of
industries is based on the subdivisional industrial
classification of the Korean Standard Industrial
Classification (sixty industries). It excludes any
industry for which shipment is below 100 million
won.

and public enterprises and began to expand business lines for industrial restructuring. Consequently, the average number of subsidiaries for the thirty largest business groups increased to 16.4 in 1987. By the 1990s, the number of affiliated companies stabilized at about twenty, and the method of growth shifted from primarily acquisition (43.3 percent) in the 1980s to a combination of merger (27.3 percent) and acquisition (33.6 percent) in the 1990s (H. R. Kim 1998b). The average number of subsidiaries has again increased in recent years, to 26.8.

In short, the seeds of modern Korean enterprise planted in the colonial period lay dormant until nurtured by specific policies of the Rhee regime—state disposal of Japanese property, allocation of foreign assistance projects, and licensing of export and import firms. Characteristics of the *chaebol*—control by owner families, close links to the state, and concentration of investment in strategic projects based on such links—derived from the Japanese *zaibatsu* tradition. This heritage carried forward into the postcolonial periods under Rhee, Park, and Chun.

The foundation of economic governance set during those formative years enabled rapid economic growth. But by the mid-1990s, the various systems and institutions of that foundation were incriminated as primary sources of economic turmoil and began to reveal vulnerabilities in Korean economic governance. The rapidly changing environments inherent in globalization and financial liberalization raise the question of whether Korean economic governance is vulnerable to collapse and replacement by an alternative.

The Structure of Korean Economic Governance

The population of businesses in the manufacturing sector has clearly expanded during the period of export-led industrialization since the early 1960s. In what follows I identify how much growth is due to establishment of new firms and how much to expansion, or branching, of existing ones.

Organizational Vitality: Age Composition. Table 5.3 expresses historical changes in age composition in terms of the number of businesses for five birth cohorts. In addition, three birth cohorts after 1985 are also presented, each characterized by a very large fraction of businesses. Overall examination of age composition indicates that the proportions for each cohort declined significantly over every five-year interval, implying that young businesses dominated the population. For example, the

Table 5.3. Age distribution of businesses

Cohort/Year	1970	1975	1980	1985	1988
Pre–1950	2,426 (10.1)	1,157 (5.1)	799 (2.6)	477 (1.1)	437 (.7)
1951–1955	1,883 (7.8)	789 (3.5)	592 (1.9)	405 (0.9)	343 (.6)
1956–1960	3,389 (14.1)	1,470 (6.5)	887 (2.9)	558 (1.3)	523 (.9)
1961–1965	6,673 (27.7)	2,655 (11.7)	1637 (5.3)	774 (1.8)	682 (1.1)
1966–1970	9,718 (40.3)	6,083 (26.7)	3,536 (11.5)	2,452 (5.6)	2,164 (3.6)
1971–1975		10,596 (46.5)	8,750 (28.4)	4,766 (10.8)	4,363 (7.3)
1976–1980			14,610 (47.4)	14,609 (33.2)	12,872 (21.5)
1981–1985				19,949 (45.3)	14,561 (24.3)
1986					7,779 (13.0)
1987					9,192 (15.3)
1988					7,012 (11.7)
Total	24,114	22,787	30,823	44,037	59,928

Source: Economic Planning Board. *Industrial Census* 1973, 1978, 1983; *Report on Mining and Manufacturing Survey*, each year.

Note: Free-standing numbers indicate number of firms in a cohort; parenthetical numbers indicate proportion. *Report on Mining and Manufacturing Survey* shows data on age composition only up to 1988.

proportion for firms ten years or younger in 1970 was 68 percent and has steadily increased to 73.2 percent in 1975, 75.8 percent in 1980, and 78.5 percent in 1985.

It is also important to examine the age composition of businesses in terms of aggregate importance. Employment share and output production over five time periods measure aggregate importance. Quick data comparison brings out striking contrasts. For example, as table 3 shows, the number of firms from the pre-1950 cohort stood at 10.1 percent in 1970 and declined dramatically to 1.1 percent by 1985. But the aggregate importance of employment share for this cohort does not show the same dramatic decline, decreasing only from 15.0 percent to 4.4 percent during the same time period. Likewise, there is a similar attenuated decline in terms of value added—for the pre-1950 cohort only from 20.6 percent in 1970 to 6.1 percent in 1985.

That all cohorts show similar patterns indicates that many old firms have disappeared, but survivors have grown significantly in size. Average level of employment and average value added per enterprise for the pre-1950 cohort grew significantly from 53 and 47 in 1970 to 223 and 3,440 in 1985 (H. R. Kim 1999). This increase in economic importance is similar for all but the younger cohorts.

Younger cohorts contributed a relatively small amount to employment and output. For example, about 45 percent of the total number of firms were less than five years old, but they provided approximately only 31 percent of total employment and 22 percent of total value added (H. R. Kim 1999). These proxies for economic importance are significantly low compared to those for older cohorts.

The fact that the share of aggregate economic importance for the younger cohorts is much lower than their actual population share probably reflects their smaller size at the time of inception than anything else. Survivors are likely to grow in size. In other words, although very young members dominate the population of firms in numbers, expansion of existing operations rather than entry of new businesses is likely the significant factor accounting for employment and output growth in the business sector since 1970.

Size Dispersion. To discover how Korean economic governance has been shaped, we also can investigate the numerical distribution of variously sized businesses. Size distribution over time is examined in three different categories: (1) proportion of businesses with a given number of employees, (2) proportion of employees in firms of various sizes, and (3) proportion of production in businesses of various sizes.

Table 5.4 shows the historical size (number of workers) distribution of firms, as a proportion. For example, between 1953 and 1960, the average size of manufacturing businesses declined by half. Much of this decline is accounted for by an increase in the proportion of very small firms employing fewer than twenty workers, from 72.7 percent in 1955 to 81.3 percent in 1960. During 1950s reconstruction, the slow expansion of economic activity occurred primarily in small-scale, self-owned, labor-intensive businesses (H. R. Kim 1998a).

However, in the 1960s and 1970s, large-scale and capital-intensive forms of organization took hold, dramatically increasing the average number of employees per firm. The proportion of the number of businesses employing more than twenty workers dramatically declined from 81.3 percent in 1960 to 58.5 percent in 1977. But since the early 1980s, the proportion has steadily increased, to 72.4 percent in 1996.

Table 5.5 shows the historical distribution of employees and production in businesses of various sizes, as a proportion. Again, the share of small-scale establishments in total employment declined from 35.5 percent in 1960 to 7.5 percent in 1977. But their share steadily increased in the early 1980s and rapidly in the early 1990s.

Conversely, the proportion of large-scale firms with more than 300 workers increased in the 1960s and 1970s, but decreased in the next two decades. At the same time, the average number of workers in this size group increased from 582.8 in 1966 to 667.3 in 1974. However, the employment share and number of businesses with 300 or more workers decreased during the 1980s and the early 1990s. The pattern of change in the proportion of production for firms of various sizes is similar to what we observed above. In the 1980s, small-scale firms reversed their employment and production decline.

Changes in the configuration of businesses as indicated by number of workers show that the proportion of employment and production provided by small-scale enterprises of fewer than 100 employees declined dramatically in the early phase of industrialization. When economic growth took off, large-scale production in a wide range of industries employing large numbers dominated industrial development. Korea has become big-enterprise oriented

Table 5.4. Proportion of the number of organizations of various sizes (%)

Year*/Size	<20	20–99	100–199	200+	Total
1953	95.9		2.5	1.5	2,368
1955**	72.7	24.4	2.0	0.8	8,628
1960	81.3	16.3	1.5	0.9	15,204
1966	80.1	16.2	2.0	1.7	22,718
1974	69.1	21.4	4.3	5.4	22,632
	<20	20–99	100–299	300+	
1977	58.5	28.5	8.9	4.1	26,726
1983	59.2	31.1	7.0	2.6	39,243
1990	60.6	32.9	4.8	1.7	68,872
1993	69.0	26.6	3.3	1.1	88,864
1996	72.4	23.7	3.0	0.9	97,144

Source: Bank of Korea, *Economic Review*, 1956; Korean Reconstruction Bank, *Final Report: Census of Mining and Manufacturing*, 1958; Ministry of Commerce and Industry/Korean Reconstruction Bank, *Final Report*, 1960; Economic Planning Board, *Report on Mining and Manufacturing Survey*, 1963; Economic Planning Board, *Report on Industrial Census*, 1983; Economic Planning Board, *Report on Mining and Manufacturing Survey*, various years.

Note: Asterisks indicate the proportion of the number of organizations with five or more workers: *as of the end of each year; **as of the end of October 1955.

Table 5.5. Proportion of employees and production in businesses of various size (%, each person, million won)

Year/ Size	<20		20-99	100-199	200+	Total
1953		57.6	9.1		33.3	101,345
1958*	32.7		34.1	11.0	22.3	260,427
	25.9		30.1	10.9	33.1	157,549
1960	35.5		32.1	10.5	21.9	275,254
	28.7		28.4	9.4	33.6	218,656
1966	25.5		24.4	10.3	39.7	566,665
	15.2		18.3	9.1	57.5	156,174
1974	10.5		16.0	10.7	62.8	1,298,384
	4.9		11.5	8.9	74.6	1,867,176

Year/ Size	<20	20-99	100-299	300+	
1977	7.5	17.5	21.0	54.0	1,918,931
	3.9	11.9	16.6	67.6	5,596,717
1983	10.1	23.8	10.9	45.2	2,215,233
	4.6	14.3	18.2	62.9	20,911,446
1990	14.0	30.1	17.7	38.3	3,019,816
	7.0	20.2	17.1	55.7	70,924,547
1993	20.1	31.1	16.7	31.1	2,885,349
	10.4	22.2	17.7	49.7	108,521,742
1996	22.1	30.8	16.3	30.8	2,897,672
	10.8	20.4	16.0	52.8	174,215,220

Source: Bank of Korea, *Economic Review*, 1956; Korean Reconstruction Bank, *Final Report: Census of Mining and Manufacturing*, 1958; Ministry of Commerce and Industry/Korean Reconstruction Bank, *Final Report*, 1960; Economic Planning Board, *Report on Mining and Manufacturing Survey*, 1963; Economic Planning Board, *Report on Industrial Census*, 1983; Economic Planning Board, *Report on Mining and Manufacturing Survey*, various years.
Notes: First row represents proportion of employees; second row, proportion of value added.
* As of end of March 1958.

much more completely and quickly than other East Asian countries such as Japan and Taiwan (H. R. Kim 1993).

Managerial Hierarchy and Concentration: Business Groups. Economic power analyzed at the firm level may misjudge the degree and source of market power in the Korean economy because a small number of *chaebol* control a substantial number of large firms. In manufacturing in 1994, the share of the thirty largest *chaebol* reached 39.6 percent of shipments, 36.9 percent of value added, and 17.7 percent of employment (H. R. Kim 1998b; Yoon and Lee 1997).

By 1987, *chaebol* also dominated in shipments of two industry groups: 49 percent share in the chemicals and petroleum, coal, rubber, and plastic products industries; and 49.2 percent in the fabricated metal products, machinery, and equipment industries (Lee 1990). These industries not only made up the largest share of the Korean manufacturing sector, but were also the fastest growing in the 1970s.

The distribution of subsidiaries of the top thirty *chaebol* shows that most were in heavy and chemical industries, textiles and apparel, and food and beverages. The top five *chaebol* showed high subsidiary concentration in fabricated metal products, machinery, and transportation equipment, but the top thirty as a whole had relatively even distribution across other industries as well (Lee 1990).

The most conspicuous *chaebol* feature is their reach across all sectors of industry: Korea's leading *chaebol* tend to be highly diversified. Study of the 108 largest *chaebol* reveals a close relationship between size and diversification strategies (Jung 1987). The ten largest *chaebol* use an "octopus-arms" strategy that reaches across unrelated products, whereas smaller *chaebol* generally have a dominant product focus. Similar to the latter, *chaebol* of the 1970s were vertically integrated in a limited number of related sectors, but more recently the trend has been toward wide reach across unrelated industrial sectors. Overdiversification leaves business groups unable to cope with changing environments and is one of the major sources of vulnerability in economic governance.

Another distinctive feature of *chaebol* is domination by the founder and his family (Shin and Chin 1989; Ungson, Steers, and Park 1997). Despite state pressure to sell shares on the stock exchange and dilute family ownership, less than 30 percent of affiliate companies were listed in the 1990s. The thirty largest *chaebol* listed only 27.6 percent of their affiliates, while the share of total capital for those listed was 63.1 percent (Fair Trade Commission 1996: 119). Nearly all unlisted firms are owned and controlled by the founding family of the *chaebol*, which often uses the group holding company or trading company to control all subsidiaries. Family ownership passes from generation to generation. Surveys show that more than 90 percent of inherited *chaebol* have passed from father to son or to other family members. Ownership and management monopoly coupled with inheritance of ownership are characteristic of *chaebol*.

Chaebol subsidiaries are owned by individual founding-family shareholders and other affiliates that these people control. It is especially striking that the greater the size of the *chaebol*, the higher the average ratio of interfirm shareholding. Furthermore, subsidiaries are managed in tandem with one another, relying on extensive cross-payment debt guarantees. Thus, the ratio of net worth for Korean companies in 1995 was 19.9 percent, significantly lower than the 51.8 percent for Taiwan in 1992, 36.4 percent for the United States in 1993, and 31.6 percent for Japan in 1992 (H. R. Kim 1998a).

The high debt-to-equity ratio of Korean *chaebol* received particular attention during the financial crisis (table 5.6). The average debts of the top thirty were more than fourfold their equity capital (Korea Stock Exchange 1998). With the business slowdown and IMF-imposed stringency, average debt-to-equity ratio of the thirty newly designated largest conglomerates soared to 517.9 percent in 1997 from 386.5 percent at the close of 1996 (Fair Trade Commission 1998). However, as a result of the IMF's directive that cross-debt guarantees between affiliates be terminated, the ratio of interfirm shareholding and debt ratio decreased to below 200 percent by the end of 1999.

Market Integrity: Linkages. Korean economic governance exhibits a relatively low level of market integrity, or cross-enterprise (in this case, *chaebol*) linkages or networks. The largest 100 firms controlled 38.5 percent of total manufacturing sales in 1966; this percentage increased slowly to 46.8 percent in 1982, before decreasing to 38.7 percent by 1994. In terms of employment, the largest 100 account for approximately 20 percent of manufacturing employment, but this ratio decreased in the 1990s (H. R. Kim 1998b; Yoon and Lee 1997).

Market structure is measured by market concentration in terms of the number of commodities and sales value. The share of

Table 5.6. Top ten *chaebol* debt-to-equity ratio (March 15, 1998) (%)

Rank	Name	Number of subsidiaries	Debt-to-equity
1	Hyundai	62 (57)	578.7
2	Samsung	61 (80)	370.9
3	Daewoo	37 (30)	471.9
4	LG	52 (49)	505.8
5	SK	45 (46)	467.9
6	Hanjin	25 (24)	907.8
7	Ssangyong	22 (25)	399.7
8	Hanwha	31 (31)	1,214.7
9	Kumho	32 (26)	944.1
10	Dong-ah	22 (19)	359.9

Source: Fair Trade Commission 1998.

Note: Figures in parentheses are for 1996.

industries characterized as monopolies increased in the 1970s, mainly because the early phase of heavy and chemical industrialization and lax enforcement of antitrust laws marked the decade. The rise of oligopolies since then indicates the tendency of *chaebol* to establish dominance in a variety of industries. Table 5.7 shows that the percentage of the number of monopolistic commodities has declined since the late 1970s, while the percentage for competitive commodities increased into 1990s.

Although not all groups competed in the major markets, the dominant pattern is oligopolistic, with each *chaebol* competing with at least one other in each of its major markets. For each of the 78 manufacturing industries in which *chaebol* are active, there were averages of 3 *chaebol* and 3.8 *chaebol* member firms operating in each industry. The oligopolistic market structure persists; shifting toward a more competitive market structure would improve the viability of the Korean economy.

Another significant determinant of economic governance is interconnections among firms. One method of interbusiness networking is subcontracting, which refers to businesses' dependency on suppliers, customers, and other industry partners. Subcontracting has never really developed in Korea because of the aggressive vertical integration and horizontal predation into other product lines by *chaebol*. Although *chaebol* are not embedded in networks of mutual obligation with outside firms in the same and related sectors, they depend heavily on banks, state agencies, and political connections. Subcontracting is much less marked in Korea than in other East Asian countries.

The lack of extra-*chaebol* interdependence is reflected in the low percentage of establishments engaged in subcontracting in manufacturing. At the establishment level, the share of subcontracting was 12.5 percent in 1978 and 21.3 percent in 1980. At the firm level, it was 11.6 percent in 1969 and 30.1 percent in 1980 (H. R. Kim 1993). *Chaebol* rely on hierarchy rather than the market to acquire small and medium-scale businesses as part of vertical integration. However, subcontracting relationships did begin to emerge after the early 1980s. The share of subcontracting by firms has in fact increased significantly, from 18.2 percent in 1978 to 42.5 percent in 1986. The proportion of subcontractors who produce more than or equal to 80 percent of total shipments for subcontracting increased from 57.4 percent in 1975 to almost 80 percent in 1986. Subcontracting networks need to be further developed to revitalize the Korean economy.

Table 5.7. Market structure in manufacturing (%)

	1970	1977	1981	1989	1994
Monopoly	29.6*	31.6	23.5	18.1	15.3
	8.7**	16.3	11.0	8.5	5.1
Duopoly	18.7	20.1	9.6	10.1	8.2
	16.3	11.0	4.7	7.2	5.6
Oligopoly	33.2	32.0	49.0	44.2	44.4
	35.1	33.9	50.9	39.3	43.4
Competitive	18.5	16.3	17.9	27.6	32.1
	39.9	38.8	33.4	45.0	45.9
Total	1,492	2,109	2,214	2,615	3,132
	1,252	13,920	44,183	140,368	281,944

Source: Yoon and Lee 1997: table 8-4.

Notes: Monopoly: $CR_1 \geq 80$ %, $S_1/S_2 \leq 10.0$; duopoly: $CR_2 \geq 80$%, $S_1/S_2 \leq 5.0$, $S_3 < 5$; oligopoly: $CR_3 \geq 60$% except monopoly and duopoly; competitive: $CR_3 < 60$%.

* Numbers in first line are percentage of the number of commodities.

** Numbers in second line are percentage of the value of shipments.

Discussion and Conclusion

Despite remarkable economic growth and export expansion, the Korean economy faces crisis. Better understanding of this juncture requires determining the origins of Korean economic governance as well as its structural characteristics over time. The sources of viability and vulnerability in Korean economic governance must also be examined to understand the historical mechanisms at work. Vulnerability exists when a form of economic governance is not able to preserve its overarching characteristics in a given circumstance. In a rapidly changing environment, a vulnerable form of governance is unable to mobilize or organize economic and political resources that would ensure continued functioning of the economy or its own self-preservation. The recent crisis, however, has led to overemphasis of vulnerabilities and weaknesses in Korean economic governance. Recent analyses have by and large excluded characteristics of viability—such as the ability of a mode of economic governance to continually adapt to changing environments. This chapter has attempted to rediscover those sources of viability that have historically existed in the structuring of Korean economic governance.

First, this study suggests that although the seeds of modern business were sown during the late Chosŏn dynasty, Korean economic governance emerged and took hold during the colonial period as well as the immediate postcolonial years of division, war, and reconstruction under Syngman Rhee. It has undergone three stages: genesis, when several indigenous enterprises were established under the colonial state; formation, when business groups, or *chaebol,* burgeoned during the Rhee regime; and growth, when large-scale *chaebol* flourished, after the early 1960s.

Second, this study's scrutiny of four interrelated dimensions of structure—organizational vitality, size dispersion, managerial hierarchy, and market integrity—illuminates the vulnerabilities and viability in Korea's economic governance. In terms of organizational vitality, Korean economic governance is quite viable in that very young members dominate the population of organizations. They are, however, greatly outweighed by older members in terms of aggregate importance. Consequently, expansion rather than entry accounts for most growth in employment and output in the manufacturing sector.

In terms of size dispersion, Korean economic governance has become conglomerate oriented. By and large, large-scale *chaebol* embracing a wide range of industries dominate, suggesting monopolistic market structure. However, recent years have brought a resurgence of small-scale businesses, as measured by employment and production. This is a sign of viability, in that small-scale enterprises provide the greater production flexibility and adaptability required to flourish in the rapidly changing economic environments of globalization and financial liberalization.

Managerial hierarchy in Korean economic governance shows bias toward bigness and toward vertically integrated large-scale *chaebol.* Control by family owners, an owner-centered obsolete management system, unrelated diversified business lines, and debt-ridden financial structures are the main characteristics of *chaebol* and are believed to be the main source of vulnerability in Korean economic governance. Thus, *chaebol* need to be restructured to specialize in a few core business lines, each led by professional managers, and also to develop sound financial policies by eliminating cross-guarantees.

Finally, as regards market integrity, subcontracting has never fully developed in Korea. Instead, aggressive vertical integration and horizontal predation have characterized interfirm relationships, creating a concentrated market structure. This lack of interdependence among independent firms (vs. *chaebol* subsidiaries) is another source of vulnerability in Korean economic governance. In a highly competitive international market, businesses and business groups need to cooperate and collaborate with each other by establishing extensive subcontracting networks and strategic alliances if they are to cope with turbulent market conditions.

To conclude, the business vitality indicated by a resurgence of small-scale businesses bodes well for the Korean economy. This vitality will assist recovery from financial crisis and needs to involve specialized business lines within business groups with sound financial structures and management systems. In addition, development of symbiotic subcontracting networks would provide another source of viability in the face of rapidly changing economic environments.

In Chinese characters, the word "crisis" comprises two elements: danger and opportunity. Danger lies in the continued Asian financial crisis, threatening meltdown of the governance system. Opportunity inheres in the chance to reform the economic governance system in a saving direction. The Korean government is taking steps to deal with globalization and market liberalization by restructuring the financial and corporate systems. At the same time, the business sector is ending the practice of mutually guaranteeing debts owed by subsidiaries of the same *chaebol,* adjusting corporate structure along more specialized lines, and beginning to hire professional managers. Although besieged by international and domestic pressures, the Korean economy may be exhibiting characteristics of change and reform that will propel it through the current crisis to a balanced position in the global economy.

References

Amsden, A. 1989. *Asia's Next Giant: South Korea and Late Industrialization.* New York: Oxford University Press.

———. 1997. "South Korea: Enterprising Groups and Entrepreneurial Government." In *Big Business and the Wealth of Nations,* ed. A. D. Chandler, Jr., R. Amatori, and T. Hikino. Cambridge: Cambridge University Press.

Balassa, Bela. 1988. "The Lessons of East Asian Development: An Overview." *Economic Development and Cultural Change* 36:273–290.

Bank of Korea. 1956. *Economic Review.* Seoul: Bank of Korea.

———. 1998. *Internal Report.* Seoul: Bank of Korea.

Chandler, Jr., A. D. 1997. *The Invisible Hand: The Management Revolution in American Business.* Cambridge: Harvard University Press.

Chandler, Jr., A. D.; F. Amatori; and T. Hikino, eds. 1997. *Big Business and the Wealth of Nations.* Cambridge: Cambridge University Press.

Cho, D. S. 1996. "Han'guk chaebol ŭi munchechŏm kwa tae chaebol chŏngch'aek ŭi kaesŏn panghyang" (The problems and policies for Korean *chaebol*). *Sasang* (Ideology), 1996:31–55.

Chung, K. H., and H. C. Lee, eds. 1989. *Korean Managerial Dynamics.* New York: Praeger.

Coase, R. 1937. "The Nature of the Firm." *Economica* 4:386–405.

Dhonte, P., and I. Kapur. 1997. "Toward a Market Economy: Structures of Governance." IMF Working Paper 97/11.

DiMaggio, P., and W. Powell. 1983. "The Iron Cage Revisited: Institutional Isomorphism and Collective Rationality in Organization Fields." *American Sociological Review* 48:147–160.

Eckert, C. 1991. *Offspring of Empire: The Koch'ang Kims and the Colonial Origins of Korean Capitalism, 1876–1945.* Seattle: University of Washington Press.

Economic Planning Board of Korea. Various years. *Report on Industrial Census.* Seoul: Economic Planning Board.

———. Various years. *Report on Mining and Manufacturing Survey.* Seoul: Economic Planning Board.

Fair Trade Commission. Various years. *The Yearbook of Fair Trade.* Seoul: Economic Planning Board.

Feldstein, M. 1998. "Overdoing It in East Asia." *Foreign Affairs,* March/April.

Frischtak, Leila. 1994. "Governance Capacity and Economic Reform in Developing Economics." World Bank Technical Paper 254.

Grajdanzev, Andrew J. 1944. *Modern Korea.* New York: John Day.

Haggard, Stephan. 1990. *Pathways from the Periphery: The Politics of Growth in the Newly Industrializing Economies.* Ithaca, N.Y.: Cornell University Press.

Hollingsworth, J. R., and R. Boyer, eds. 1997. *Contemporary Capitalism: The Embeddedness of Institutions.* Cambridge: Cambridge University Press.

Jacobs, N. 1985. *The Korean Road to Modernization and Development.* Urbana, Ill.: University of Illinois Press.

Jones, L. P., and I. Sakong. 1980. *Government, Business, and Entrepreneurship in Economic Development: The Korean Case.* Cambridge: Harvard University Press.

Jung, K. H. 1987. *Growth Strategy and Managerial Structure of Korean Businesses.* Seoul: Korea Chamber of Commerce and Industry.

Kang, M. H. 1996. *The Korean Business Conglomerate:* Chaebol *Then and Now.* Korea Research Monograph 21. Berkeley: Institute of East Asian Studies, University of California.

Kim, E. M. 1997. *Big Business, Strong State.* Albany: State University of New York Press.

Kim, H. R. 1993. "Divergent Organizational Paths of Industrialization in East Asia." *Asian Perspective* 17:105–135.

———. 1994. "The State and Economic Organization in a Comparative Perspective: The Organizing Mode of the East Asian Political Economy." *Korean Social Science Journal* 20:91–120.

———. 1998a. "Colonial Origins of Economic Governance in Korea." Working paper. Institute for Modern Korean Studies, Yonsei University.

———. 1998b. "The Evolution of the Korean Business System." *Sangnam Forum* 1:81–109.

———. 1999. "Ecological Dynamics of Industrial Organizations in South Korea." *Asian Pacific Business Review* 6(2):39–43.

———. 2000. "Fragility or Continuity?: Economic Governance of East Asian Capitalism." In *Politics and Markets in the Wake of the Asian Crisis*, ed. R. Robison, K. Jayasuriya, M. Beeson, and Hyuk-Rae Kim, 99–115. London: Routledge.

Korea Stock Exchange. 1998. *Inside Report.* Seoul: Korea Stock Exchange.

Korean Reconstruction Bank. 1958. *Final Report: Census of Mining and Manufacturing.* Seoul: Korean Reconstruction Bank.

Lee, Y. K. 1990. "Conglomeration and Business Concentration in Korea." In *Korean Economic Development*, ed. J. K. Kwon. New York: Greenwood Press.

———. 1997. *The State, Society, and Big Business in South Korea.* London: Routledge.

Maurice, M.; A. Sorge; and M. Warner. 1980. "Societal Differences in Organizing Manufacturing Units." *Organization Studies* 1:59–86.

McNamara, D. 1990. *The Colonial Origins of Korean Enterprise, 1910–1945.* Cambridge: Cambridge University Press.

Ministry of Commerce and Industry/Korean Reconstruction Bank. 1960. *Final Report.* Seoul: Ministry of Commerce and Industry.

Ministry of Finance and Economy. 1998. *Inside Report.* Seoul: Ministry of Finance and Economy.

Shin, E. H., and S. W. Chin. 1989. "Social Affinity among Top Managerial Executives of Large Corporations in Korea." *Sociological Forum* 4:3–26.

Sorge, A., and M. Warner. 1986. *Comparative Factory Organization.* Aldershot: Gower.

Ungson, G.; R. Steers; and S. H. Park. 1997. *Korean Enterprise: The Quest for Globalization.* Boston: Harvard Business School Press.

Wade, R. 1990. *Governing the Market: Economic Theory and the Role of Government in East Asian Industrialization.* Princeton, N.J.: Princeton University Press.

Whitley, R. 1992. *Business Systems in East Asia: Firms, Markets and Societies.* Newbury Park, Calif.: Sage Publications.

———. 1994. "Dominant Forms of Economic Organization in Market Economies." *Organization Studies* 15:153–182.

Williamson, O. 1996. *The Mechanisms of Governance.* New York: Oxford University Press.

Wong, S. L. 1985. "The Chinese Family Firm: A Model." *British Journal of Sociology* 36:58–72.

World Bank. 1992. *Governance and Development.* Washington, D.C.: Government Printing Office.

———. 1993. *The East Asian Miracle: Economic Growth and Public Policy.* Oxford: Oxford University Press.

Yoon, C. H., and K. U. Lee. 1997. *Sanŭp chojikron* (Industrial organization). Seoul: Bupmoonsa.

Young, A. 1994. "Lessons from the East Asian NICS: A Contraction View." *European Economic Review* 38:964–973.

SIX

From Take-off to Drop-off?: Postwar Economic Development and Industrialization

KARL J. FIELDS

The twentieth century descended upon South Korea (hereafter Korea) with stunning intensity, bringing to a dramatic and certain end its former "hermit" status. Brutal colonization, devastating wars (hot and cold), foreign and civil and less tragically (but not the less transformative) hyper-rapid industrialization, and thoroughgoing socioeconomic change irrevocably transformed this East Asian nation. Korea's remarkable postwar industrialization was arguably the centerpiece of this drama. The largest of East Asia's miracle minidragons, Korea has had the most mercurial postwar developmental experience.

The destruction and division of both the Pacific War (1937–1945) and the Korean War (1950–1953) left Korea among the poorest countries of the world. War damage destroyed nearly two-thirds of its production facilities, infrastructure, and even much of its housing, and claimed by one estimate the lives of nearly one-tenth of the population (Halliday and Cumings 1988 as cited by Lie 1998). By 1961, per capita income was still only US$82 (in current prices), inflation persisted in the double digits, and social unrest and political instability plagued the country.

The next three decades witnessed an industrial development program of rapid (though somewhat uneven) growth in Korea that outpaced the efforts of almost all other postcolonial developing countries.[1] From 1962 to 1969, the real growth rate averaged

---

[1] The only other exceptions among developing countries that have demonstrated comparable growth rates are the remaining East Asian "tigers" or "mini-dragons," which include Taiwan, a political economy with which Korea is frequently and favorably compared, and the entrepôts of Hong Kong and Singapore.

nearly 9 percent per annum and slowed only slightly during the 1970s and 1980s, still averaging more than 8 percent during both decades. The pace slowed only slightly again to 7.5 percent during the 1990s in the years before the 1997 financial crisis (see table 6.1). By 1996, Korea had become the world's eleventh largest economy, boasted a GDP per capita of over US$10,000, and had earned membership in that most exclusive of rich nation's clubs, the Organization for Economic Cooperation and Development (OECD).

By the following year, however, the Asian financial crisis, which brought much of Asia (and subsequently other regions of the globe) to its knees, pushed Korea to the brink of financial meltdown, and compelled it to accept radical reform measures at the hands of the International Monetary Fund. GDP contraction for 1998 in Korea has been estimated at 5.4 percent with a midyear unemployment rate of 7.6 percent, up from 2.5 percent in 1997 (Chang 1998: 437). This signals a more severe contraction than that experienced in 1980 in the wake of two global oil crises and Korea's own political crisis.

While optimists point to the recent upturn in the Korean stock market as evidence that the postcrisis Korean economy has turned the corner and is regaining momentum, many observers remain pessimistic. Writing of the unraveling of the Korean economy in the final weeks of 1997, one scholar describes it as "the final, inglorious end of the Korean economic miracle" (Chang 1998: 437). Some go further, arguing that the so-called miracle was little more than a mirage and that sown in the institutions, inefficiencies, and irregularities of its economic take-off were the seeds of its inevitable drop-off.

Such dramatic, and until recently, largely successful transformation in a country whose cohort of developing nations has too often been characterized by persistent stagnation has not gone unnoticed. There has been no shortage of explanations of Korean industrialization and economic development, if little consensus among these accounts. The economic crisis of the late 1990s likewise generated a great deal of both discussion and controversy. This chapter chronicles the flow and recent ebb of Korea's developmental experience and examines competing explanations for this transformation.

These alternative explanations for both the postwar rise and more recent decline of Korea are broadly grouped into market, statist, and cultural approaches. This chapter concludes, however,

Karl J. Fields

Table 6.1. Selected principal economic indicators, 1962–2000

Year	Economic growth rate (GNP)	Inflation rate (CPI)	Per capita national income (GDP US$)	Exports (custom clearance) (US$ mil.)	Imports (custom clearance) (US$ mil.)
1962	2.2	--	87	54.8	421.8
1963	9.1	--		86.8	560.3
1964	9.6	--		119.1	404.4
1965	5.8	--		175.1	463.6
1966	12.7	11.2		250.3	716.4
1967	6.6	10.8		320.2	996.2
1668	11.3	10.4		455.4	1,462.9
1969	13.8	12.9		622.5	1,823.6
1970	7.6	15.6	253	835.2	1,984.0
1971	9.4	13.5		1,067.6	2,394.3
1972	5.8	11.5		1,624.1	2,522.0
1973	14.9	3.2		3,225.0	4,240.3
1974	8.0	24.5		4,460.4	6,851.8
1975	7.1	25.2		6,081.0	7,274.4
1976	15.1	15.3		7,715.3	8,773.6
1977	10.3	10.2		10,046.5	10,810.5
1978	11.6	14.5		12,710.6	14,971.9
1979	6.4	18.3		15,055.5	20,338.6
1980	-4.8	28.7	1,597	17,504.9	22,291.7
1981	6.6	21.3		21,253.8	26,131.4

Table 6.1 cont.

1982	5.4	7.3		21,853.4	24,250.8
1983	11.9	3.4		24,445.1	26,192.2
1984	8.4	2.3		29,244.9	30,631.4
1985	5.4	2.5		30,283.1	31,135.7
1986	11.0	2.8		34,714.5	31,583.9
1987	11.0	3.1		47,280.9	41,019.8
1988	10.5	7.1		50,696.4	51,810.6
1989	6.1	5.7		52,377.2	61,464.8
1990	9.0	8.6	5,883	65,015.7	69,843.7
1991	9.2	9.3		71,870.1	81,524.9
1992	5.4	6.2		76,631.5	81,775.3
1993	5.5	4.8		82,235.9	83,800.1
1994	8.3	6.3		96,013.2	102,348.2
1995	8.9	4.5	10,037	125,058.0	135,118.9
1996	6.8	4.9	10,548	129,715.1	150,339.1
1997	5.0	4.4	9,511	136,164.2	144,616.4
1998	-6.7	7.5	6,723	132,313.1	93,281.8
1999	10.9	0.8	8,551	143,685.5	119.752.3
2000	9.3	2.3	9,628	172,267.5	160,481.0

Sources: Bank of Korea, *Principal Economic Indicators, 1962-86* (Seoul: Republic of Korea, 1988); Bank of Korea, *Principal Economic Indicators, 1987-2002* (http://www.bok.or.kr/index_e.html), accessed May 2002); Koreascope, *Economic Growth and National Income* (http://www.koreascope.org/english/sub/1/index3-a.htm), accessed May 2002.

that monocausal explanations are not only inaccurate but potentially dangerous. The most persuasive explanations are ecumenical and may be labeled institutional, falling in the interstices of
these broad divisions. In sum, no useful explanation of the
Korean developmental experience can ignore the role of unique
traditional Korean elements, market forces, or the profound
influence of the Korean state.

The following section briefly summarizes each of these competing accounts for Korean industrial development and proposes an
alternative synthetic institutional framework as the most satisfac-
tory explanation. The third section examines the evolving strategies, shifting policies, and structural consequences of this industrialization program from before its take-off in the 1960s to the
seeming drop-off at the end of the century. The final section then
revisits the categories of explanation, in an effort to account for
the more recent downturn and once again utilizes an institutional
framework for understanding both the crisis in Korea and the obstacles and opportunities for Korea to survive and thrive in a
postcrisis Asian and global economy.

Competing Accounts for Development

Causal explanation is the ultimate goal of all scientific enterprise, from the cell biologist's search for a cure for cancer to the
economist's efforts to predict inflation. The nature of the human,
and particularly the social, condition, however, has made the
discovery of such explanations in the scientific study of societies
(what we call the social sciences) particularly elusive and the
debate over contending claims hotly contested. Few debates are
as contentious (and undetermined) as that over a potential "cure"
for underdevelopment in less-developed countries (LDCs).

The remarkable postwar growth experience of a handful of
East Asian political economies including Korea's has provided a
rich laboratory for a host of social scientists working in the disciplines of economics, politics, sociology, and anthropology (among
others). Although there is even substantial disagreement within
disciplines, three broad paradigms for explaining East Asia's
exceptional postwar capitalist development have emerged.[2] The

---

[2] I use the term "paradigm" intentionally, indicating my belief that in Kuhnian
terms, the branch of social science concerned with economic and political development is still in a stage of "pre-science" or pre-paradigmatic inquiry. See Kuhn
1970 and Barnes 1982.

three contenders examined in this section champion markets, states, and culture, respectively, as the key ingredients in explaining Korean development. I examine each in turn, before offering a hybrid institutional alternative.

Markets: Laissez-Faire Capitalism

The most influential of these paradigms is that put forth by neoclassical economists who, like their classical predecessors Adam Smith and David Ricardo, saw virtue in markets and vice in most government or state hindrances to the free flow of these markets. These market advocates argue that unfettered and therefore competitive markets for goods and services maximize the efficiency of the myriad exchanges that take place, thereby maximizing growth and ultimately human (consumer) welfare. For neoclassical economists, the laws of supply and demand (as expressed in the price mechanism) are much more effective at guiding the rational choices of both producers and consumers than the most well meaning and carefully reasoned policies of government bureaucrats. More troubling is that political leaders can and often do restrict market forces in ways that distribute largesse to, or create unproductive rents for, favored groups in exchange for political support.

To escape the deleterious effects of state intervention, with its inevitable inefficiency and probable "crony capitalism," the neoclassical prescription for development is one of openness and market discipline. This policy has been highly influential, monopolizing official development policy in the West and the institutions charged with carrying out these policies in LDCs, such as the World Bank, International Monetary Fund, and the United States Agency for International Development. Because the free market paradigm was the dominant postwar program for promoting LDC development, analysts naturally turned to it as the logical explanation in accounting for the remarkable developmental success of the East Asian tigers following their rags-to-riches takeoff beginning in the 1960s.[3]

The key to Korea's economic success, according to the neoclassical explanation, was that the Korean state intervened less in the market than was the case in other developing economies. The key

---

[3] This section, and the subsequent discussion of the statist paradigm, draws on Amsden 1989, Kang 1995, Chang 1993, and Evans 1992.

transition occurred during the early 1960s, with a strategic shift from inward-looking or import-substituting industrialization to an outward-looking or export-led growth strategy. The protective economy of the 1950s, characterized by inefficient firms sheltered from competition by high tariff walls and discouraged from exporting by multiple exchange rates, gave way to a more open economy with lower tariffs, uniform and realistic exchange rates, and less interference in both labor and commodity markets. These policies spurred dramatic economic growth by making exporting profitable, thereby allowing Korea to pursue its comparative advantage in labor-intensive industries, and exposing domestic producers to the competitive pressures of the international market, thereby improving the efficiency of the economy.

Although this explanation may have made good theoretical sense, close observers of the Korean development experience were quick to point out that the Korean state intervened consistently, extensively, and pervasively in the marketplace, even, or perhaps particularly, as the Korean economy shifted to a more export-oriented strategy. Compelled to reconcile this apparent paradox, neoclassical proponents responded in two ways. One argument held that the coincidence of growth and state intervention did not mean that intervention was beneficial, but rather that had there been even less of it, growth would have been even greater. A second, more nuanced argument acknowledged that some state intervention, although distortative, was in fact positive because it offset distortions caused by other policies. Although distorting to the economy, in the case of Korea such distortions led to a canceling out of positive and negative interventions with the net result being a "virtual" free market or free trade regime with a neutral incentive structure. In sum, the neoclassical paradigm characterizes the state's role as harmless at best, but too often harmful.

States: Developmental Capitalism

As on-the-ground accounts of Korean development accumulated, it became increasingly difficult to deny the presence and even contribution of the state in this industrialization process. As economists and others drew on the cases of Korea, Japan, Taiwan, and other Asian high-growth economies, a second paradigm emerged; it contended that the state, far from being harmful or even harmless, was in fact playing a positive or developmental role in the industrialization process.

This "statist" literature denied neither the potential for government-inspired distortion and corruption nor the key role of market forces, but afforded not just a regulatory, but also a developmental role for the state in the process of industrialization. That is, instead of watching from the sidelines or serving as referee, the state was acting as coach and in many cases the star player in the game of industrialization. Proponents contended that because state formation typically preceded industrialization in these late-developing nations and given the particular demands and opportunities of "catch-up" industrialization, the neoclassical account had become both empirically inaccurate in accounting for East Asian high-speed growth and prescriptively inappropriate for developing countries in general.

In the case of Korea, proponents argued that in order to overcome its relative backwardness and achieve the national goal of an "independent economy," political leaders supported by skilled bureaucrats assumed the responsibility of guarding the gate to and from the international political economy, accumulating capital, and deciding what, when, and how much and to produce and in some cases even who was to produce it. In fact, rather than trying to lower or prevent market distortions, the state offered cheap loans and other subsidies to large private conglomerates (*chaebol*) to deliberately "distort relative prices in order to stimulate economic activity." In exchange for these subsidies, the state then imposed "performance standards" on these *chaebol* (Amsden 1989).

To sustain long-run growth and international competitiveness, the state employed these and a host of other carrots and sticks collectively referred to as industrial policy. Proponents of this paradigm argued that developmentally oriented states employed these interventionist policies to deliberately "get prices wrong" in an effort to create for Korea a "dynamic comparative advantage" in industries that static neoclassical theory would argue were beyond Korea's comparative advantage. These industrial leaps, they argued, required levels of capital investment, technological sophistication, and entrepreneurial risk far greater than a free market could sustain. In Korea's case, this required an interventionist state willing and able to subsidize, shield, and even prod private firms to take these leaps. This developmental state role is a far cry from the free or self-directed market perspective offered by economists.

But even if such rapid structural change required an interventionist state, what is to prevent this government meddling from turning into predatory political enrichment and the subsidies and shielding from turning into the collusive coddling of inefficient producers so feared by the free market advocates (as seemed to be the case elsewhere in the developing world)? In short, what prevents a powerful developmental state from becoming a predatory one (Evans 1992)?

While there is certainly evidence of corruption and crony capitalism in Korea, developmental state proponents argue that it was not sufficient to derail development in Korea as it did in most other developing countries.[4] They point to several historical and international factors that gave the Korean state a degree of autonomy or insulation from the political pressure of powerful private agents, the discipline to focus on national developmental goals rather than the particularistic enrichment of politicians or industrialists, and the capacity to then impose its will upon, and gather crucial information from, these private actors.

These theorists argue that it is not a coincidence that both Taiwan and Korea (and to a certain extent Japan) share a similar developmental story. Both experienced Japanese colonialism and created elitist bureaucratic institutions patterned after the Japanese model. Following the end of colonial occupation, both faced mortal threats from Communist (though fraternal) neighbors, bolstering a national vision and long-term commitment to transforming and strengthening their economies while largely ignoring social welfare and excluding labor, consumers, and other social interests from the political process.

Korea, Japan, and Taiwan all had societies leveled first by war and then by U.S.-advised and U.S.-imposed land reform that redistributed income and weakened or wholly eliminated powerful landed elite who otherwise would have likely stood in the way of structural change (as has been the case in most other developing countries). All three fell under the aegis of American cold-war protection, in which the American mentors turned a blind eye to both the political authoritarianism and economic protectionism of these developmental states and showered the regimes with crucial

---

[4] Chang concludes that "[t]he abuse of bureaucratic power, political favoritism, and corruption are hardly rare in Korea. And the country by no means lacks stories of rent-seeking activity. The puzzle is to explain, then, why in the case of Korea these dangers did not inhibit rapid industrial development" (1993: 145).

aid, investment, technology transfers, and unfettered American markets. These specific historical legacies and situational imperatives, it is argued, strengthened these developmental states and gave them the discipline, focus, and insulation to limit collusive ties and channel the efforts of both foreign and local capital in promoting economic development.

Culture: Confucian Capitalism

Proponents of a cultural explanation acknowledge the regional similarities of Northeast Asian economic development, but argue that it is not so much international or exogenous political variables, but rather endogenous cultural similarities among these East Asian nations that explain their success. These "Asian values" are oftentimes now associated with an ideological movement championed by a number of Asian political leaders and much criticized by both political and economic liberals (primarily but not exclusively in the West) as an ethnocentric cloak for denying the individual rights of citizens and consumers. The original literature behind the term, however, emerged particularly among Asian scholars in seeking an "oriental alternative" to Weber's Protestant ethic as a crucial factor to capitalist success in East Asia.

Weber argued that Calvinist Puritans, through their treatment of profit making as a religious duty and idleness and profligacy as sins, generated a social ethic that served as the foundation for Western liberal capitalism. The economic triumph of East Asia has led some of its observers to attribute this success to a functionally similar social ethic within East Asia. Confucianism provides a common cultural heritage for some though certainly not all of Asia. Not surprisingly, proponents point out, this Confucian (or more accurately neo-Confucian) influence has been greatest in Japan, Korea, and the regions of the Chinese diaspora (Taiwan, Hong Kong, Singapore) that have led postwar global economic growth rates.

Advocates of this cultural paradigm point to Confucian ethics such as the importance of benevolent and moral government, filial and familial piety, and a this-worldly emphasis on the perfectibility and educability of humans. While perhaps not embracing the neo-Weberian thesis entirely, others point to the "post-Confucian" characteristics of East Asian societies as both evidence of a lasting (albeit evolved) Confucian legacy and the wellsprings of a potent combination for developmental purposes. These virtues include an expectation of meritocratic (and bureaucratic) governance, a quiescent attitude toward authoritarian rule, diligence in work, frugality in consumption, and a commitment to education, family prosperity, and social stability.

Many scholars of Korean development have pointed to the specific impact of Korea's traditional values on its economic success. They argue there was much in traditional Korea that prepared it for takeoff and that the neo-Confucianism fostered during the five-century Yi dynasty prior to Japanese colonization promoted egalitarian literacy, respect for hierarchic and authoritarian personal relations, and bureaucratic, even technocratic, service and rule (Cumings 1997; Kang 1995).

And although critics argue that some of these "virtues" owe their origin not to a distant Confucian past, but rather to a contemporary political and economic elite whose interests lie in a diligent and quiescent labor force, this still raises the question of why this has succeeded in Korea and other economies within the region of Confucian influence but not elsewhere in the developing world. Thus, proponents contend, when authoritarian president Park Chung Hee claimed that "a society that puts national interest above the interests of the individual develops faster than one which does not" (Tai 1989: 17), this dictum fell on receptive and responsive ears that could accept the legitimacy of his claim for both cultural and empirical reasons.

Seeking a Synthesis: New Institutionalism

This section has presented market, statist, and cultural explanations for Korean development. Kang describes the development debate between market and state as becoming "old and potentially irresolvable" (Kang 1995: 559). Similarly, *The Economist* writes extremely critically about any potential link between Confucian values and economic development but concludes, "Nobody has come up with an alternative grand theory that satisfactorily identifies the origins of the East Asian success" (January 21, 1995: 39).

While the contest among these competing paradigms has at times taken on an almost religious fervor, the passage of time and intellectual developments on the margins of this debate have fostered a new generation of scholarship that seeks to synthesize the virtues of each into a more complex but empirically more accurate explanation of economic development. The common denominator of these studies has been a focus on institutions or the economic, political, and sociocultural patterns of interaction that have structured the developmental process. These institutions can range from formal governmental agencies and civic and economic organizations to familial ties and simple social norms or customs.

Inherently interdisciplinary, this "new institutionalism" offers a particularly rich alternative for explaining economic development in Korea. The statist and cultural correctives to the neoclassical account were efforts to introduce historical legacies, political institutions, and sociocultural norms into the ahistorical and static formalism of ideal neoclassical markets. Economists working in the field of "new institutional economics," on the other hand, recognize that institutions arise in markets and that such institutions can reduce uncertainty and economize transaction costs under imperfect market conditions (e.g., Williamson 1985).

Though political scientists, sociologists, and anthropologists typically needed little persuasion to examine institutions, they have become more willing to employ models of public choice, agency, and transaction costs, formerly the province of economics. The best work on Korea now reflects this eclecticism. Amsden concludes in her important study of Korean development that in order "to understand variations in growth rates among late-industrializing countries... one must explore two key institutions: the reciprocity between big business and the state... and the internal and external behavior of the diversified business group" (Amsden 1989: 150–151). Lee argues that the Korean state and *chaebol* comprise a "quasi-internal organization" governed by a Confucian ethos that has reduced communication costs, uncertainty, and opportunism, allowing the state to efficiently implement developmental policies (C. Lee 1992). Kang calls for examining the political institutions behind Korea's economic development within the context of both historical and cultural legacies and constraints imposed by the international system (Kang 1995).

Although lacking the elegance of neoclassical explanations or the simple certainty of other monocausal theories, these explanations hold much promise for explaining Korean development. Korean entrepreneurs are and have been embedded in a sociopolitical environment in which duties and obligations to both family and state (and now also international agencies) have exerted great influence on the nature and outcome of economic activities. As the following section reveals, cultural norms, social relations, and, often most important, state-imposed institutions have done much to shape the course of Korean development.

From Takeoff to Drop-off: Four Decades of Industrial Growth

This section provides a brief overview of postwar Korean development, identifying the primary strategies, goals, policies, and structural consequences of each of five decades of growth beginning in the 1950s. Perhaps more than any other developing country, Korea exemplifies the costs and benefits of state-led development. Moreover, there is an integral link between state legitimacy and economic development. Successive regimes from the 1960s through the 1980s were compelled to define legitimacy in terms of economic development both domestically, because of illicit means of coming to power, and internationally, to quench a burning nationalist desire to establish Korea as a significant player in the global economy.

Prologue to Take-Off: The 1950s

The decade of the 1950s began in war and dire poverty and ended in industrial stagnation, political corruption, and widespread social unrest. Consumed by the nationalist goal of reunification with North Korea and an intense hatred of Japan, President Syngman Rhee was unable or unwilling to understand the relationship between economic growth and the attainment of his own goals. His anti-Japanese stance "retarded the resumption of trade with a natural and traditional partner and his yearning for reunification was carried to the extreme that there was an unwillingness to build up the South as an independent and integrated economy"(Mason et al. 1981: 253). War devastation and political exigencies compelled a development strategy that relied almost entirely on U.S. assistance and benefited primarily a handful of well-placed industrialists.

U.S. assistance in the form of food, raw materials, capital goods, and cash proved essential for short-term recovery but debilitating in the longer run. For the period 1953–1961, Korea received some US$2.3 billion in foreign aid, which financed over two-thirds of all Korean imports. This assistance went far in rebuilding Korea's war-torn infrastructure, but it inhibited indus- trialization and fostered a collusive symbiosis between state patrons and their dependent industrial clients. A system developed in which politicians and bureaucrats dispensed U.S.- funded loans and commodities to well-connected capitalists in exchange for generous campaign donations and other kickbacks.

Confirming the neoclassical fear of government intervention, Rhee's authoritarian regime used its considerable clout to shelter favored industrialists in a default strategy of import-substitution industrialization (ISI), substituting protected domestic production for imports. These protectionist policies included an overvalued currency, multiple exchange rates, and the fire sale of Japanese enterprises to local (and politically influential) entrepreneurs. Officials awarded lucrative government contracts to these favored industrialists and merchants who reaped windfall gains by becoming exclusive producers or importers of valuable consumer commodities. These monopolists also came to form the core of Korea's powerful *chaebol* business class.

Rhee and his political associates were much more concerned with staying in office and facilitating the flow of U.S. aid than they were with economic development as an end in itself. Consequently, waste and inefficiency plagued bureaucratic management of the economy, and entrepreneurs learned that the quickest route to prosperity lay in seeking government rents, not pursuing productive profits.

Despite these structural problems, the Korean economy by the late 1950s was far from desperate. In it were the seeds of the industrial takeoff that would follow. By far, the greatest boon was land reform implemented by Rhee with American urging. It virtually eliminated Korea's centuries-old landed elite class, increased rural productivity, broadened the distribution of this production, gave Korean peasants a stake in the new economy, and removed key obstacles to industrialization (Lie 1998). In addition, for all its faults, U.S. aid assured a relatively rapid postwar recovery, providing Korea's educated and able workforce with an infrastructure comprised of state-of-the-art technologies from which the industrial takeoff was launched.

Takeoff: The 1960s

Beginning in the 1960s, Korea experienced within one generation perhaps the most profound and "condensed" industrial transformation the world has ever known. This thirty-year period was characterized by unprecedented growth rates, high inflation rates (particularly in the 1960s and 1970s), rising export and diminishing unemployment rates, and rapid structural transformation through expansion of the manufacturing sector. The manufacturing sector itself also witnessed profound change, from labor-intensive light industries in the late 1950s and early 1960s to heavy and chemical industries in the 1970s and an increasing acceleration since the 1980s into electronics, semiconductors, and other advanced technologies (Cho 1994: 16).

This industrialization process took off during the 1960s following General Park Chung Hee's seizure of power in a military coup in May of 1961. Coming to power through illicit means, he sought legitimacy and the support of a growing urban middle class by championing economic growth and justified his authoritarian and interventionist state in the name of anticommunism. Park faced opposition from neither a landed aristocracy nor organized labor. Coming to office with promises to punish big business for its "illegal and unfair profiting" during the 1950s, he arrested but then quickly cut deals with Korea's biggest tycoons, recognizing them as the only viable agents for developing the country.

The Park government implemented the first of a series of five-year industrial plans in 1962. The first plan was hastily prepared, overly ambitious, and subsequently revised downward, but it nonetheless reflected Park's conception of industrial development, a vision that both characterized succeeding plans and paced Korea's industrial development in subsequent decades. The fundamental principles underlying this vision included (1) promoting rapid economic development through industrialization, proceeding from light to heavy industrialization as soon as possible; (2) privileging national growth over both price stability and income equity (across either regions or classes); (3) fostering large private businesses, but with firm government control and guidance; (4) controlling the cost and maintaining a steady supply of labor; and (5) inducing the inflow of foreign capital and promoting exports to increase employment and repay foreign debts (Cho 1994: 31–32).

The most significant shift during this decade was the piecemeal adoption of a strategy of export-oriented light industrialization (albeit in conjunction with continued import substitution). The Park government implemented a series of policies designed to foster industrial exports and expose Korea's export regime to the discipline of the global market. These measures included devaluing the currency, unifying exchange rates, improving basic infrastructure including the establishment of economic processing zones (EPZs) and trade promotion agencies, and instituting export incentives such as subsidized export loans and tax breaks.

Market discipline and government policies notwithstanding, the success of this transition to export-led development during the 1960s may owe less to policy factors than it did to several external contingencies, including a resurgent Japanese economy, the onset of the Vietnam War, and an expanding U.S. open market. Normalizing economic and diplomatic relations with Japan in 1965 may have been difficult politically for Korea, but it proved financially very beneficial. Japan provided Korea with over US$800 million in grants, loans, and trade credits and rapidly stepped up its investments in Korea. These investments led to both the diffusion of Japanese technology and business expertise and the reintegration of this former colony into a Japanese-led regional division of labor (Lie 1998: 60–61).

And although U.S. foreign economic assistance declined during the 1960s, the flow of American dollars into the Korean economy actually increased during this period as a result of income gen erated through Korean participation in the Vietnam War effort. This included the earnings of soldiers, technicians, and workers as well as income from industrial exports to Vietnam in support of the U.S. cause and to an increasingly voracious American consumer market.

However crucial these external events may have been, one should not discount the ability of Park and his technocratic advisers to seize the opportunities made available by these events and utilize these windfalls in crafting an industrial takeoff. Park created a host of interventionist institutions and staffed them with a meritocratic bureaucracy, remarkable for both its policy-making efficiency and its insulation from private capital, if not from the military dictator. Park assumed the role of Confucian patriarch of the nation and called upon the Korean people to embrace the Confucian virtues of obedience, loyalty, thrift, and diligence. By the end of the 1960s, developmental success, if not yet prosperity, had earned for Park a remarkable degree of political support, if not yet legitimacy.[5] However, a combination of stepped-up industrial deepening and political dirigisme under conditions of global economic downturn during the following decade would erode this support and ultimately prove the downfall of the Park regime.

---

[5] Korea's level of development should be kept in perspective. Despite laudable progress, by the end of the 1960s, Korea's per capita GNP was still less than Japan's had been in 1951, and its economic production still likely lagged behind that of North Korea (Lie 1998: 74).

Industrial Deepening: The 1970s

Besieged by external trade and security pressures and his near defeat in the 1971 presidential election, Park sought to enhance both national self-sufficiency and the legitimacy of his military rule by launching an industrial great leap forward into heavy and chemical industries. This HCI drive was to bring about "epoch-making increases in exports" and rapidly narrow the gap between Korea's industrial structure and that of the developed countries (Cho 1994: 38).

To enable this industrial deepening, Park in 1972 declared martial law and promulgated the Yushin Constitution, granting himself lifetime tenure and sweeping powers to rule by decree. This combination of authoritarianism and growth during the 1970s demonstrated both the upper limits of nonsocialist intervention in promoting capital accumulation and the trade-offs associated with state-led development. Rapid growth in GNP and exports paced a concurrent climb in inflation and decline in investment efficiency as the decade wore on. Increased industrial self-sufficiency came at the cost of rising foreign indebtedness and at the expense of "repressed workers, exploited farmers, [and] silenced citizens" (Lie 1998: 76). The clearest winners of this HCI strategy were the *chaebol* conglomerates, the dependent agents of Park's industrial drive and conscious products of his push for capital concentration. Sales of the ten largest *chaebol* climbed from 14 percent of GNP in 1974 to 48 percent in 1980 and over 67 percent by 1984 (Amsden 1989: 116).

The Park government placed priority on six industries—steel, petrochemicals, shipbuilding, industrial machinery, nonferrous metals, and electrical industries—and mobilized all available policy instruments in its industrial promotion efforts, including fiscal, monetary, credit, trade, and labor policies. The state controlled prices and protected the local economy from foreign investment and competition, promoting protectionism under the guise of free-trade rhetoric. The military regime imposed political stability by silencing the opposition and ensured a cheap and docile labor force by controlling wages and squelching the labor movement.

Above all, the state bankrolled the HCI drive. It became the primary source of capital and credit in funding the industrial deepening, and in so doing appropriated the investment decisions and assumed the investment risks of private firms. The Park government attracted foreign loans and mobilized all available local funds at banking institutions through the state-sponsored

National Investment Fund. These funds were then channeled to the *chaebol* in the form of subsidized "policy" loans, which carried rates during the 1970s that were less than half both the regular bank rate and the inflation rate. Offering what were in essence negative loan rates (as well as tax credits and other subsidies) to preferred customers, the government assured the compliance of the conglomerates and their trading companies in carrying out the government policies of industrialization and export (see Fields 1995: chap. 4).

Although the role of state patronage during the 1970s was overwhelming, the economic and sociocultural foundations of *chaebol* entrepreneurship should not be dismissed. Korea had a growing pool of educated and talented economic elites eager and able to succeed in business. At the same time, the traditional Confucian disdain for commerce had declined, and familial control of *chaebol* ownership and management had proven conducive to *chaebol* growth. The *chaebol* nonetheless quickly learned that the most effective way to grow was to expand into as many government-sponsored spheres as possible and to cultivate ties and personal networks with the state through family, military, school, and regional connections.

This price distortion rent seeking, and other collusive behavior, can nonetheless be distinguished from similar activities of the 1950s by the Park regime's capacity to impose strict performance standards on private firms that received the subsidies (Amsden 1989: 145). The government was clearly in the position of patron and had the capacity to demand superior production and export performance on the part of its industrial clients.

This growth-first model or "sword-won alliance" (Cheng 1990) contained, however, a number of structural problems that became increasingly apparent as the decade progressed, particularly with the external challenges Korea was facing. HCI favored the *chaebol* at the expense of other firms and led to rising disparities in income and wealth. Another serious problem was the continued exploitation of workers, made possible by proscriptions on effective labor organization and the steady oversupply of labor through agrarian underdevelopment (S. H. Lee 1998: 99). Rapid industrial expansion predictably also led to growing shortages of physical, human, technological, and financial resources, which in turn led to jumps in wages and prices and spiraling inflation. And although Korea survived the 1973 oil crisis and subsequent international stagflation relatively well, the second oil crisis in

1979 hit Korea hard. Korea's balance of payments worsened, and its foreign debt ballooned.

Economic crisis and political unrest culminated in the October 1979 assassination of Park and the collapse of his Yushin regime; these in turn led to further political, social, and economic crisis. As in 1960, an abortive process of democratization was replaced by Chun Doo Hwan's military seizure of power in 1980 with calls for economic stabilization and social justice.

Liberalization: The 1980s

Like his predecessor, Chun too came to power through illegitimate means and sought to overcome the legitimacy gap by distancing his regime from old policies and programs. In economic terms, this meant promises of price stability, increased social expenditures, decreased economic intervention, the privatization of finance (if not its liberalization), and an end to preferential treatment and dominance of the *chaebol.*

In some of these regards, the Chun government succeeded quite well. It successfully stemmed inflation, which dropped from 39 percent in 1980 to just over 20 percent in 1981 and to less than 1 percent by the mid-1980s (Cho 1994: 48). The government privatized commercial banks and toned down many of the more extreme and overt measures of intervention in both the financial and industrial sectors. The government nonetheless retained firm control over finance, particularly banking policies and personnel.

It also toned down the frenetic pace of export promotion, and as a balance of payments surplus emerged and grew during the 1980s, Korea felt increasing pressure from the United States and other trading partners to liberalize its import market and the economy in general. Particularly in the wake of the 1985 Plaza Agreement, as the pace of liberalization and market opening throughout Asia and the world picked up, the Chun regime began to respond with stepped-up liberalization measures. Perhaps not surprisingly, Chun was much less successful in fulfilling his pledge to curb the giant *chaebol* and wean them from government assistance. In fact, liberalization actually enhanced the conglomerates' financial autonomy and economic clout and "contributed to a rise, not a decline, in economic concentration" (Amsden 1989: 136).

From 1982 onward, Korea managed to pull itself out of economic crisis and by mid-decade had experienced a remarkable turnaround. In the years from 1986 to 1988, the Korean economy witnessed an unprecedented boom, expanding at a rate of more than 12 percent for three consecutive years (Clifford 1998: 236). The economy grew as the *chaebol* successfully exported higher-value-added products inherited from Japan in the product cycle and made competitive by the *chaebol*'s access to favorable credit and cheap labor. Economists, with some justification, have pointed to Chun's retreat from HCI interventionism and his liberalizing measures as the source of the recovery (Stern et al. 1995: 276). Others point to external factors, chiefly the blessings of the so-called three lows that characterized Korea during the mid-1980s: low interest rates, a devalued won (particularly after the yen's rapid appreciation after 1985), and a return to lower oil prices.

This return to economic prosperity brought with it rising popular expectations for more equitable sharing of this wealth and increased demands for political democracy and social justice. President Roh Tae Woo was elected to office (with the barest plurality of votes) in 1987 amidst huge public demonstrations and unprecedented appeal for change. In response to popular demand, Roh promised to carry out reforms regarding land tenure (in the wake of skyrocketing real estate prices and speculative *chaebol* profiteering), the concentration of economic power in the hands of the conglomerates, and labor-management relations.

Reflecting the growing power and autonomy of the *chaebol*, the Roh government's efforts to curb the conglomerates by compelling them to rein in the speculative real estate investments and shed subsidiaries outside designated core areas failed completely. Workers did not wait to see if the Roh government would carry out labor reforms, choosing rather to take matters into their own hands. Unceasing labor unrest and social foment marked the final three years of the decade. Nearly one-third of all firms with more than 300 employees were struck in 1987 alone, and more than one million workers were involved in strikes between June and October of 1987 (Clifford 1998: 276). Between the summer of 1987 and late 1989, there were more than 7,100 strikes, and the number of independent workers unions nearly tripled (Bello and Rosenfeld 1992: 41).

The Roh government had little choice but to weigh in on the side of labor, and its actions led to a rapid rise in real wages. This rise, combined with appreciation of the Korean won and a ballooning of domestic real estate prices, weakened considerably the price competitiveness of Korean exports and dampened prospects for economic growth as the decade ended.

Liberalization and Drop-off: The 1990s

Growth regained momentum in the early 1990s, partially as a result of Roh's successful efforts to "internationalize" the Korean economy, opening up trade and ultimately diplomatic relations with a host of Communist and formerly Communist countries in Europe and Asia. But the continued decline in competitiveness of exports, rising capital costs, and increased domestic demand slowed growth and threatened both domestic price stability and Korea's balance of payments.

Kim Young Sam's government took office in 1993 as the first civilian government since 1961 and made dramatic moves to end the old system established by three decades of military rule. Chief among these reforms were sweeping liberalization efforts, including unprecedented "sunshine" measures for the public disclosure of financial assets and transactions and "a new leap toward a new economy," calling for a move from government intervention and regulation of the economy to market competition.

These liberalization measures included privatizing state-owned enterprises, deregulating interest rates, ending the program of government-regulated credit (the so-called policy loans), granting more managerial autonomy to banks, and relaxing the regulations regarding foreign borrowing (particularly short-term borrowing) (Chang 1998; Lee and Sohn 1994). Kim dismantled the Economic Planning Board (the pilot agency of state intervention in the economy), took measures to open the economy to foreign investment (to meet requirements for entrance into the OECD), and liberalized foreign currency rules (Lee and Sohn 1995).

The Korean economy experienced robust economic growth and surging export volumes during the mid-1990s. Some attributed this growth to the liberalization measures; others pointed to declines in labor unrest (on the heels of a fivefold increase in wages over twelve years) and substantial appreciation of the Japanese yen. By 1996, Kim had achieved his goals of boosting GDP per capita to more than US$10,000 and securing Korea's membership in the OECD.

Anticipated as a year of reckoning for Hong Kong (because of its retrocession to China), 1997 proved to be a much more fateful year for Southeast Asia and subsequently Korea because of the financial crises that swept the region. The so-called Asian crisis became a contagion and then a conflagration that proved to be a time of reckoning for Korea. The crisis also led to much finger pointing and generated conflicting explanations for the dramatic drop-off. It provides us with an opportunity to revisit the explanatory paradigms introduced at the beginning of this chapter.

Accounting for the Crisis

In May of 1997, Thailand experienced a financial meltdown that spread to much of the rest of Asia and ultimately reached much of the world, giving new significance to the notion of globalization. What began as foreign currency crises in Southeast Asia hit Korea a series of blows: skyrocketing interest rates, plummeting stock prices, free-falling devaluation of the won, and evaporating foreign currency reserves. In domino-like fashion, Korean corporations (including seven *chaebol*) either declared bankruptcy or were forced into court-ordered receivership (Park 1998). Most humiliating, in December of 1997, following agonizing negotiations, the Kim Young Sam government signed a very severe economic adjustment package with the International Monetary Fund, which provided Korea with $57 billion in rescue funds in exchange for fundamental and far-reaching changes in Korea's export-dependent, state-led, *chaebol*-centered developmental model (S. H. Lee 1998: 210).

Conflicting explanations for Korea's economic plight abound, with the only consensus among market, statist, and cultural accounts being that the roots of the crisis in Korea began long before the summer of 1997. Neoclassical economists pointed to the crisis as proof that the "inherently inefficient and corrupt state-led economic system had finally reached its limits." They argued that despite liberalization efforts earlier in the 1990s, the structural legacies of three decades of state interventionism persisted, as shown by proliferating evidence of cronyism and corruption scandals involving government and business and grandiose diversification and extravagant investment schemes on the part of Korean companies. The solution, they contended, would require thoroughgoing liberalization of the financial, trade, and labor markets and the establishment of a genuine market economy (Chang 1998: 437; S. Lee 1998).

Proponents of Korea's developmental state countered that in fact the cause of Korea's crisis was too much openness, or at least poorly designed liberalization policies implemented earlier in the 1990s. These policies included the drastic liberalization of the financial sector, which led to overinvestment and a huge expansion of foreign borrowing by both financial institutions and private corporations no longer intermediated by the state. The government couldn't be blamed for pushing overleveraged companies into risky or poor investments, they claimed, because the government had been out of the business of industrial policy since the mid-1990s. Bureaucrats no longer formulated five-year plans, had shed their tools of sectoral industrial policy, and no longer directed or even coordinated private investment decisions (Weiss 1998; Mathew 1998; Chang 1998).

Increasing numbers of Asian officials and even scholars have too become disillusioned with the virtue of market openness. At worst, some have charged that Asia in general and Korea in particular are the "victims of a massive conspiracy of Western governments, the IMF, financial markets, and industrial corporations" (L. Lim 1998: 37). These co-conspirators first forced liberalization, then manipulated asset values of Asian banks and corporations in order to be able to scoop up these assets at fire-sale prices following the massive devaluation associated with the crisis. Less ominously, many have concluded that Western-style unregulated financial markets (both international and domestic) are ill-suited to Asia (if not universally ill-advised).

One silver lining (though not the only one) of the crisis has been to compel some intellectual accounting in this debate over East Asian development. The debate is no longer simply one of taking credit for success. Partisan theorists advocating their favored explanation for Korea's developmental miracle must now, arguably with the same set of tools, also account for the more recent apparent failures.

If free markets have been the driving force behind the Korean economic miracle, as the neoclassical economists would have us believe, why did the stepped-up liberalization in the years immediately prior to the 1997 crisis not spare Korea from the crisis and its contagion? If, on the other hand, the Korean state deserves the lion's share of credit for the rapid industrial development, doesn't this same apparatus now have to take responsibility for the recent downturn? And finally, if Korea has succeeded, like its neighbors, because of its Asian values, surely these deeply ingrained cultural norms have not changed so substantially in the intervening years as to excuse culture from shouldering some of the blame.

This chapter concludes, predictably, that the best explanation is somewhere in the middle. As Linda Lim concludes, "Both openness and statism have contributed not only to the Asian miracle, but also to the Asian meltdown" (1998: 34). Few would disagree that Korea can benefit from economic and social reform. The key now will be to draw from these competing paradigms in constructing and implementing a reform program not to assuage egos or justify ideologies, but to prepare Korea for a prosperous and peaceful twenty-first century.

References

Amsden, Alice. 1989. *Asia's Next Giant.* Oxford: Oxford University Press.

Barnes, Barry. 1982. *T. S. Kuhn and Social Science.* New York: Columbia University Press.

Bello, Walden, and Stephanie Rosenfeld. 1992. *Dragons in Distress: Asia's Miracle Economies in Crisis.* San Francisco: Food First.

Chang, Ha-Joon. 1993. "The Political Economy of Industrial Policy in Korea." *Cambridge Journal of Economics* 17:131–157.

———. 1998. "South Korea: Anatomy of a Crisis." *Current History,* December, 437–441.

Cheng, Tun Jen. 1990. "Political Regimes and Developmental Strategies: South Korea and Taiwan." In Gary Gereffi and Don Wyman, eds., *Manufacturing Miracles.* Princeton, N.J.: Princeton University Press.

Cho, Soon. 1994. *Dynamics of Korean Economic Development.* Washington, D.C.: Institute for International Economics.

Clifford, Mark. 1998. *Troubled Tiger: Businessmen, Bureaucrats, and Generals in South Korea.* Armonk, N.Y.: M. E. Sharpe.

Cumings, Bruce. 1997. *Korea's Place in the Sun.* New York: Norton.

Evans, Peter. 1992. "The State as Problem and Solution: Predation, Embedded Autonomy, and Structural Change." In Stephan Haggard and Robert Kaufman, eds., *The Politics of Economic Adjustment.* Princeton, N.J.: Princeton University Press.

Fields, Karl. 1995. *Enterprise and the State in South Korea and Taiwan.* Ithaca, N.Y.: Cornell University Press.

Halliday, Jon, and Bruce Cumings. 1988. *Korea: The Unknown War.* New York: Pantheon.

Kang, David. 1995. "South Korean and Taiwanese Development and the New Institutional Economics." *International Organization* 49 (Summer): 555–587.

Kuhn, Thomas S. 1970. *The Structure of Scientific Revolutions.* Chicago: University of Chicago Press.

Lee, C. H. 1992. "The Government, Financial Systems, and Large Private Enterprises in the Economic Development of South Korea." *World Development* 20 (February): 187–197.

Lee, Chong-Sik, and Hyuk-Sang Sohn. 1994. "South Korea in 1993: The Year of the Great Reform." *Asian Survey* 34 (January): 1–9.

Lee, Su-Hoon. 1998. "Crisis in Korea and the IMF Control." In Eun-Mee Kim, ed., *The Four Asian Tigers.* San Diego, Calif.: Academic Press.

Lie, John. 1998. *Han Unbound: The Political Economy of South Korea.* Stanford, Calif.: Stanford University Press.

Lim, Linda. 1998. "Whose 'Model' Failed?: Implications of the Asian Economic Crisis." *Washington Quarterly,* Summer, 25–42.

Mason, Edward, et al., eds. 1981. *Studies in the Modernization of the Republic of Korea: 1979–81.* Cambridge: Harvard University Press.

Mathews, John A. 1998. "Fashioning a New Korean Model out of the Crisis." *Japan Policy Research Institute Working Paper* 46 (May): 1–14.

Park, Tong-Whan. 1998. "South Korea in 1997: Clearing the Last Hurdle to Political-Economic Maturation." *Asian Survey* 38 (January): 1–10.

Stern, Joseph J.; Ji-Hong Kim; Dwight H. Perkins; and Jung-Ho Yoo. 1995. *Industrialization and the State: The Korean Heavy and Chemical Industry Drive.* Cambridge: Harvard Institute for International Development and Korea Development Institute.

Tai, Hung Chao. 1989. *Confucianism and Economic Development.* Washington, D.C.: Washington Institute Press.

Weiss, Linda. 1998. "The Myth of the Powerless State." *Japan Policy Research Institute Critique,* May, 1–2.

Williamson, Oliver E. 1985. *The Economic Institutions of Capitalism.* New York: Free Press.

SEVEN

Family, Gender, and Sexual Inequality

SEUNG-KYUNG KIM

The recent interest in family and women's studies in Korea marks the beginning of a process of self-examination within Korean society. Scholars considering issues of family cohesion, traditional values, and modern society have raised important questions about the future of Korean family structures and gender relations. Understanding the meaning of family requires examining it as an inherently gendered set of relationships and exploring how these gendered relationships have changed within the family and within the society as a whole. This chapter provides an overview of the changing gender roles; and by outlining the various movements under way to address issues of gender inequality, it maps out the rise of gender issues in Korean society and the increasing demands of women for greater participation in the decision-making process in society.

The meaning attached to the word "family" has changed tremendously over the past century. From being a conservative patrilineal and patriarchal institution that had as its most important function the continuation of the family line through a male heir, "family" has become a more individualized nuclear unit, which exists within a transformed society where economic production takes place away from the household. Nevertheless, contemporary Korean families retain cultural factors rooted in earlier periods. Specifically, many aspects of women's position in contemporary South Korean society are rooted in neo-Confucianism, which was Korea's state ideology under the Yi dynasty (1392–1910). Although Confucianism no longer occupies a formal position in the ideology of the state, it continues to be a core element of Korean cultural tradition (H. J. Cho 1986; Kihl 1994; Kim and Finch 2002; Robinson 1991; E. Yi 1993).

Three institutionalized norms that structured women's status during the Yi dynasty have continued to circumscribe contemporary Korean women's position within the family and the society at large. These are patrilocal marriage based on a rigid rule of exogamy, an inheritance system based on male primogeniture, and the ideology that males and females properly occupy separate spheres. I will first discuss how these principles determined women's position during the Yi dynasty, a monarchy based on Confucian patriarchy. Second, I will examine how these norms were altered during the oppressive colonial period and the turbulent war period. Third, I will analyze how these norms have changed in contemporary Korean society as a result of rapid industrialization and urbanization. In mapping the changes in these three principles, I will discuss the first wave of the women's movements and examine the rise of the second wave of the women's movements in contemporary South Korea.

Confucian Patriarchy and Gender Ideology during the Yi Dynasty

The imposition of neo-Confucian state ideology during the five hundred years of the Yi dynasty shaped Korean society in ways "that have continued to influence the lives of Korean women to the present day" (Deuchler 1977: 1). The neo-Confucian philosophy of the Yi dynasty literati-officials asserted that "the human world and the cosmic order had to be in equilibrium" (Deuchler 1977: 2). To maintain this equilibrium, people needed to observe five rules of moral imperative (inlyun): "the relationship between sovereign and subject guided by righteousness (ŭi), the relationship between father and son guided by parental authority (ch'in), the relationship between husband and wife guided by the separation of their functions (pyŏl), the relationship between elder and younger brothers guided by the sequence of birth (sŏ), and the relationship between senior and junior guided by faithfulness (sin)" (Deuchler 1977: 2). Neo-Confucian ideology provided Korean society with an exceptionally thorough blueprint for social life, but its effects spread unevenly through society, with only the upper echelons able to afford to adhere fully to its moral precepts. The yangban, or gentry class, became strongly Confucianized, while the lower ranks of the peasantry often failed to meet Confucian standards.

As Korean society came to adhere more closely to neo-Confucian orthodoxy, women's roles became more narrowly circumscribed within the limits of a male-focused family system that featured patrilineal inheritance, patrilocal residence, clan exogamy, and primogeniture. By 1700, the middle of the period of Yi-dynasty rule, inheritance had become strictly patrilineal and adhered to a strict rule of primogeniture (see Haboush 1991). Neo-Confucianism asserted "the superiority of the primary eldest son as the legitimate heir to the patriarchal family over other offspring" (Moon 1994: 194). In earlier periods, according to Deuchler, a daughter was eligible to inherit the same share of her parents' property as her brothers: "The inheritance usually consisted of fields, or the income of certain fields, and slaves... Toward the end of the dynasty, daughters seem to have lost their right of inheritance. They received a dowry upon getting married and then had no further economic claims on their natal lineages" (1977: 28).

The continuation of the basic social unit of the family was seen as especially important. Neo-Confucian philosophy asserted that "all human relations are rooted in the union between man and woman," and this relationship was structured by the view that "heaven (*yang*) dominates earth (*yin*), and correspondingly, male has precedence over female" (Deuchler 1977: 3). The precedence of male over female provided the basis for "specific codes of gender relations institutionalized in patrilocal marriage, patriarchal family, and patrilineal kinship" (Moon 1994: 188). The asymmetrical relationship between male and female was inculcated in early childhood: boys and girls should not be together after the age of seven. In *yangban* families, boys studied Confucian classics to prepare for taking the civil service examination, whereas girls were taught "womanly behavior" and domestic tasks such as "embroidery and the cultivation of silkworms, and were initiated into the intricacies of preparing sacrificial food for ancestor ceremonies" (Moon 1994: 6). The most important book for upper-class girls was *Naehun* (Instruction for women), compiled by the mother of King Songjong in 1475. To be a properly refined woman, a girl was required to learn the four basics of womanly behavior: moral conduct, proper speech, proper appearance, and womanly tasks. *Naehun* also emphasized the proper role of a married woman: to be a good daughter-in-law, an obedient and dutiful wife, and a wise and caring mother (Deuchler 1992: 257).

Daughters were regarded not as true members of the family, but as temporary guests and future outsiders. Becoming a wife was the central event in a woman's life, and her essential role in the patrilineal family was to bear sons who could continue her husband's family line. A marriage was arranged as a transaction between "two surnames," and followed a strict rule of exogamy: "The two surnames must not share a family name and an ancestral seat" (Moon 1994: 193). The rule of strict clan exogamy persisted into the 1990s. Marriages were patrilocal, and as a woman married into her husband's family, she was also required to curtail her ties to her family of origin in order to ensure her loyalty to her husband's family (Deuchler 1977; Harvey 1979; Peterson 1983). New brides were exceptionally isolated and powerless, as they were cut off from their friends and kin, but women gradually amassed power within the new family as they became mothers of sons.

Rigid adherence to patrilineal descent principles resulted in strict control over all aspects of women's lives. From the moment a new bride entered an upper-class household, "her freedom of movement was curtailed so that she virtually lost contact with the outside world" (Deuchler 1977: 23). Aristocratic married women were secluded in the inner quarters of the house and were allowed to venture out only in covered sedan chairs (Deuchler 1977: 2). So completely was a woman's identity absorbed into that of her husband that if she became widowed she was expected to remain chaste, or even to kill herself (H. J. Cho 1988: 72). In the interest of public morality, the state strove actively to expand family control over women and even instituted "special economic measures" to subsidize chaste widows (Deuchler 1977: 38).

During the Yi dynasty, status differentiation among women became increasingly important, as it affected not only the women themselves, but also their descendants. The government acknowledged the "primary wife" (ch'ŏ) as the only woman who could provide a man with a "rightful heir," and she was given social and economic prominence accordingly. A "secondary wife" (ch'ŏp) was treated as unimportant, and "her attachment to a man's domestic group [was] precarious and often only temporary" (Deuchler 1977: 30). The status difference between primary and secondary wives resulted in differing statuses for their sons: "From the middle of the dynasty, all descendants of secondary sons were barred from taking the civil service examinations and were thus unable to climb to political prominence" (Deuchler

1977: 33–34). The insecure status of a secondary wife was reflected in her having neither parental authority over her biological children nor ritual obligation toward her husband's ancestors (Deuchler 1977: 33–34).

Only husbands could dissolve a marriage, and then only under extraordinary circumstances. A man was allowed to expel a wife who committed one of the "seven instances of extreme disobedience—disobedience toward the parents-in-law, failure to produce a son, adultery, theft, undue jealousy, grave illness, and extreme talkativeness" (Deuchler 1977: 34–35). Women were, however, protected by a rule that even with these grounds, a woman could not be expelled "if the family fortune had improved greatly during the marriage, if the wife could not return to her own family," or "if she had mourned for either or both parents-in-law" (Deuchler 1977: 34–35).

Although women were publicly subordinate to men, many scholars have observed that women were far from helpless (Brandt 1971; Kendall 1985; M. H. Kim 1993; Osgood 1951). Women were able to enhance their positions within their husband's household by giving birth to sons and by being virtuous, and they could become powerful masters of the inner sphere. Their contribution to maintaining harmonious family life was recognized and the court gave *yangban* women "honorary titles ... on the basis of their husbands' official ranks" (M. H. Kim 1993: 72). Women in powerful families were also able to exert considerable behind-the-scenes influence on their husbands and sons through personal skills and strong personalities, and could manipulate social networks to help their sons and husbands to advance (Park 1985).

Cho Hae-Joang argues for the importance of the power women could wield within families (1988). As the label *anchuin* (inside master) signifies, a woman was able to build her own power and autonomy within the private sphere and to become "a financial manager symbolized by the right to carry the family keys to rice and other food storage areas" (Lee 1975 cited in M. H. Kim 1993: 72). Within the household there was a female-dominated space where "women had opportunities to fulfill their needs and desires by creating a culture of their own" (M. H. Kim 1993: 71). Furthermore, "access to economic resources, the ability to withdraw goods and services, and even sheer defiance gave the woman unassigned power, or increased her influence over her husband and her sons" (Park 1985, cited in M. H. Kim 1993: 72).

Cho Hae-Joang also observes that women played the central role in perpetuating the system of male preferences and that playing that role was based on women's survival strategies rather than a product of formal familial ethics. Mothers formed stronger emotional bonds with their sons, who would remain in their social sphere, than with daughters, who could be expected to leave (1988: 81).

Upper-class Korean women, as Kim Myung-Hye notes (1993), lived paradoxical lives in that they were able to exercise significant power within their households, but beyond their households they could act only indirectly through the influence they had on powerful men. Only by behaving in accordance with the female subservience required by the neo-Confucian value system could women achieve access to power. *Yangban* women "won power, status value, and autonomy by stressing their differences from men, and by accepting and elaborating upon symbols and expectations associated with their cultural definition" (Rosaldo 1974, cited in M. H. Kim 1993).

Women's real contribution to the economy during the Yi dynasty—either as upper-class women managing property or households or as lower-class women toiling at farm work, doing household chores, sewing—was obscured by the ideology of female superfluousness and scarcely acknowledged (Son 1993: 374–375). Especially important were lower-class women whose families were unable to forgo their labor and who worked in the fields alongside the men. Besides working as farm labor, taking care of children, and doing household work, peasant women also participated in other productive labor such as weaving and needlework for pay, thus contributing to the household economy. However, neither upper-class women nor peasant women were allowed to be active in public organizations and local communities either socially or economically, and their contribution was acknowledged only in the private sector, within the family (Son 1993: 375).

Exceptions to this confinement of women during the Yi dynasty were women who were considered outside the "proper" category of women, such as *kisaeng* (entertainers). The rigid rules of confinement restricting upper-class women's activities were not applied to these women. They enjoyed economic independence (although they depended on aristocratic patrons), relative freedom of movement, and the chance to become literate. *Kisaeng* were given training in painting, poetry, and music, but their education was different from that provided to upper-class women. Shamans were another category of women that existed outside the boundaries of polite society. Despite their exceptional freedom and spiritual importance, they were nonetheless looked down on as low class and marginalized.

During the first few centuries of the Yi dynasty, the neo-Confucian regulation of the status hierarchy became increasingly rigid, but later it began to suffer from internal contradictions. By the last century of the dynasty, "change was taking place in a number of directions, some of them of fateful significance" (Eckert et al. 1990: 180). These changes were reflected in (1) the increasing number of "fallen" *yangban*, who were born into *yangban* lineages but unable to maintain their claims to that status; (?) the decay of the distinction between legitimate and illegitimate lines of descent; and (3) the growing strength of provincial gentry, who had been less favored than capital elites (Eckert et al. 1990: 180–182).

At the end of the nineteenth century, when foreign goods and culture were imposed on the Korean kingdom, "traditional" Korean society was forced to adapt. Western ideology and economic organization clashed violently with the values of the indigenous Confucian farming society, and the territorial aggression of its neighbors forced Korea into the international political arena, where its weakness left its destiny in the hands of outside powers. This turbulent period, however, also offered Korean women new perspectives on their social and economic position. One of the most important innovations for Korean women was the modern education system that was introduced by Western religious organizations. The missionary Mary Fitch Scranton founded Korea's first school for women, Ewha Haktang, in 1886, and this was soon followed by a number of other missionary schools for women.

During this period, progressive male intellectuals also advocated women's rights. The first nongovernmental liberal journal, *Tongnip Sinmun* (Independence), published editorials advocating equality between men and women. In an 1896 editorial, the paper argued that "women are not inferior to men; men are so uncivilized that they mistreat women without any humane considerations or just cause. Isn't it a sign of primitiveness that they oppress women merely by their physical superiority?" (Y. C . Kim 1976: 214). The paper also urged education for girls, arguing that

> if women are educated and develop interests in society, they would realize that their rights as human beings are equal to men's.

They would also find a way to stop the brutality of men. We ask, therefore, that women be educated even better than men in order to educate other women and become an example of behavior to men (Y. C. Kim 1976: 215, quoted in Jayawardena 1986: 220).

In 1898, a group of one hundred upper-class women formed a secular woman's organization, Ch'anyang-hoe, and started the first nonreligious girls' school, the Sunsong Girls' School. This school's mission statement called for women's education, "not only as an end in itself but also as a means of achieving for women the same civil rights as were enjoyed by men" (Y. C. Kim 1976: 249–250 quoted in Jayawardena 1986: 221). This was the start of girls' education in Korea, and its success prompted the founding of other private girls' schools in the early 1900s.

Graduates of this education system, armed with Western education and Western values, sought to replace the patriarchal value system of Yi-dynasty Korea with gender equality and the ideology of democracy. In particular, Christianity's relative gender equality raised Korean women's awareness of their subordinate position within Confucian ideology. Women educated by Christian schools and universities became the leaders of Korea's first women's movement and also played key roles in the independence movement during the subsequent colonial period.

The Colonial Period and Korean Women

The early 1900s was a chaotic period that saw the demise of the nation and its incorporation into the growing Japanese empire. In 1905 Japan forced Korea to become a Japanese protectorate, and in 1910 it annexed Korea and established a colonial government. The colonial regime was to last for thirty-five years, during which Korea experienced varying degrees of political repression as its weak farming economy was absorbed into Japan's capitalist economy. In addition to reorganizing rural production under Japanese auspices, the colonial regime also expanded mining and manufacturing in service of the Japanese economy. The regime also oversaw an increasing urban population and the continued expansion of education. The system of compulsory universal education implemented by the colonial government in Korea gave women increased access to education.

The Japanese takeover coincided with the introduction of Western liberalism based on a philosophy of individualism and the first generation of Korean women to receive a Western-style education. These mostly upper-class, educated women sought to replace the Confucian ideal image of Korean women with an alternative modern image of women, *sinyŏsŏng* (new woman). Their progressive essays published in new magazines and newspapers advocated "women's self-realization" and "free choice in marriage" (H. J. Cho 1988: 96). Some of these early *sinyŏsŏng* regarded it as their pioneering duty to oppose the traditional family system and tried to live according to their beliefs. These modern women felt they should be free to form relationships based on love, rather than being legally bound into an arranged marriage.

The new ideology of *sinyŏsŏng* was expressed in 1922 in a characteristic editorial in the magazine *Puin* (Woman). The editorial urges its readers to transform themselves completely, not just superficially:

> Should we only use the word civilization and not adopt its content;...should we only be intoxicated by the beautiful words of male and female equality and not cultivate our capacity for equality;...should we only adopt Western hairstyles...and dress and not create the situation that requires it;...should we only be proud that we do not do sewing and not learn more important skills; and should we only be proud of escaping from ordinary kitchen work and not learn more important work? (Park 1977: 109–110)

Kim Won-Ju, a well-known poet and writer, advocated the new sexual morality of the *sinyŏsŏng* in her article "Our Ideal": "We need to protest against the old sexual morality that disregards our individuality and character.... We need to get rid of the old idea that if a woman lost her virginity, her love is no longer pure" (Pak 1985, 47 cited in H. J. Cho 1988: 97). Kim had a notorious love affair with Yi Kwang-Su, a married man who was a leading writer of their time, but after the affair ended, she retreated from her avant-garde stance and completed her life as a Buddhist nun.

Some *sinyŏsŏng* in the 1920s became concubines or went into second marriages and became targets of public criticism for their impulsive behavior regarding marriage and divorce. The term *sinyŏsŏng* was first used by women who had received modern education to refer to themselves; but by the end of the 1920s, it came to designate women with loose sexual morality, and in the extreme, implied a high-class call girl. Thus educated women began calling themselves "inteli" women, to distinguish themselves from the others. These first-generation women's liberationists faded out at the end of 1920s without having made noticeable

gains for women in society and under attack from both conservatives and progressives (H. J. Cho 1988: 97–98).

In addition to women who sought women's liberation through
greater personal freedom, many women were active participants
in political movements during the colonial period. Women students who were educated at the Ewha Haktang played an especially important role in the anticolonial movement, "forming an
underground society called Patriotic Women's League"
(Jayawardena 1986: 222). Ewha students were prominent in the
March First Movement in 1919 against Japanese occupation, leading many of the demonstrations. The young woman who became
emblematic of the independence struggle was an Ewha student,
Yu Kwan-sun, who led the demonstration at her hometown in
Ch'ungch'ŏng province. She was arrested and tortured to death
by the Japanese at age sixteen. Christian women who participated
in the March First Movement became more aware of nationalist
ideology, but the colonial government's suppression prevented the
churches from developing into an overt political movement.
Faced with Japanese repression, Christian women backed away
from direct confrontation with the Japanese, but they continued
their nationalist work underground through proselytizing and
organizing night classes (Lee 1996: 159).

Women were also important in organizations based on socialist
ideas, first introduced to Korea by students educated in Japan (A.
Yi 1989: 264–265). The Korean Communist Party was founded in
1925, and its early leadership included one notable woman, Chong
Chong-Myong. Women in this and other socialist organizations
set their main goal as national liberation, and since such organizations directly challenged Japanese rule, they were suppressed
nearly as quickly as they formed (H. J. Cho 1988: 98–99).

In 1927, a coalition of missionary and socialist women formed
Kŭnuhoe, an important new women's organization. Kŭnuhoe
advocated progressive positions on a variety of social issues and
declared in its mission statement that the "oppression of Korean
women is caused by both Confucian patriarchy and the contradictions of modern capitalism" (A. Yi 1989: 268). Their seven guidelines were (1) the abolition of legal and social gender discrimination, (2) the abolition of patriarchal customs, (3) freedom of marriage and the abolition of early marriage, (4) the abolition of pros-
titution, (5) advocation of rights for rural women, (6) paid mater-
nity leave and the abolition of wage discrimination for women's
labor, and (7) the abolition of dangerous labor and nighttime labor

for women and minors (A. Yi 1989:268; Son 1993:376). Kŭnuhoe advocated rights for women, worked at exposing the terrible working conditions endured by Korean women workers, and advocated national independence from Japan. Kŭnuhoe struggled with both internal division and external oppression for four years, before breaking up in 1931 (A. Yi 1989: 269–271; S. Yi 1994: 235–236). Kŭnuhoe is important in that it was the first women's organization that tried to represent the whole "ten million Korean women" and was the first alliance of progressive missionary-educated women and progressive socialist women.

The Japanese colonial regime also made use of women's organizations to rally support for itself. As Japan mobilized the resources of Korea for its war effort, it established several procolonial government women's groups, such as Puin kyemong toknyŏban (1938) and Chosŏn imjŏnbokukdan puinhoe (1942) to recruit women to support the war. Young women recruited by these groups were among those who ended up as "comfort women," military prostitutes serving the Japanese Imperial Army (Son 1993: 376).

Throughout the colonial period, women's direct participation in the wage labor market increased. As colonial Korea was drawn into Japan's war efforts, men were drafted into the military and forced to provide labor for factories and mines. Rural women were forced to take over a greater share of farm labor, while urban women took on new roles as wage laborers in factories. The textile industry employed more than 50 percent of these women industrial workers.

Although the colonial period was marked by increases in women's role in the formal economy and the beginning of women's overt participation in political and social movements, overall the lives of most women remained within the "traditional" family-centered sphere (Son 1993: 377). Under neo-Confucian ideology women were responsible for the household economy, so even the removal of male household heads for military service did not necessitate new ideological forms for ordinary Korean women. Hae-Joang Cho argues that even when women's economic activity necessarily involved them in the public sphere, the ideology of patriarchy did not weaken noticeably, and women continued to strongly uphold the patriarchal ideology even in the absence of male authority figures (1988: 91–94).

In line with trends in Japan at this time, with the introduction of capitalism and growing urbanism, neoconservatives sought to develop an ideology to define women's roles within the nuclear family. The idea that a woman should be a "good wife and wise mother" (*hyŏnmo yangch'ŏ*) was imported, translating the Japanese term *ryosai kenbo*. The ideological basis for *hyŏnmo yangch'ŏ* is not unlike neo-Confucian prescriptions for women's behavior, but it has been recast to emphasize the nuclear family. *Hyŏnmo yangch'ŏ* came to be the ideology of "elite women," distinguishing their modern individual-oriented marriages from old-fashioned extended-family-oriented ones. They saw their role as a complementary one supporting their husbands' role as modern salarymen. Thus, the ideology of *hyŏnmo yangch'ŏ* has taken root among middle-class women (H. J. Cho 1988: 99–100).

Women's Role between 1945 and 1960

During the last years of Japanese colonial government, national liberation movements were forced underground, and the Korean women's movement effectively disappeared. After liberation, however, women's organizations were among the many social and political movements that sprung up in the contest to define Korea's future (Cumings 1997: 185ff.). On August 17, 1945, women activists representing a broad range of ideologies established the first postwar women's organization, Konkuk punyŏ tongmaeng.

As its more conservative members departed, Konkuk punyŏ tongmaeng moved steadily to the left. In December, it renamed itself Chosŏn punyŏ ch'ongdongmaeng, affiliated with the Communist party, and began mass organization. It renamed itself again in 1947 Namchosŏn minju yosŏng tongmaeng, recasting itself as a parallel organization to the North Korean Pukchosŏn minju yosŏng tongmaeng. In 1946 the American military government in South Korea banned it along with other left-wing organizations, and it remained illegal after the South Korean government was established in 1948 (S. Yi, 1994: 244–246).

More-conservative women including some who had collaborated with the Japanese also founded several organizations during the period of American military government. These right-wing women's organizations sought to establish a unified, sovereign, and anti-Communist Korea, but they did not receive much mass support because of their leaders' pro-Japanese history (S. Yi 1994: 240–243). The right-wing organizations put forth platforms that advocated "better status for women," "gender equality rights," and "expanding women's rights in order to achieve gender equality" (S. Yi 1994: 247). Both left- and right-wing women's organizations thus supported gender equality, but whereas the right wing advocated a narrow agenda of gradual reform and nurturing women politicians, the left wing sought a much more sweeping "complete liberation in the political, economic, and social arena[s]" (S. Yi 1994: 247).

When the Republic of Korea was established in 1948, the Constitution guaranteed women equal rights with men, including the right to vote and stand for election. Nevertheless, women were almost completely excluded from political life. "The membership of the first National Assembly (1948–1950) consisted of 199 men and one woman" (Soh 1993: 2). Eighteen women ran for the National Assembly, but the first woman to win a seat was Yim Yong-Sin, who won "the special election held in Andong in January 1949, to fill a vacancy" (Soh 1993: 60). The first generation of South Korean woman politicians came mostly "from the ranks of Christian women who were educated during the Japanese colonization of Korea" (Soh 1993: 59). Soh traces the political activism of these "pioneer women" to "the larger process of the resistance against Japanese rule, especially the March First Movement of 1919, which proved to be the turning point in the lives of the women legislators of the pioneer generation" (Soh 1993: 59).

The Korean War (1950–1953) left the Korean peninsula "a smoldering ruin" (Cumings 1981: xix). The three years of civil war ruined both the southern and northern parts of the country.

> The toll in human lives was staggering. In the South alone, the combined total of military and civilian casualties—Koreans who had been killed, executed, wounded, kidnapped, or gone missing—was about 1.3 million people. Nearly half of the industrial capacity and a third of the housing in the south were destroyed along with much of the public infrastructure (Eckert et al. 1990: 345).

The lingering effects of the devastating war lasted at least a decade, leaving people in extreme poverty; "it also left its scars on an entire generation of survivors, a legacy of fear and insecurity that continues even now to affect the two Koreas both in their internal development and in their relations with each other" (Eckert et al. 1990: 346).

During the period of the Korean War and the ensuing political chaos, Korean women were forced to take on additional economic responsibilities to help their families survive. Women usually bore sole responsibility for their families as they fled the war front and became refugees. Cho Hae-Joang describes Korean women during this period as "strong, able mothers" who sustained their families without relying much on men. She notes that novels about wartime portray men as symbolic figures, who are often absent from the family, while the "mother figure" takes on great importance. She argues that the period of the Korean war established the image of a "strong Korean woman" and contrasts this period's "matrifocal" (*mojungsim*) family, where a mother was the central structural and emotional figure in the family, with the "uterine" (*hagung*) family of the Yi dynasty, where women formed the emotional center of the family within a larger patriarchal structure (1988: 102, 103).

Despite the absence of patriarchs, Korean families retained most of their patriarchal ideology, with women hoping to reconstitute "proper" families headed by their sons when the chaos ended. Thus the ideological change during this period was relatively slight. After the end of the war, leftist organizations remained outlawed, and political conservatism was mandated by the staunchly anti-Communist regime of Syngman Rhee. Increased American influence contributed to the strengthening of women's rights within the family, but the society's core value for women remained a variation of the *hyonmŏ yangch'ŏ* ideology. As the society struggled to overcome poverty, mothers strove to improve the lives of their children (H. J. Cho 1988: 104).

Rhee's regime became increasingly dictatorial as he clung to power by rigging elections and amending the constitution in order to hold on to the presidency. Student demonstrations against rigged elections led to Rhee's forced resignation and the founding of the short-lived Second Republic. The student revolution of April 19, 1960, established the student movement as a significant political force in South Korean politics, and students have remained prominent in the prodemocracy movement since then.

Contemporary Gender Relations

The military dictatorship of Park Chung Hee, who seized power in 1961, continued Rhee's anticommunism. While Park's regime was even more openly antidemocratic than Rhee's, it inaugurated a new approach to the economy based on the goal of economic development. Park's economic policies focused totally on growth and disregarded "imbalances in income distribution" and "unevenness in industrial development across geographical regions" (S. Cho 1994: 32). Park argued that a powerful central government was needed to coordinate the economic forces required for development (Amsden 1989: 50), although he also promised that the benefits of development would eventually reach everyone and asked the people's support to build "a nation without hungry people."

Authoritarian military government, concentrated economic expansion, and the rapid urbanization of rural society characterize South Korea during this period. With Park's first Five-year Economic Plan for government-driven and export-led development, the country entered a period of intense "late industrialization" (Amsden 1989). "Late industrial capitalist development" has had wide-ranging effects on all aspects of society and notably "in both gender processes and class processes" (M. H. Kim 1993: 73). South Korea was transformed from a society made up predominantly of rural peasants into one made up of urban workers. The separation between the public work sphere and the private family sphere also increased as society became more urban and more pervasively capitalist.

Park's regime ended in 1979 with his assassination, but it was quickly replaced by another military dictatorship, headed by General Chun Doo Hwan. Chun continued most of Park's political and economic policies, but his repressive regime was even less popular than Park's. The specter of the Kwangju massacre, which accompanied Chun's seizure of power, lingered over his regime and provided a rallying point for political opposition. Opposition to Chun came to a head in 1987, with nationwide demonstrations for democracy and workers' rights. Although the opposition to Chun was widespread, it was not united, and after forcing direct presidential elections, the opposition split its votes, letting Roh Tae Woo, Chun's designated successor, win a plurality of votes in the election. In subsequent presidential elections, both of Roh's opponents became president. Kim Young Sam was elected in 1992, Kim Dae Jung in 1997, and with each change in government, the country has become progressively more open and democratic.

Social movements played a crucial role in shaping Korean society throughout this gradual process of democratization. Under the military regimes of Park and Chun, only organizations that were approved by the government could operate openly. During this period the leading women's organization was Han'guk yŏsŏng tanch'e hyŏbŭihoe (Korea Council of Women's

Associations; KCWA), founded in 1959. This organization was made up of middle-class women, including both housewives and professional women. It advocated women's status, and service to the society and the country, but it did not directly challenge the regime's priorities. As opposition to Chun Doo Hwan increased, a more radical women's organization was formed. Han'guk yŏsŏng tanch'e yŏnhaphoe (Korea Women's Associations United; KWAU) was founded in 1987 with a platform that advocated "democratization and autonomy of the Korean society and achieving women's liberation" (S. Yi 1994: 313). The KWAU cooperated with labor and democratic organizations as part of the *minjung* (common people) movement of the 1980s that brought about the end of authoritarian dictatorship.

The division of contemporary South Korean women's groups into two camps was deepened by the legacy of civil war and military dictatorship. Decades of polarizing political struggles forced women's groups into either pro- or antigovernment positions. A willingness to engage gender issues in isolation from other social issues implied an acceptance of the status quo, while a broader engagement of social issues brought groups into direct conflict with the authoritarian government. The *minjung* movement brought together groups based among intellectuals and groups of working-class activists who were united more by their opposition to authoritarianism than by a common agenda.

In South Korea, organizations such as KCWA that remained narrowly focused on women's issues were vulnerable to government co-optation and were often criticized by other social movements for being conservative and even reactionary. Those advocating far-reaching reform of society have argued that the impact of liberal women's organization was trivial and compromised by its cooperation with the government (Chong 1993: 164). However, KCWA and its affiliated organizations attracted large followings during the 1960s and 1970s and succeeded in accomplishing a revision of Family Law and other reforms.

In the relatively democratic society of the mid and late 1990s, the broad coalition of social movements advocating the rights of the disenfranchised (women, workers, farmers, and the urban poor) was replaced by a less militant and more fragmented set of civil organizations. By 1998 there were nearly two hundred of these civil organizations dealing with women's issues (President's Special Committee on Women's Issues 1998). Abelmann says, "It has become clear that 1990s activism cannot be easily subsumed under a singular aesthetic or narrative of dissent. With civilian rule the objects of dissent are more dispersed and the narratives and organization of the dissent are more fragmented. In the 1990s, a discourse of *simin* (civil) movements has become central to the public discourse of dissent" (1996: 227).

Industrialization and urbanization substituted the urban, couple-centered nuclear family for the rural, extended patrilineal family, and as these trends accelerated through the 1970s and 1980s, this structure became dominant. The change in family structure is reflected in the decrease in the number of household members, separate nuclear family households, changes in gender roles, and the decrease in the number of children. Son describes how this change in family structure has also modified relationships within families from a vertical and authoritarian system that emphasized the broader kin group to a more egalitarian and individual-oriented system (Son 1993: 379).

The emphasis placed on the nuclear family by contemporary urban couples frequently brings them into conflict with their parents who still hold "traditional" beliefs about extended family relations, having raised their children in the expectation that they would provide them with emotional and economic security in their old age. Kim Myung-Hye (1993: 78) describes how old and new definitions of family coexist among the urban middle class:

> The term "family" (*chip*) in the upper middle class has at least two levels of meaning. One is normative: husband, wife, and children are relatives who should live together (the nuclear family). The other meaning includes a more extended network of kin relations that people may activate selectively. Living apart does not necessarily mean autonomy and the independence of a married son and his family from his parents.... Nuclear families are under cultural constraints to appear as both autonomous and interdependent, and private and communal simultaneously. The ideal autonomy of an independent nuclear family is constantly being contrasted with the realities of extended kin networks, in which resources must be shared and faces must be saved (*ch'emyon yuji*).

Associated with the decrease in family size and development of separate nuclear family residence has been a steady rise in the age of marriage for both men and women. Young women now participate in higher education at rates approaching those of men, and generally marry only after completing their education. The average age of women at the time of their first marriage increased from 21.6 in 1960 to 26.1 in 1995 (President's Special Committee on Women 1998: 122). Men are also marrying later. Lett reports that "upper- and middle-class men did not usually marry until after they had completed not only their three-year military obligation but also at least four years of college" (1998: 81).

Another important change has been in the meanings attached to marriage: from two families cooperating to ensure the continuation of the patrilineage to an ideal based on "romantic love" between husband and wife who unite to pursue their own happiness. Young women and men are increasingly selecting their spouses on their own, sometimes going against their parents' wishes, and premarital dating has become an essential part of the process of selecting a spouse. Kendall, in *Getting Married in Korea,* discusses how not only the marriage, but also the marriage ritual has changed as South Korean society has changed. Her monograph describes how marriage rituals "serve to construct an image of 'bride' and 'wife' and how this image has shifted through the twentieth century"(1996: 18).

Along with the increasing importance of romantic love, Western ideas of "masculinity" and "femininity" expressed with English loan words have become important. Men are expected to display masculine traits, such as being "strong, energetic, and intelligent," and women are expected to be feminine, displaying such traits as being "emotional, subservient, and weak" (H. J. Cho 1988: 106). As the younger generation seeks the perfect romantic love, women become more "feminine" and men more "masculine." Women are thus brought into nuclear families as part of a novel but still male-centered and male-dominated gender system. Cho argues that the current system rationalizes the separation of gender roles by emphasizing the psychological difference between genders (H. J. Cho 1988: 106).

With the increasing prevalence of the nuclear family and the expansion of industrial capitalism, women's familial roles have been idealized as "good wife, wise mother." Middle-class women have become full-time housewives who perform the household chores, provide emotional support for their husbands, and educate their children to become successful. While gendered specialization of men as breadwinners and women as mothers and housewives has been prevalent, women have, nevertheless, been active in a wide-ranging variety of economic activities that relate in some way to their primary roles as mothers and wives. These range from formal-sector employment of women as schoolteachers to a much broader range of informal-sector activities including tutoring, selling real estate, investing in rotating credit associations,

and investing in the stock market. Thus, "middle-class women
are perceived as immersed in the fury of the marketplace, dealing
with the hands-on pragmatics of stocks, high-interest loans, and
real estate, and sometimes besting their husbands' paychecks"
(Kendall 2002: 11; see Nelson 2000). Working-class housewives
also engage in supplementary economic activities ranging from
preparing food to door-to-door sales to doing subcontracted factory work in their homes (Kim and Finch 2002; Nelson 2000).

The cheap labor of Korean women provided the foundation of
Park Chung-Hee's drive for export-led industrialization, and as
the country industrialized, factory jobs for women increased
rapidly. In 1960, women had been only a small part of the
manufacturing labor force, comprising a mere 160,000, but by
1990, the numbers of women workers in the manufacturing sector
increased to over two million (Economic Planning Board, cited in
M. H. Kim 1992: 158). Female workers were most important in the
labor-intensive light manufacturing. Through the end of the 1970s
these light industries produced most of South Korea's exports, and
female workers comprised more than half of their work force
(Choi 1983: 83–84). Female factory workers were predominantly
young, single women working from the time they completed their
schooling until they got married. These women could be hired for
extremely low wages, and companies benefited enormously from
low labor costs, which made their products competitive on the
world market. Wages paid to women averaged less than half
those paid to male industrial workers (K. S. Kim 1986: 73; Korean
Association of Women Workers 1987: 32). Since women workers
formed a distinct segment of the workforce, their experience in the
labor movement has been somewhat separate from that of male
workers, and women have had little role in the formal institutions
set up by the government to co-opt labor (see Tongil pangjik
pokjik t'ujaeng wiwonhoe 1985: 32).

Throughout the period of Park Chung-Hee's presidency, while
male workers were co-opted by the system of government-run
unions, women workers became increasingly important within the
more radical informal labor movement (Tongil pangjik pokjik
t'ujaeng wiwonhoe 1985:22–25). Women worked mostly in small
to medium-size factories in light industry, and because their collective actions were generally spontaneous responses to issues that
arose in specific factories, women's activism tended to be episodic
and discontinuous, with little immediate effect on national politics.
Nevertheless, the disconnected actions taken by women in

factories across the country were linked together by church groups and by a growing sense of working-class consciousness. Women's collective actions also provided the labor movement with historical continuity because the combination of repression and co-optation nearly extinguished activism among male workers during the most repressive phases of Park's regime. Women's unions are generally credited with leading the labor movement during the 1970s (Choi 1993: 37; Koo 1993: 140, 156; Lee 1989: 264–271; Pak 1983; Sin 1985: 49–60).

During the 1980s women workers formed unions that cooperated with other social forces as part of the broad-based *minjung* movement. The progressive women's movement organization of the 1980s, the KWAU, also supported women workers in their struggle, "envisioning the future of women's liberation with human liberation through struggling against the dominant power in which women workers are the central force" (KWAU 1988: 22, cited in J. H. Cho 1996: 9). In the 1990s, the women's movement flourished along with other *simin* movements, and the number of nongovernmental organizations (NGOs) increased tremendously.

Gender Policy and Women's Status

The South Korean Constitution states that women and men are equal before the law, and although the Constitution's provision of gender equality should overrule all other lower laws, many lower laws contain obstacles to gender equality. Thus, in order to achieve the gender equality granted in the Constitution, there is a need to bring the lower laws into line with the Constitution, and there is a need for the government to work toward eliminating the conditions that block gender equality. Different regimes have formulated gender policies to cope with these contradictions within the legal system.

For a long time, the government treated women-related affairs within the social and cultural areas and placed women's affairs under the Ministry of Health and Welfare. Until 1980, gender policy was narrowly defined and applied to only a few categories of women (e.g., wage workers, pregnant women, women prostitutes), rather than addressing the needs of women in general. Furthermore, there was no systematic plan to improve women's status. Gender policy was first given a formal recognition in the cabinet in 1988, when President Roh Tae Woo established the Second Ministry of Political Affairs to concentrate on women's issues.

Gender policy has focused on three areas: equality between women and men, expansion of women's participation in society, and improvement of women's welfare. In addition to overall policy changes, women's legal status has been subject to gradual transformation. The government has enacted and revised various laws relevant to women related to these three areas of focus.

The expansion of women-related organizations and the establishment of women-related laws are closely linked and have been important factors in the development of the government's gender policy. The women-related laws that are the basis of establishing gender policy can be put into three categories: laws related to gender equality, laws related to securing and expanding women's social participation, and laws related to improving women's welfare. The laws related to gender equality are the Constitution and the Family Law. The laws to promote women's social participation are the Labor Standard Law and the Gender Equality Employment Act. The laws related to improving women's welfare include the Prevention of Sexual Violence against Women Law and the Victims Relief Act. Among the women-related laws, the two most important laws that affected the development of gender policy are the Gender Equality Employment Act of 1987 and the revision of the Family Law in 1989 (see E. Kim 2000; Moon 1998). The enactment and revision of these various laws reflect changes in the social perception of Korean women's issues.

In the 1997 election campaign, one of Kim Dae Jung's slogans was "Establish equal participation of men and women in society in order to realize gender equality." After his election, his government's gender policy sought to bring about a society with gender equality, to increase women's participation in society, and to improve women's welfare. This policy aimed at establishing a social system in which men and women participate equally and are responsible equally for healthy families, nation, and society. President Kim's gender policy was reflected in his inaugural address, where he announced he would "secure women's rights and aggressively develop women's abilities" and "work to eliminate the gender discriminatory behavior within the family, work and society" (Chong 2001). His government has stressed gender mainstreaming, representation, competitiveness, and cooperation. These became concrete through expanding women's recruitment goals, securing women's participation in administrative committees, and improving unemployment compensation for women.

With a large number of new and revised women-related laws, the Kim Dae Jung government has moved the nation toward gender equality. The government promulgated significant laws to promote gender equality and eliminate discrimination including the Prevention of Domestic Violence against Women Act in 1998, the Revision of People's Pension Program in 1998, the Prevention of Sexual Violence against Women and Relief Act Revision in 1998, the Special Law for Supporting Women's Business in 1999, the Gender Discrimination Prevention and Relief Act in 1999, and the Revision of the Gender Equality Employment Act in 1999. This strong record of legislation is, however, diluted by the government's inability to provide adequate resources and personnel to carry out its agenda for gender equality.

In January 2001, three years after taking office, President Kim Dae Jung fulfilled his campaign promise and established a Ministry of Gender Equality (Yŏsŏngbu). The first minister appointed to head this office was Han Myong-Suk, a long-time activist with an indisputable record of working for Korean women's issues. By appointing Han as the minister, President Kim fulfilled one of his most important campaign promises and satisfied political constituents with a wide range of political backgrounds. The newly established ministry exemplifies the government's commitment to strive for gender equality in Korean society and makes South Korea one of the few countries in the world where gender equality is addressed at the cabinet level.

Conclusion

Gender relationships within Korean society have made many adjustments as the country has transformed from a closed dynasty that followed the rigid gender codes of Confucianism to an industrialized country with a Ministry of Gender Equality to provide women equal status to men. Nevertheless, although "late industrial capitalist development" has had wide-ranging effects on all aspects of society and notably "in both gender processes and class processes" (M. H. Kim 1993:73), it remains the case that "gender asymmetry is manifest in many domains of social practice, from the significant under-representation of women in all branches of government to the difficulties that women face when they apply for passports" (Kendall 2002:6). More than twenty years after the enactment of the Gender Equality Employment Act (Namnyŏ goong p'yongdung pŏp) of 1988, discrimination against women in hiring continues to be rampant. It is no longer legal, but nonetheless, many advertised jobs still specify "men only" or, more subtly, require applicants to have "completed military service" (*Han'guk Ilbo*, October 25, 2001).

In order for Korean women to achieve genuine gender equality, legal change and changes in government policy need to be combined with the changes in people's perception and attitudes. The changes already made in law and government policies have provided a starting point from which cultural changes may occur, but they cannot guarantee women full equality with men. The everyday lives of South Korean women continue to be shaped by cultural sentiment and societal norms that are a legacy of premodern Korea. However, changes are taking place in many different arenas, most importantly in women's ideology, and the future will undoubtedly see continuing transformation in the role of women within South Korean society.

References

Abelmann, Nancy. 1996. *Echoes of the Past, Epics of Dissent: A South Korean Social Movement.* Berkeley: University of California Press.

Amsden, Alice. 1989. *Asia's Next Giant: South Korea and Late Industrialization.* New York: Oxford University Press.

Brandt, Vincent. 1971. *Korean Village: Between Farm and Sea.* Cambridge: Harvard University Press.

Cho, Hae-Joang. 1986. "Kabujangjeui pyŏnhyŏngkwa kŭkbok" (The transformation of the Korean patriarchal family). *Han'guk yŏsŏnghak* (Journal of Korean women's studies).

———. 1988. *Han'gukŭi yŏsŏngkwa namsŏng* (Korean women and men). Seoul: Munhakkwa chisŏngsa.

Cho, Joo-Hyun. 1996. "Yŏsŏng chŏngch'esŏng ŭi chŏngch'ihak: 80–90 nyŏndae han'guk ŭi yŏsŏngundong ŭl chungsimŭro" (Gender identity politics: The case of the women's liberation movement in Korea in the 1980s and 1990s). *Han'guk yŏsŏnghak* (Journal of Korean women's studies).

Cho, Soon. 1994. *The Dynamics of Korean Economic Development.* Washington, D.C.: Institute for International Economics.

Choi, Jang-Jip. 1983. "Interest Conflict and Political Control of South Korea: A Study of the Labor Unions in Manufacturing Industries, 1961–1980." Ph.D. dissertation, University of Chicago.

————. 1993. "Political Cleavages in South Korea." In Hagen
Koo, ed., *State and Society in Contemporary Korea.* Ithaca, N.Y.:
Cornell University Press.

Chong, Hyon-Baek. 1993. "Pyŏnhwahanŭn segyewa yŏsŏng hae-
bang undongronŭi mosaek" (Changing world and the search
for the theory of the women's liberation movement).
Yŏsŏngkwasahoe (Women and society), 4:138–165.

————. 2001. "Comprehensive Evaluation and Policy Suggestions
on Kim Dae Jung Government's Gender Policy for the Past
Three Years." Paper presented at the "Workshop on the
Evaluation of Kim Dae Jung Government's Gender Policy for
the Past Three Years and Policy Suggestions." February 23.
Seoul.

Cumings, Bruce. 1981. *The Origins of the Korean War.* Princeton,
N.J.: Princeton University Press.

————. 1997. *Korea's Place in the Sun: A Modern History.* New
York: W. W. Norton.

Deuchler, Martina. 1977. "The Tradition: Women during the Yi
Dynasty." In Sandra Matielli, ed., *Virtues in Conflict: Tradition
and the Korean Woman Today.* Seoul: Royal Asiatic Society.

————. 1992. *The Confucian Transformation of Korea: A Study of
Society and Ideology.* Cambridge: Council on East Asian Studies,
Harvard University.

Eckert, Carter; Lee Ki-Baik; Lew Young Ick; Michael Robinson;
and Edward W. Wagner. 1990. *Korea Old and New: A History.*
Seoul: Ilchokak.

Haboush, Ja-Hyun Kim. 1991. "The Confucianization of Korean
Society." In Gilbert Rozman, ed., *The East Asian Region: Confucian Heritage and Its Modern Adaptation.* Princeton, N.J.: Princeton University Press.

Harvey, Young-Sook Kim. 1979. *Six Korean Women: The Socialization of Shamans.* St. Paul, Minn.: West.

Jayawardena, Kumari. 1986. *Feminism and Nationalism in the Third
World.* London: Zed Books.

Kendall, Laurel. 1985. "Ritual Silks and Kowtow Money: The
Bride as Daughter-in Law in Korean Wedding Rituals." *Ethnology* 24:253–267.

————. 1996. *Getting Married in Korea: Of Gender, Morality, and
Modernity.* Berkeley: University of California Press.

————. 2002. *Under Construction: The Gendering of Modernity,
Class, and Consumption in the Republic of Korea.* Honolulu:
University of Hawai'i Press.

Kihl, Young-Whan. 1994. "The Legacy of Confucian Culture and South Korean Politics and Economics: An Interpretation." *Korea Journal* 34:37–53.

Kim, Elim. 2000. "The Decade since the Enforcement of the Gender Equality Employment Act: The Achievements and Tasks." *Women's Studies Forum* 16:5–23.

Kim, Kum-Su. 1986. *Han'guk nodong munche ŭi sanghwang kwa insik* (The circumstances and interpretation of the Korean labor Problem). Seoul: P'ulbbit.

Kim, Myung-Hye. 1992. "Late Industrialization and Women's Work in Urban South Korea: An Ethnographic Study of Upper-Middle-Class Families." *City and Society* 6:156–172.

———. 1993. "Transformation of Family Ideology in Upper-Middle-Class Families in Urban South Korea." *Ethnology* 32(1):69–85.

Kim, Seung-Kyung. 1997. *Class Struggle or Family Struggle?: The Lives of Women Factory Workers in South Korea.* Cambridge; and New York: Cambridge University Press.

Kim, Seung-Kyung, and John Finch. 2002. "Living with Rhetoric, Living against Rhetoric: Korean Families and the IMF Economic Crisis." *Korean Studies* 26(1):120–139.

Kim, Yung-Chung, ed. 1976. *Women of Korea: A History from Ancient Times to 1945.* Seoul: Ewha Womans University Press.

Koo, Hagen. 1993. "The State, *Minjung*, and the Working Class in South Korea." In Hagen Koo, ed., *State and Society in Contemporary Korea.* Ithaca, N.Y.: Cornell University Press.

Korean Association of Women Workers. 1987. *Han'guk yŏsŏng nodong ŭi hyŏnjang* (The scene of Korean women workers). Seoul: Paeksan Sŏdang.

Lee, Hyo-Chae. 1989. *Han'guk yŏsŏng undongsa* (A history of the women's movement in Korea). Seoul: Ch'ongusa.

———. 1996. *Han'gukŭi yŏsŏngundong: ŏjewa onŭl* (Women's movement in Korea: Yesterday and today). Seoul: Ch'ongusa.

Lett, Denise P. 1998. *In Pursuit of Status: The Making of South Korea's "New" Urban Middle Class.* Cambridge: Harvard Asia Center.

Moon, Seung-Sook. 1994. "Economic Development and Gender Politics in South Korea: 1963–1992." Ph.D. dissertation, Brandeis University.

———. 1998. "Begetting the Nation: The Androcentric Discourse of National History and Tradition in South Korea." In Elaine Kim and Choi Chung-Moo, eds., *Dangerous Women: Gender and*

Korean Nationalism. New York: Routledge.

Nelson, Laura C. 2000. *Measured Excess: Status, Gender, and Consumer Nationalism in South Korea.* New York: Columbia University Press.

Osgood, Cornelius. 1951. *The Koreans and Their Culture.* New York: Ronald Press.

Pak, Young-Mi. 1983. "The Role of Labor Unions in the Female Labor Movement in South Korea." *Korea Scope* 3(3):3–12.

Park, Yong-Ock. 1977. "The Women's Modernization Movement in Korea." In Sandra Matielli, ed., *Virtues in Conflict: Tradition and the Korean Woman Today.* Seoul: Royal Asiatic Society.

————. 1985. "Yukyojŏk yŏsŏngkwanŭi chaejomyŏng" (A reexamination of the Confucian view of Korean women). *Han'guk yŏsŏnghak* (Journal of Korean women's studies), 1:7–55.

Peterson, Mark. 1983. "Women without Sons: A Measure of Social Change in Yi Dynasty Korea." In Laurel Kendall and Mark Peterson, eds., *Korean Women: A View from the Inner Room.* New Haven, Conn.: East Rock Press.

President's Special Committee on Women. 1998. *Yŏsŏng paeksŏ* (White paper on women). Seoul: Han'ullim.

Robinson, Michael. 1991. "Perceptions of Confucianism in Twentieth-Century Korea." In Gilbert Rozman, ed., *The East Asian Region: Confucian Heritage and Its Modern Adaptation.* Princeton, N.J.: Princeton University Press.

Sin, In-Ryong. 1985. *Yŏsŏng, nodong, pŏp* (Women, labor, and law). Seoul: P'ulbbit.

Soh, Chung-Hee Sarah. 1993. *Women in Korean Politics.* Boulder, Colo.: Westview Press.

Son, Chang-Kwon. 1993. "Kyŏngje palchŏnkwa yŏsongŭi chiwi" (Economic development and women's status). In H. S. Im and K. S. Pak, eds., *Ŏnŭlŭi han'guk sahoe* (Korean society today). Seoul: Nanam.

Tongil pangjik pokjik T'ujaeng wiwŏnhoe. 1985. *Tongil pangjik nodongjohap undongsa* (History of the Tongil textile labor union). Seoul: Tolbegae.

Yi, Ae-Suk. 1989. "Chong chong-myong ŭi samkwa t'ujaeng" (The life and struggle of Chong Chong-myong). *Yŏsŏng* 3:255–280.

Yi, Eun-Hee Kim. 1993. "From Gentry to the Middle Class: The Transformation of Family, Community, and Gender in Korea." Ph.D. dissertation, University of Chicago.

Yi, Sung-Hui. 1994. *Yŏsŏngundongkwa chŏngch'i iron* (The women's movement and political theory). Seoul: Noktu, 1994.

EIGHT

Population Changes and Urbanization

KYE-CHOON AHN

Demographic transition generally refers to changes in features of a given population over a particular interval. These changes do not take place inside a vacuum, but are rather a culmination or outgrowth of varying forces that shape society and its people: war, peace, famine, and financial success. These multifaceted changes take place in numerous places all over the world, and the Korean peninsula is no exception.

This chapter focuses on levels of selected Korean demographic elements—population size and population composition as described by age, gender, religion, and urbanization—during a period of economic development and industrialization.

Demographic Transition

Transition during periods of development usually starts with a decline in mortality followed considerably later by a decline in fertility. Because of the time lag, however, the rate of population growth is high throughout most of the period. This is typical of most countries that experience varying degrees of industrialization.

South Korea's industrialization has been a rapid, compressed process that has taken place within the years following the Korean War. Beginning most notably with the Park Chung Hee regime in the 1960s, South Korea began a rapid development of its technology and industry. South Korea's economy has produced a much higher standard of living than was imaginable in the era before the intensive economic reforms began. However, one must take note of the fact that this change followed, as has been mentioned elsewhere, both a devastating war and a protracted period of colonization. These forces have all combined to shape the development of Korea's demographic makeup. Demographic transition in Korea began early in the twentieth century (figure 8.1). Mortality rates steadily declined after 1920, while fertility rates began to decline in 1960. Korea is now in the final stage of demographic transition. This section scrutinizes changes in mortality, fertility, and population size.

Decline of Mortality

Korea introduced Western medicine and public health programs around the turn of the century. However, their benefits began to reduce mortality rates only around 1920 under Japanese colonial rule. Mortality then steadily declined until 1950, followed by an abrupt drop during the rapid industrialization after the Korean War. Unlike most Western developed countries—where improved living standards initiate mortality decline—Korean declines came first through improvements in medicine and public health programs and accelerated later through economic development.

Declines in mortality rates are reflected in increased life expectancy at birth after 1910. Table 8.1 shows that life expectancy was generally low from 1910 to 1945, the period of Japanese colonialism, although it steadily increased to 44 years by 1942. By 1960 it had reached 53 years and continued to increase. Life expectancy in 1995 (73.5 years) was much higher than the average (63 years) of developing countries and very close to the average (75 years) of developed countries.

Decline of Fertility

Under Japanese colonial rule, fertility rates among Korean women were relatively high. The crude birth rate was more than 40 per 1,000 population, and total fertility rate was more than 5 children per woman most of the time. Although some improvements were made in maternal and child health, poor access to modern contraception was the primary reason for fertility remaining high until 1950.

Fertility reached its historical peak in Korea between 1955 and 1960 at 6 children per woman, mainly as a result of the post–Korean War baby boom. Table 8.2 reveals an ensuing drastic decline. Until 1985, age-specific fertility rates decreased almost uniformly, and total fertility rates declined to 1.08 in 2005,

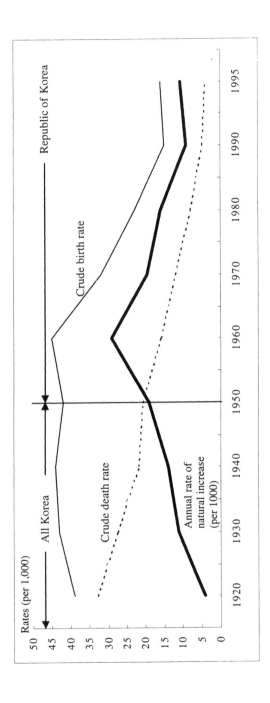

Figure 8.1. Demographic transition in Korea, 1920–1995

Table 8.1. Life expectancy at birth, 1910–2003

Period	Both sexes	Male	Female
All Korea			
1906–1910	23.5	22.6	24.4
1911–1915	25.0	24.0	26.0
1916–1920	27.1	25.8	28.2
1921–1925	29.6	28.3	30.8
1926–1930	33.6	32.4	35.0
1931–1935	37.1	36.3	41.5
1936–1940	42.6	40.6	44.7
1938–1942	43.8	42.5	45.0
Republic of Korea			
1955–1960	52.6	51.1	53.7
1966	61.9	59.7	64.1
1970	63.2	59.8	66.7
1978–1979	65.8	62.7	69.1
1985	69.0	64.9	73.3
1991	71.6	67.7	75.7
1995	73.5	69.5	77.4
2003	77.5	73.9	80.8

Adapted from ESCAP 1975; Korea National Statistical Office 1991, 2005.

Table 8.2 Age-specific and total fertility rates, 1950–2005

Year	Age-specific fertility rate (per 1,000 women)							Total fertility rate (per woman)
	15–19	20–24	25–29	30–34	35–39	40–44	45–49	
1950–1955	95	269	277	207	138	54	10	5.2
1955–1960	114	303	311	237	163	64	12	6.0
1965	21	200	299	212	136	66	-	4.7
1970	14	173	297	191	101	34	4	4.0
1976	15	159	239	119	46	16	4	3.0
1980	12.4	135.9	242.7	114	40.2	15.1	5.6	2.83
1985	10.1	118.7	159.1	41.1	8.8	2.2	0.5	1.67
1990	4.2	83.2	169.4	50.5	9.6	1.5	0.2	1.59
1995	3.6	62.9	177.1	69.6	15.2	2.3	0.2	1.65
2000	2.5	39.0	150.6	84.2	17.4	2.6	0.2	1.47
2005	2.1	17.9	92.3	82.4	19.0	2.5	0.2	1.08

Adapted from ESCAP, 1975; Korea National Statistical Office 1999; *Annual Report on the Live Births and Deaths Statistics*, 2005.

lowest in the world. In world demographic history, it is difficult to find a comparably steep 25-year decline. Fertility has remained below replacement with little fluctuation since. The decline of fertility is associated with three factors: rise in age at first marriage, implementation of the National Family Planning Program, and wide use of abortion.

Mean ages at first marriage were 26.4 and 21.6 respectively for men and women in 1960, and 28.6 and 25.5 in 1990 (Lee 1994). The rise appears to be associated with increased educational attainment for both sexes. Adoption of the draft system after the Korean War may also be a factor.

The Korean government launched the National Family Planning Program along with the Economic Development Plan in 1961. It made modern contraception available, including male and female sterilization. Contraception proved to be widely popular, winning the program worldwide recognition as one of the most successful of its type.

Were the program truly successful, we might expect reduced use of abortion for birth control. However, the proportion for married women who had induced abortion greatly increased after 1965, despite its illegality and the availability of alternatives. For a short period in 1991, the proportion reached 54 percent for all married women.

Population Growth

During the period of Japanese colonialism (1910–45), the Korean population continued to grow in numbers and rate of increase, with the exception of 1935–40 (see table 3). The increased number of Korean emigrants to Japan and Manchuria during World War II can explain the exception.

Table 8.3 also provides population figures for the Republic of Korea (South Korea) after World War II and the division of the peninsula into North and South. The high growth rate between 1944 and 1949 occurred when overseas Koreans returned and refugees flooded in from North Korea. The estimated number of net migrants was about 3,323,000, or 85 percent of the total population increase. The rate drop between 1949 and 1955 is mainly due to casualties and partly to reduced birth rates during the Korean War (1950–53), despite a large influx of refugees from the North.

Between 1955 and 1960, the population growth rate swelled to 2.88 percent. This increase reflects the postwar baby boom and

Table 8.3. Trends in population growth, 1925-2030

Year of census	Total population (in 1,000)	Annual growth rate (%)
All Korea		
1925	19,020	1.45
1930	20,438	1.63
1935	22,208	1.18
1940	23,547	1.82
1944	25,120	
Republic of Korea		
1944	16,244	
1949	20,189	4.40
1955	21,502	1.02
1960	24,994	2.88
1966	29,160	2.71
1970	31,435	1.90
1975	34,688	1.99
1980	37,436	1.56
1985	40,448	1.52
1990	43,411	0.99
1995	44,609	1.01
2000	46,125	0.67
2010	50,618	0.53
2020	52,358	0.21
2030	52,744	-0.04

Adapted from ESCAP 1975; Korea National Statistical Office 1998 also reduced death rates won by improved public health and medical services. As demographic transition proceeded, growth rates plunged. During the 1990s it fluctuated about 1 percent. As of 2000, the population was estimated at 46.1 million, with a density of 462/km^2. According to the Korea National Statistical Office (KNSO), the growth rate will continue to drop until it reaches zero about 2030, stabilizing the population at about 52.7 million.

Changes in Population Composition

Naturally, the forces that helped shape the populace's numbers in terms of net gains and losses affected the relative cultural, social, and economic layers of society as well. That is, just as much as the overall numbers fluctuated as a result of the aforementioned causes of colonialism, war, and industrialization, so too did the nation's inner workings shift as a result of these pressures. This section discusses changes in the population structure as measured by age and sex, educational attainment, religion, industry, and occupation.

Age and Sex

A simple method to examine age and sex composition simultaneously is the population pyramid. Figure 8.2 reveals tremendous changes in composition during the last three decades of rapid demographic transition. Relatively high fertility and mortality rates account for the standard pyramid shape in 1960, as is typical of many developing countries. The high dependency ratio (population under 15 plus population over 64 divided by population 15–64) was derived from the higher proportion of population under 15 years of age.

The bell-shaped figure in 1990 is typical in many developed nations. The dependency ratio had declined to 41 percent by 1995, mainly because of the decreasing proportion of population under 15 years of age. According to KNSO projections, the proportion of the elderly (usually age 65 or over) will increase at a higher rate than ever, and Korea will become an aged society by 2020.

Korea's sex composition is imbalanced from birth. The sex ratio at birth peaked in 1993 at 115 (115 males per 100 females) and declined thereafter to 107.7 in 2005 (Korea National Statistical Office 2005). The imbalance derives mainly from selective abortion of female fetuses. The imbalance should continue to diminish

Figure 8.2. Age and sex composition, 1960–2020

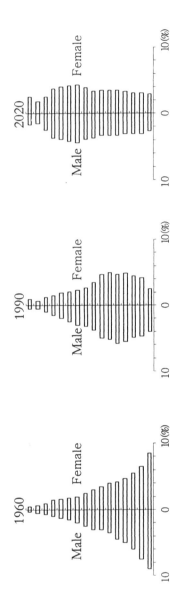

in the future because of stricter enforcement of laws proscribing selective abortion.

Educational Attainment

As table 8.4 reveals, educational attainment levels have risen significantly since 1975. In 1975, 66 percent of the population had only primary schooling; 6 percent were college graduates. By 1995 the figures were 27 percent and 20 percent. As the proportion completing only primary school plummeted, the proportions graduating from high school and college soared. These changes may well reflect high student and parent aspirations and increased numbers of institutes of higher learning.

Although males and females show considerable differences in educational attainment, both follow the same pattern of change. Although the proportion of female high school and college graduates was still much lower than that of males in 1995, the rate of improvement for females has been much higher. Equal attainments should be realized in the near future.

In 1998, students enrolled in colleges, universities, and graduate schools numbered about 2.5 million. At 5.3 percent of the total Korean population, this proportion is among the highest for developed countries. However, the Korean economy is too small to provide jobs for all of this highly educated population, exacerbating unemployment.

Religion

Perhaps the longest-running trend in the demographic makeup of Korea has been its religious affiliation. As a result of Buddhist, Confucian, and the historically recent Christian influences—all tempered by Korea's own nascent shamanistic background—Korea's denominational makeup is perhaps the most forgiving. Koreans absorb most religious systems into society's norms without too much contention rather than exhibiting intolerance for others' belief structures. Thus, the effect of religion on the demographic makeup of Korean society was insignificant compared to the various other external and internal factors.

The Korean Constitution recognizes religious freedom as a basic human right, but about half of Koreans ages 15 and above have no religious affiliation (table 8.5). The proportion of the religious decreased from 57.4 percent in 1985 to 46.9 percent in 2005.

Table 8.4. Composition by highest educational attainment (population over 25 years old) (%)

Level of education	1975			1995		
	Total	Male	Female	Total	Male	Female
Primary school graduates and under	65.5	53.1	77.1	26.6	17.8	35.0
Middle school graduates	14.8	17.7	12.1	15.7	14.2	17.1
High school graduates	13.9	19.7	8.4	38.0	41.4	34.8
College, university graduates and over	5.8	9.5	2.4	19.7	26.6	13.1

Source: Korea National Statistical Office 1975, 1995

Table 8.5. Changes in composition by religion (in %)

	1985	1995	2005
Buddhist	19.9	23.2	22.8
Protestant	16.1	19.7	18.3
Catholic	4.6	6.6	10.9
Confucian and others	1.8	1.3	1.0
No religion	57.4	49.3	46.9

Source: Korea National Statistical Office 1985, 1995, 2005.

Among those who are religious, the major religions are Buddhism, Christianity (Protestant and Catholic), and Confucianism.

According to the Korea National Statistical Office, Buddhism, among the oldest of the religions, made up 22.8 percent of the total population aged 15 and above in 2005, while Protestants and Catholics were 18.3 percent and 10.9 percent of that population. Those espousing Confucianism and other religions were less than 1.0 percent.

Industry and Occupation

Of course, Korea's phenomenal growth under the state-directed management of the 1960s and beyond was not without certain inevitable consequences. Most countries that face a marked turn from an agrarian society into a newly industrialized country will naturally see a related and necessary shift in the labor force.

Table 8.6 shows the drastic change in Korea's industrial composition in the period 1965–2000. In the early 1960s, primary industry dominated, but by 1995 it stood at only 12.5 percent. Tertiary industry swelled, dominating by 1995 and comprising more than two-thirds of those employed by 2000. Secondary industries also advanced until 1985, but then remained about the same level as a result of a downturn in mining. These dramatic changes stemmed from rapid industrialization since the 1960s and created vast social changes in other social dimensions.

Changes in industrial composition are reflected in occupational composition. As table 8.7 shows, the proportion of workers in primary industries declined dramatically in the 1964–2000 period, while that in the remaining occupations increased. Increases were particularly great for professional and kindred workers, semiskilled workers, and laborers. Occupational changes are closely related to changes in social stratification.

Urbanization

Overall Trends

Another major feature of social changes in Korea is urbanization, a common aspect of industrialization. Overall trends in urbanization can be examined in terms of the number of cities, the proportion of the population that is urban, and the annual urban growth rate (table 8.8).

Table 8.6. Changes in industrial composition, 1965–2000 (in %)

	Year				
	1965	1975	1985	1995	2000
Primary industry (agriculture, forestry, and fisheries)	58.6	45.9	24.9	12.5	10.9
Secondary industry (mining and manufacturing)	10.3	19.1	24.4	23.6	20.2
Tertiary industry (SOC and others)	31.1	35.0	50.6	64.0	68.9
Total employed persons (in thousands)	8,206	11,830	14,970	20,377	21,061

Source: Korea National Statistical Office 1965–2000.

Table 8.7. Changes in occupational composition, 1964–2000 (in %)

	Year				
	1964	1977	1985	1995	2000
Professional, technical, administrative, and managerial workers	2.8	4.2	7.3	16.4	18.6
Clerical and related workers	3.8	7.6	11.5	12.3	11.2
Sales workers	10.9	12.3	15.5	21.9	23.9
Service workers	6.0	6.7	10.8	11.7	10.2
Agriculture, forestry, and fisheries workers	61.6	41.8	24.6	11.7	10.2
Production, transportation, equipment operation and laborers	14.9	27.5	30.3	37.7	35.0
Total employed persons (in thousands)	7,779	12,929	14,970	20,377	21,061

Source: Korea National Statistical Office 1964–2000.

.

Table 8.8. Trends in urbanization

Year	Number of cities	Proportion of urban population (%)	Annual urban population growth rate (%)
1945	15	12.9	13.5
1949	19	17.1	6.6
1955	25	24.5	5.4
1960	27	28.0	5.7
1966	32	33.6	7.0
1970	32	41.1	5.2
1975	35	48.2	4.8
1980	40	57.3	4.2
1985	50	65.4	4.1
1990	73	74.4	1.6
1995	73	78.5	1.0
2000	79	79.7	NA

Source: Korea National Statistical Office 1949–2000.

When liberated from Japan in 1945, South Korea had only fifteen cities, and the urban population (usually defined as those living in the areas called cities [*shi*] in Korea, but since the 1995 census denoting only those who live in the smaller *dong* areas of cities) was only 13 percent of the total population. During the next four years, the urban growth rate soared. As noted above, this increase mainly reflects the clustering of Koreans returning from overseas and refugees from the North. Even between 1949 and 1955—which includes the Korean War—the urban population grew at a much higher rate than that of the total population. Most refugees from the North poured into the southern cities after the war, and during the war rural people were drawn to urban areas. Korean urbanization from 1945 to 1960, then, had little to do with industrialization and mainly was fueled by historical events such as liberation and the Korean War. Rapid urbanization so transformed Seoul that it already showed signs of overurbanization.

Rapid industrialization greatly encouraged urbanization after 1960. New industrial sites built around urban centers were a magnet for surplus rural labor. Industrial cities such as Ulsan and Koomi were built. During the past forty years, the number of cities has increased from twenty-seven to seventy-nine. About 80 percent of the total population inhabited urban areas in 2000. Urban growth rates were particularly high in the 1960s, when five-year economic development plans were initiated. Although the urban growth rate began to decline after 1975, it remained much higher than that of the total population. After 1985 we see deceleration beginning, and urbanization seems likely to level off in the future.

Components of Urban Growth

With conditions changing so quickly in the latter part of the twentieth century, there was an ever-constant gain for urban areas over rural ones in the race to develop the nation's infrastructure and manufacturing sectors. The urban areas benefited and in turn attracted a large number of people seeking to share in this newfound wealth.

The urban population boom derived from three factors: net rural to urban migration, natural urban population increase, and changes in the boundaries of existing urban areas, as well as an increase in the number of areas classified as urban. As table 8.9 shows, rural-to-urban migration played the greatest role in

Table 8.9. Components of urban population growth

	Total urban growth (in 1,000)	Contribution of each component (%)		
		Net migration	Natural increase	Boundary changes
1960–65	2,338	41.3	30.5	28.2
1965–70	3,594	75.5	24.5	-
1970–75	3,841	51.5	38.5	10.0
1975–80	4,640	58.1	32.7	9.2
1980–85	5,009	38.6	39.2	22.2
1985–90	5,866	27.0	36.3	36.7
1990–95	2,727	7.0	72.8	20.2
1995–2000	1,719	12.9	62.2	24.9

Source: Adapted from Kwon and Kim 1990.

urbanization until about 1980. At that point, natural increase
became the primary influence. As the number of cities increases,
the third component will also come to contribute more to urban
growth.

Urban Concentration in Seoul and the Capital Region

Korean urbanization has been concentrated in Seoul and its
surrounding area. Seoul, the capital since the Yi dynasty, has
swelled since 1960. In 2000, its population was 9,861,000, or 21
percent of the total population. Seoul typifies a primary city. It
has reached a saturation point and stopped growing in recent
years. Table 8.10 shows that its population began to fall after
1990, mainly as a result of out-migration to new suburban cities
such as Ilsan and Bundang in Kyŏngki province. Consequently,
Seoul's negative population growth rate has not affected the population growth of the capital region.

Growth rates of the capital region have been very high since
1960, particularly in Inch'on and other cities in Kyŏngki province.
High urban Kyŏngki growth rates and low or negative rural rates
are two sides of the same coin. In fact, many Kyŏngki towns were
redesignated as cities. Despite decreases in Seoul and rural
Kyŏngki, the population in the capital region continued to grow.
Although the region's growth rate plummeted after 1990, it
remained greater than the national average. In the 2000 population census, the capital region embraced 46 percent of the total
population.

Heavy concentration in Seoul and the capital region has
created urban problems of various kinds. Early in the 1970s, the
Korean government initiated various doomed administrative
measures to mitigate capital region growth. Seoul and its sur-
roundings still dominate Korean society in every respect, and
population concentration is likely to persist as long as such dominance continues.

Table 8.10. Capital region population growth rate (%)

Year	Total	Seoul	Inchon	Kyŏnggi	
				Urban	Rural
1960–66	5.92	7.32	4.50	13.36	0.85
1966–70	4.72	8.98	4.68	6.28	0.30
1970–75	5.90	4.75	4.65	23.66	-0.12
1975–80	3.93	3.88	6.07	8.45	1.33
1980–85	3.47	2.84	4.93	10.71	0.20
1985–90	3.22	1.92	5.41	12.22	-4.33
1990–95	1.65	-0.73	4.77	7.28	-1.60
1995–2000	1.12	-0.66	1.40	1.62	

Source: Korea National Statistical Office 1960–2000.

References

Chang, Yun-Shik, et al. 1974. *A Study of the Korean Population.* Seoul: Population and Development Studies Center, Seoul National University Press.

Kim, Kyong-Dong, ed. 1988. *Korean Society.* Seoul: Seoul National University Press.

Kim, Seung-Kwon et al. 2000. *Chǒn'guk ch'ulsan mit kachok pogǒn chosa pokosǒ* (National fertility and family health survey report). Seoul: Korean Institute for Health and Social Affairs.

Korea National Statistical Office. Various years. *Reports of Population and Housing Census.* Seoul: Bureau of Statistics.

––––––. 1964–2000. *Economically Active Population Survey.* Seoul: Bureau of Statistics.

––––––. 1991, 2004. *Life Tables for Korea.* Seoul: Bureau of Statistics.

––––––. 1998. *Social Indicators in Korea.* Seoul: Bureau of Statistics.

––––––. 2003. *Annual Report on the Live Births and Death Statistics.* Seoul: Bureau of Statistics.

Kwon, T. H. 1977. *Demography of Korea.* Seoul: Seoul National University Press.

–––––– and Kim D. S. 1990. *Inku ǔi ihae* (Understanding population). Seoul: Seoul National University Press.

––––––, et al. 1975. *The Population of Korea.* Seoul: Population and Development Studies Center, National University Press.

Lee, Hung-Tak. 1994. *Inkuhak* (Demography). Seoul: Pobmunsa.

United Nations. Economic and Social Commission for Asia and the Pacific (ESACP). 1975. *Population of the Republic of Korea.* Bangkok: ESACP, UN.

NINE

Social Grievances and Social Protests against the Oppressive State

DONG-NO KIM

Hyundai, a leading engine of economic development in Korea for four decades, stood on the verge of bankruptcy in January 2001. Curiosity about how the situation would resolve ran high. Not only were people reminded of the economic crisis that had struck three years before when two conglomerates, Hanbo and Kia, became insolvent. They wondered whether the state would respond in a way that matched the free market rhetoric it espoused to satisfy the IMF (International Monetary Fund) policy guidelines imposed for financial assistance in the previous crisis. To the contrary, Institute of Financial Supervisory Service officers announced that financial institutions could renew the corporation's existing loans and supply new subsidies only under government conditions designed to address management problems.

The announcement was not completely unexpected, as it reflected the custom of decades. It was, however, a disappointment, since collaboration between political leaders and business groups had brought on the economic crisis in the late 1990s. Evidently, the then-new government, led by Kim Dae Jung, who campaigned against such collaboration for decades before he captured power, would keep with tradition.

The Korean State and Society

In Korea, an alliance between the state and economic elites has a long history, reaching back far beyond industrialization. As early as the Chosŏn dynasty the state and economic elites united to control the general population. The state occasionally sparred with *yangban* (the traditional ruling class) elites to obtain greater economic resources (Palais 1975), but common political interests generally united the ruling blocs: the king needed the ideological backup *yangban* scholars could provide to secure political legitimacy, while *yangban* elites enjoyed local political power as proxies of the king. Such reciprocation of political legitimacy required tight collaboration to effectively maintain the dominant ruling structure at the expense of the broader public.

In modern Korean society, the alliance was reestablished with the onset of industrialization in the early 1960s. Political leaders headed a nation of extreme poverty inherited from Japanese colonial rule and devastation from the Korean War. They needed an economic partner to achieve rapid economic development that would compensate for their lack of political legitimacy, which originated from their ascendance to the power through an illegitimate military coup. To that end, they granted subsidies, including direct financial assistance and tax privileges, to a selected group of business enterprises that later became gigantic conglomerates, or *chaebol*. The alliance served the two power groups' reciprocal interests so effectively that popular resistance was taken seriously and resulted in harsh oppression. Mutual benefit did not, however, incur an equal relationship between the allies. Rather, it has mainly been the state's discretion to establish the alliance and to pick up appropriate partners from the business sector. As industrialization proceeded and increased their economic power, some business groups dared to challenge direct state economic intervention and seek independence. Such dissent was short-lived, however. The state simply punished the rebellious and made alliances with newly emerging firms. Dissolution of *chaebol* that outlived their usefulness to the state was commonplace.

Because this partnership derives from Korean structural conditions, not simply personal illegitimate ties, it is not easy to dissolve. Even democratic regimes established in the last decade have failed in the effort. Indeed, the newly established democratic government also drew on this coalition as it sought to lay the foundation for reconciliation of the two Koreas. It subsidized corporations, principally Hyundai, willing to launch ventures in North Korea. As such businesses failed to make a profit, it fell to the state to reciprocate the risk taking by bailing them out. The Hyundai case clearly testified to how the time-honored alliance between the ruling groups still persisted even with substantial progress of political development.

Even though alliance between the two ruling parties has remained intact for so long, it has not been without serious and fierce challenges from below. Popular rebellion through various forms of collective behavior, violent and nonviolent, has repeatedly threatened to disrupt the status quo when its injustice and malpractices grew particularly severe. The formidable coalition between the state and the economic ruling class, dominated by the former, had to constantly confront the resistant society.

The complex history of this confrontation defies generalization, but we can detect four major protest groups: peasants, laborers, students, and citizens. I intend to examine in this chapter the nature of each—why they protested, what they hoped to achieve, and what their effect has been on Korean society, past and present. In this investigation I will employ a historical-sociological approach to find out the general trend and peculiarity of social movements in Korea. One distinctive feature I am concerned with is that in most cases the protestors expressed their grievance against the state, even though they were engaged in a class struggle against the economic ruling groups. This obliges me to focus on the question of how and why they protested against the state and what they attempted to achieve through their protests against the state.

Peasant Movements

Before industrialization, the peasant majority was Korea's most important social group. Until the late nineteenth century, rural Korea was relatively stable despite state despotism and economic strain. However, peasant rebellion that erupted in the Chinju region in 1862 brought great repercussions. Rebellions became routine after the opening of the country in 1876 and culminated in the monumental Tonghak peasant war in 1894. Peasant rebellions in the late nineteenth century shared a common grievance: peasants protested against excessive taxes and their administration. As table 9.1 shows, uprisings targeting corrupt officials and petty functionaries who practiced extortion in the taxation and other administrative processes accounted for about 85 percent of the total. This contradicts the general belief of some scholars who contend that the main targets were landlords and that peasants were mainly concerned with tenancy disputes.

The Tonghak peasant war in 1894 typifies protests of the period. It was the first national popular protest in Korean history,

Table 9.1. Peasant rebellions in the late-nineteenth century

| Year | Target of peasant protests | | | | |
	Local officials	Petty functionaries	Landlords	Status system	Other
1862-80	4	2	1	1	1
1881-90	13	12	2	1	0
1891-93	16	8	2	0	2
Total (%)	33 (51)	22 (34)	5 (8)	2 (3)	3 (5)

Sources: National History Compiliation Committee, *Chosŏn wangjo sillok* (The veritable records of the Chosŏn dynasty).

lasting about eight months beginning in March. The war started in Paeksan, where peasants gathered by the thousands to deliver the Righteous Statement (Ch'angǔi mun) of their uprising, endorsed by three rebel leaders, Chun Pong-Jun, Sohn Hwa-Jung, and Kim Kae-Nam. Declaring their aim "inwardly to punish corrupt officials and outwardly to drive away foreign barbarians" (Oh 1940: 112), peasants launched their campaign against state corruption and spread it nationwide.

After victory in several critical battles against government forces, the peasant army negotiated a peace agreement lest the rebellion develop into an international war drawing in military intervention by countries such as China and Japan to assist the government. The compromise placed the peasant army in charge of local administrative duties in Chŏlla province and inaugurated the short-lived ruling period of the Tonghak war. However, after swift victory over China in the Sino-Japanese War, the Japanese army entered southern Korea to suppress the peasant army, an action that caused the second uprising of the peasant army. Peasant forces, though 167,000 strong, were no match for the Japanese equipped with modern military technology. The decisive battle of Kongju in the second uprising brought final defeat to the peasant army.

The second uprising differed from the previous one in that it was an anti-imperial struggle against the Japanese army. Official documents describing the event abound in nationalist rhetoric. In contrast, the first uprising and period of peasant self-rule were motivated by grievances against state bureaucrats and petty functionaries involved in taxation and the commercialization of agriculture. Most of all, peasant demands suggested in the peace agreement with the government confirm this. Politically, the peasants demanded, foremost, punishment of corrupt and exploitative bureaucrats and abolishment of government apparatuses implicated in administrative abuse. Economically, demands focused on the tax system and commercialization of agriculture. Demands included retaining current tax law but returning to old rates, prohibiting collection of taxes already paid, and exempting uncultivated land from taxes (D. N. Kim 1994: 178–180). In addition to political and economic demands, they made social demands. These centered on the social inequalities born of the rigid social status system and included ending slavery and discrimination against outcasts, allowing widows to remarry, and appointing governmental officials by merit rather than heritage.

In sum, the Tonghak peasant war and most other peasant protests of the period targeted the state, not the economic ruling class.
This is a strong indication that the landlord system was still
characterized by the extreme fusion of political power with
economic wealth, implying underdevelopment of the economic
landlord system in which peasants mainly confronted the landlords, who exploited them solely with economic means. Their
struggles against the state and state bureaucrats thus testify that
peasants' primary self-identity had not yet shifted from the nation
to economic class.

The nature of peasant movements, however, changed considerably during the colonial period. We can generally characterize
several stages: relative calm in the 1910s and 1940s, tenancy
disputes in the 1920s and early 1930s, and the Red Union Peasant
movement in the 1930s. The most typical peasant movements of
the period were tenancy disputes. Not only did more peasants
participate in such disputes across more regions; their voices
registered more clearly than in the ideologically and regionally
restricted Red Union Peasant movement.

Tenancy disputes of the colonial period were marked by
antipathy toward landlords, both Japanese and Korean (Asada
1984: 52), not the state, as before. We might have expected that
peasants would resist the state more fiercely than ever, given that
it was an imposed, colonial government. The reality is contradictory to this expectation, as tenancy disputes dominated social protests of the period. Tenancy disputes increased in number but
decreased in intensity as Japanese colonial rule consolidated
because the colonial government introduced measures that institutionalized conflicts between landlords and peasants in the early
1930s, such as the Tenancy Arbitration Ordinance (Sochak
chojǒngryǒng) in 1932 and the Land Ordinance (Nongchiryǒng) in
1934 (see Shin 1996). Direct physical confrontation virtually ended
because the measures provided a means for orderly and peaceful
conflict resolution (Government-General of Korea 1940: 26, 33).

However, active protests of peasants in various forms failed to
improve their economic lot. Their demands for tenancy-rights
guarantees, rent reduction, and elimination of the land tax and
transfer of water fee regularly failed to topple landlord interest
bolstered by support of the government-general. Furthermore,
colonial state interest in economic exploitation increased as the
state mobilized resources for World War II. As the colonial period
closed, income per capita fell below subsistence level, economic

distance among classes widened, and the proportion of tenants increased. Despite these economic conditions, the strict control of the heavily militarized colonial government kept the peasants generally silent in the last phase of the colonial period.

Only when control from above attenuated did the peasants take collective action to register grievances. This opportunity came when Korea was liberated from Japanese colonial rule. Japanese withdrawal from the peninsula left a power vacuum and presented an opportunity for rigorous protest. As the American military government struggled to check dominance by Communist and leftist organizations and stabilize an economy lacking even basic staples, peasants were forced to accept minimum compensation for their collected rice, sometimes below production cost. The American military government even used aggressive police force to collect rice, expecting the show of arms to quell peasant protests.

However, such agricultural policies, especially the forced collection of staples, had unexpected consequences. In time, peasants united in violent opposition to the American military government forces before they could reestablish and control the means of physical violence in the occupied territory. The first monumental protest, known as the October Uprising, broke out in 1946 in the midst of severe conflict between the Left and Right over the issue of trusteeship. The American military government had tightened its grip on the Left to assure that the southern peninsula remained free of Communist leanings. The Left lashed back with a general strike. When the flame of protest spread from the September railroad workers strike in Pusan to Taegu, police suppression martyred a protester on October 1, transforming the strike into a general mass uprising comprising fifteen thousand at its peak.

As military intervention quelled protest in Taegu, it spilled across the rest of Kyŏngsangbukdo province and then the entire southern peninsula. In places, violent protestors seized police stations and massacred police and government bureaucrats in charge of rice collection. Some allege that Communist organizations were central in organizing peasants and leading the movement (see, e.g., Shim 1991). Notwithstanding some fragmentary evidences showing the dispatch of leftist leaders to rebel provinces, however, any connection of peasants to these organizations was still far from substantial (D. N. Kim 1998). Rather, the People's Committees (Inmin wiwŏnhoe), the voluntary local organizations composed of aborigine activists, were the more active and central protest leaders (Cumings 1981: chap. 10). This is confirmed by the fact that peasant demands during the protest focused on their economic adversity, primarily due to rice extortion, and not on ideological concerns of the left or right.

Peasant hopes for economic remedy through protest were dashed when the American military government refortified its position with military and police power. December brought a virtual end to the round of protest, and peasants withdrew from the protest arena with the inception of industrialization, even as new industrial workers and students assumed the baton.

Labor Movements

Large-scale labor organizations and movements began in post-liberation Korea when leftists formed a national umbrella labor organization, the National Council for Trade Unions in Korea (Chosŏn nodongchohap chŏnkuk p'yŏungŭihoe, or Chŏnp'yŏng). Inheriting the legacy of labor disputes in the colonial period, the NCTUK rapidly expanded its base, establishing two thousand branches with close to 550,000 members by the end of 1945. Threatened by such huge leftist organizational capacity, the American military government nearly destroyed it to the level of thirteen branches with 2,500 members in 1947 and instead established a new para-governmental labor organization, Taehan noch'ŏng.

After more than a decade of working-class silence, labor movements revived in the 1960s when industrialization produced a major contingent of urban industrial workers. Movements in the 1960s and early 1970s were largely unorganized and rudimentary. They hoped to improve miserable working conditions and extend the legality of labor organizations, strictly limited after the 1961 military coup banned social protest. The state not only restricted workers' right to bargain with and protest against the capitalists, but also, more fundamentally, limited their right to organize. It officially prescribed the workers' right to organize trade unions, but in reality frequently failed to observe the authorized law. It is in this social context that Chŏn T'ae-Il, a young, small garment-factory worker in Seoul's P'yŏunghwa Market, immolated himself to publicize workers' suffering, demanding "Abide by the labor standard laws!"

The state was rarely moved by the violent, desperate working-class protests. Since it sought its political legitimacy in economic development, it needed to tame labor forces in order to attract

foreign capital essential for sustained economic growth as industrialization advanced (Koo and Kim 1992: 130–131).[1] Labor's
anemic organizational base in this period required outside assistance if it was to have any impact. The church and then students
filled that need. Among several church groups involved in labor
organization since the early 1970s, the most influential was the
Urban Industrial Mission (Tosi sanŏp sŏnkyohoe). The UIM was
especially active in helping female workers form grassroots trade
unions in textile and electronic factories, the two main industrial
sectors in the early stage of industrialization. It is estimated to
have assisted about 20 percent of the newly organized trade
unions of the 1970s.

Students also formed a coalition with industrial workers. Pro-
claiming a worker-student alliance (*nohak yŏndae*), thousands of
students became "disguised workers" in plants in order to
enlighten laborers concerning their legal vulnerability and to
organize them into labor movements.[2] Such subterfuge was
required because laws prohibited third-party involvement in
disputes between workers and entrepreneurs. As fellow laborers,
they effectively awakened workers' class consciousness and organized them to mount labor disputes. Only through such outside
church and student support could the labor movement survive the
highly oppressive Chun Doo Hwan regime.

The labor movement proliferated when its desperate efforts to
improve working conditions and economic compensation coincided with structural cleavage in the political realm in the final
days of the Chun regime. Its heyday began in 1987 when political
democratization created structural opportunity for various social
movements to thrive. Thus, it may be that the factor most responsible for the prevalence of labor movements and formation of the
working class was the weakened state oppression, not workers'
objective economic conditions (Choi 1997: 358). Massive citizen
rallies that began in June and lasted for about a month demanded
direct presidential elections, creating huge momentum for change.
Immediately after the June 29 declaration, which involved

---

[1] This structural condition for economic development in Korea in the 1970s
resembles that of Latin American countries. Such states sought to exclude the
working class from the corporatist ruling bloc in order to channel foreign investment in the blocs, thus forming a triple coalition among the state, bourgeoisie, and
foreign capital. See, for example, Evans 1979.
[2] The number of "disguised workers" peaked in the three thousands in the
mid-1980s. See Park and Cho 1989.

substantial democratic concessions by the oppressive regime, labor
activists wasted no time in organizing independent labor unions
qualitatively different from those that had prevailed previously.
With the enhanced organizational capacity of labor unions, workers were eager to register their grievances through violent protest.
Table 9.2 depicts the trend of labor organization and labor
disputes in this period. It shows a mushrooming of labor organizations reminiscent of the period immediately following liberation.
However, consolidation of political democratization under the Roh
Tae Woo regime and subsequently the Kim Young Sam and Kim
Dae Jung civilian governments provided labor with an unprecedented congenial climate. Labor now had formal, state-
sanctioned mechanisms through which to pursue goals. These
encouraged all workers—white- and blue-collar—to actively participate in labor organizations, creating a high rate of organization
even among middle-class workers. Blue-collar radicalization of
the labor movement, however, caused some white-collar workers
to retreat from the movement and assume a more conservative
position. Thereafter, manual workers in heavy industry primarily
led the movement, mounting more violent protests compared with
those that female workers in light industry had initiated years earlier.

Loosened state control over working-class organization and
protest after 1987 did not mean, however, that the state was
indifferent to worker predominance at the bargaining table with
capitalists. The state still intervened between the two classes and
helped the capitalists secure the greater control. They primarily
did so by resisting revision of labor laws that gave the state and
bourgeoisie superiority vis-à-vis the working class, allowing only
minor changes in 1987 and 1988. Consequently, the labor law of
1992, which followed extensive working-class effort to amend the
law in its favor, retained all of the important restrictive clauses. It
still proscribed "third-party" involvement in labor activity (to
prevent political activists from penetrating the labor arena),
allowed only single unions based in single corporations (to
prevent independent unions able to oppose company-based
unions), disallowed union political activity, and denied teachers
and civil servants the right to organize (Koo 1993: 159).

Although the state incrementally eased restrictions and provided a freer space for labor organizations and movements, it
would not grant the working class equality with the political elite
and economic ruling class. The exclusionary nature of labor

Table 9.2. Labor movements since the 1980s

Year	Union members	Number of unions	Unionization rate (%)*	Number of disputes
1980	1,119,572	2,618	14.7	206
1985	1,004,398	2,534	12.4	265
1987	1,267,457	4,086	13.8	3,749
1988	1,707,456	6,142	17.8	1,827
1989	1,932,415	7,861	18.7	1,616
1990	1,886,884	7,676	17.4	322
1991	1,803,408	7,656	16.0	234
1992	1,734,598	7,505	15.1	235

Source: Recalculated from D. C. Kim 1995: 58, 67.
* Unionization rates were measured by dividing the total number of union members by the number of total employees.

policy was again evident during economic restructuring following the IMF economic crisis since 1997. To meet the crisis, state propaganda urged all constituents of Korean society to share in the economic hardship that economic efficiency would require. In truth, the working class bore the brunt of adversity. Massive layoffs accompanying economic restructuring of financial institutions and corporations, private and public, ignited labor protests. It seems, however, that worker resistance enjoyed less public support than previously. This may be partly because, when all feel vulnerable, they have limited sympathy for others, and partly because labor became more focused on class interests, and less on general social interests. The narrowed focus of labor movements on class interests, in particular, reduced the moral legitimacy they enjoyed when resisting dictatorial regimes in the past. Struggle for survival still continues in several important factories, but it will take time to learn how matters will resolve in the global economy.

It appears, then, that labor movements since the 1940s in Korea were struggles against the state, not against capitalists directly. Class struggles between laborers and the bourgeoisie ultimately became nonclass confrontations between the state and the working class. Again, this situation derived from state omnipresence and omnipotence in all realms of society. It has never completely loosened its grip on labor and maintains its power to control labor law. Despite political democratization since the late 1980s, the state has minimally eased and sometimes added labor restrictions. It still prohibits some labor organizations, virtually limiting labor disputes and wage increases (D. C. Kim 1995: 178).

Thus, although labor disputes sought to improve economic conditions for workers, the workers had to protest against the state because it kept intervening in the labor relations. Prior to 1987, the working class required state approval to organize against the capitalists, a virtually unobtainable outcome. Denial of the right to organize and protection of capitalist economic interests necessarily impaired relations between the state and the working class. As stated above, even after 1987, when democratization took hold and workers agitated with renewed rigor, the impasse essentially remained. Until quite recently, labor law—the critical element in the relationship among the state, capitalists, and working class—was always central in labor disputes (D. N. Kim 1997: 125). As the law stood, labor's efforts to improve its economic lot were by definition illegal and thus were concentrated on the revision of the impartial labor law.

Because the state was the target of worker ire, interactions were violent. Unlike confrontations between the bourgeoisie and workers, which involved economic rather than physical measures since both lacked legitimate means of physical violence, the state held a physical-force advantage vis-à-vis protesters, and it did not hesitate to brandish that weapon. Labor disputes were accordingly more violent and radical than in other industrializing East Asian countries, such as Taiwan and Singapore. Disputes were less frequent in Korea except for the extraordinary years of 1987–1989, but averaged more participants and longer duration (table 9.3).

Student Movements

Students, like peasants and laborers, have been among the most active agents in changing Korean society. At critical junctures throughout modern Korean history, college students have formed social movements determined to tear down old systems and establish better ones. In 1960, they rose up to fell the dictatorial regime of the first president, Syngman Rhee. Their fleeting victory, aborted by military coup in a year, was the first show of student power to shape Korean society. President Park Chung Hee's military regime practiced harsh student oppression for almost two decades until Park's assassination in 1979.

Even during those years, however, students staged intermittent demonstrations. For example, students protested against normalization of diplomatic relations with Japan in 1965. When Japan gave economic aid for Korea's industrialization, the Korean state willingly adopted a diplomatic treaty with Japan without acquiring due apology and proper compensation for colonial rule. This insult ignited nationalist feelings that led to broad protests, which included students, against the regime. The succeeding generation of students in the 1970s inherited this activist tradition. Though the number of student movements before 1979 was modest, their intensity and moral authority were exceptional and posed the only serious challenge to the dictatorial regime. For instance, in 1975 an organization of underground student movements, the Alliance of Democratic Students (Minch'ŏng hakryŏn), proved so threatening to Park Chung Hee that he sought through martial court to execute its leaders.

Table 9.3. Labor disputes in Korea and Taiwan

Year	Dispute frequency		Number of participants (thousands)		Loss of workdays (thousands)	
	South Korea	Taiwan	South Korea	Taiwan	South Korea	Taiwan
1980–86	204.7	1,060.9	28	10	5.2	0.0
1987–89	2,412.7	1622.0	655	34	643.1	2.1
1990–94	229.4	1,858.8	125	22	212.4	0.5

Source: Recalculated from Kuk 1999, 100, 103, 105.

Following Park Chung Hee's assassination by one of his top aides, students seized the moment to institutionalize a democratic political order. During the Seoul Spring, students were the main contenders against an emerging military group conspiring to confiscate power from civilian politicians. When the military coup succeeded in 1980, the students again fiercely attacked the regime's legitimacy during the Kwangju democratization movement in 1980. The Kwangju movement, in which the military massacred hundreds, represents one of the greatest tragedies in modern Korean history. The massacre inspired students to accelerate their activism, drawing on the populist legacy of student movements of the 1970s and armed with the theoretical teachings of neo-Marxism, dependency theory, and liberation theology. Because the United States tacitly approved of the harsh suppression of the Kwangju uprising by the military junta, the massacre implicated the United States as a supporter of a dictatorial regime willing to serve U.S. interests. Students now began to question their trust in the United States as an advocate of democratization. In this way, student movements in the 1980s became characteristically anti-imperial, anti-American campaigns.

The Kwangju massacre set the tone for the initial period of Chun Doo Hwan's new military regime. Facing severe oppression from that regime, students used the years to enhance their capacity for effective social action and to wait for the weakening of control from above, arming themselves with new theoretical understandings of Korean society. Their opportunity to act came in 1984 when the government introduced measures that encouraged college student self-rule, including legalization of campus student activities. The government's motive was to strip student movements of the moral legitimacy that originated from their struggles against the dictatorial regime by exposing them as radical and pro-Communist (Pae 1999: 97–98). To the government's chagrin, official sanction and public exposure provided a breathing space, and energized the movements.

New radical social theories also served to revitalize student movements in this period by stimulating investigation into the nature of Korean society, particularly what constitutes its main contradictions and how to solve them. Intense debate arose among social activists and social scientists concerning the social formation of Korea (Park and Cho 1989). The debate divided student activists into three camps in the early 1980s: the National Democratic Revolution (NDR), the People's Democratic Revolution

(PDR), and the Civil Democratic Revolution (CDR). The CDR proposed an all-inclusive alliance among oppressed groups to wage struggles against the dictatorial political regime. Though it constituted one of the three most influential student movement groups at the time, it did not have a lasting effect. The NDR believed that the main contradiction lay in the antagonistic relationship between the military dictatorship and the general population. The student movement therefore needed to depose the regime by forming a close alliance with the opposition party. In contrast, the PDR contended, without fully negating the position of the NDR, that the main problem for Korea was further complicated by its control by foreign imperialists, more specifically, the United States. The student movement should thus concentrate on Korea's liberation from foreign domination, together with the struggles against the fascist state.

The split temporarily resolved when movement leaders incorporated the basic principles of the NDR and PDR and developed a more inclusive ideology embracing the three *mins: minjok* (nation), *minju* (democracy), and *minjung* (populace). Led by the Council for the Achievement of Three Min Principles (Sammint'u), students protested against the political regime and the economic ruling class in 1984–1985. They established a worker-student alliance to awaken workers' class consciousness and mobilize workers for the democratization movement. In addition, they occupied the American Cultural Council in the center of Seoul, the first real challenge to U.S. dominance on the Korean peninsula. This incident constituted an important turning point in the social movement history of Korea, providing the critical momentum to lead the student movements toward the campaign against the United States by officially dubbing it the enemy of Korea's democratization.

The united student front was short-lived. In 1986, some student movement leaders launched a full-scale attack against U.S. imperialism. They formed a new group, the Council for the Struggle for Anti-American Independence and Anti-Fascist Democracy (Chamint'u; NLPDR), which judged Korea's main problem to be U.S. imperialist penetration into Korean politics and economy, making it a U.S. colony on the periphery of a dominating world system. The prerequisite for solving Korea's problems was anti-imperialism. In opposition, another group of students organized the Council for the Nationalist and Democratic Struggle against the Dictatorial and Fascist Regime (Minmint'u), which emphasized the internal contradictions stemming from coalition between the dictatorial political regime and monopoly capitalism. The two groups collided in 1986 over the general election and revision of the constitution. The radical Minmint'u proposed forming a Constitutional Assembly to create a new, populist constitution, rather than forming a coalition with the opposition party. Chamint'u took a more compromising approach, temporarily halting anti-imperialist activities and promoting a united front of all social forces interested in institutionalizing democracy in Korea.

Chamint'u adopted a more resilient strategy by mitigating radicalization and violence of the student movement and sought to broaden popular support through nonviolent demonstrations. Most college student associations withdrew from Minmint'u because of its radical position. The Konkuk University Incident, which produced numerous student and police injuries, also sobered many students. With this incident, they supported the more moderate strategy, making it central in student activism in the 1980s and afterward.[3]

January 1987 marked a critical juncture in the development of student movements. Through the death of a Seoul National University student, Park Chong-Ch'ol, by police torture and conspiracy to conceal it, the government forfeited all moral authority. In addition to committing these crimes, the government suspended discussion of democratic amendment of the constitution. Popular sentiment against the government flared, and student movement leaders seized the moment to mobilize students and ordinary citizens alike in protest. Student organizations, especially those allied with Chamint'u, formed a coalition with other dissidents to wage street campaigns and played a central role in the formation of the National Coalition for a Democratic Constitution. After a month-long struggle against the dictatorship, protestors finally obtained some concessions. In the June 29 declaration the regime agreed to employ limited democratizing measures, including holding direct presidential elections, by which the political regime could secure much enhanced moral authority and political legitimacy. High expectations were dashed when election outcomes in December 1987 placed Roh Tae Woo—a Chun Doo Hwan crony and central figure in the 1980 military coup—in the presidential office.

---

[3] For the debates between Chamint'u and Minmint'u, see Ilsongchong 1988: 109–130.

The student movement shifted its focus following the election. Rather than protesting against the dictatorial regime and imperial forces, it turned to the need for national reunification. It formed a new national umbrella organization in 1988, the Council for the Representatives of College Students in Korea (Chŏndaehyŏp). However, conflict among student movements remained and sporadically erupted over the issue of the main obstacle to national reunification. The Council of the Representatives of College Students in Seoul (Sŏdaehyŏp), endorsing Chamint'u ideology, considered the United States as the main antagonist and launched anti-American, antinuclear campaigns. Conversely, the Council for the Formation of All Alliances of College Students in Seoul (Sŏkonch'u), ideologically Minmint'u loyalists, argued that state monopoly capitalism perpetuated division of the peninsula: students should concentrate on demolishing monopoly capitalism and state dictatorship. The disharmony between the two camps was mitigated by their joint attempt to hold a conference of college students in South and North Korea.

Persistent student activism centered on reunification placed students in the vanguard of Korean social transformation. Students championed a new way to achieve a long suppressed social agenda, seen at the time as radical and frequently costing them popular support. Voices such as theirs, urging national reunification by peaceful means and talks with North Korea, were branded pro-Communist or pro–North Korean. Public support especially waned when they acknowledged the legitimacy of *juch'e* (self-reliance) ideology, the official state doctrine of North Korea. Such steps finally strayed too far from the conservative mainstream. The state eagerly sought to paint the student movement as pro–North Korean radicalism in order to isolate it from the public; this effort was generally successful because of the enhanced legitimacy of the political regime after the June 29 Declaration and subsequent democratization process.

In the face of this crisis, student activists accordingly strove to reorganize the student movement as the Federation of All College Student Associations in Korea (Hanch'ongryŏn). This attempt proved futile, however, since the new umbrella organization adhered to previous organizational principles and political ideology. Public support became irrecoverable as state propaganda portrayed students as lackeys of North Korea. Ironically, the fatal blow to the student movement came when the state embraced the reunification agenda and initiated talks with North Korea, the "sunshine" policy that earned the former South Korean president, Kim Dae Jung, international accolade in the form of the Nobel Peace Prize. The student movement thereby lost its agenda in addition to public support.

College campuses across Korea are currently peaceful. Student demonstrations occur, but rarely draw more than a hundred together. Most students are indifferent or antipathetic to the student movement, and some criticize student political activism on campus (see, e.g., http://user.chollian.net/~wealive and http://www.yonhak.com/yeonhak/movement.htm). Rather, their concern centers on cultural events more than political protest against the state, monopoly capitalism, and foreign imperial forces, the causes that captured their predecessors' passion.

Civil Movements

The demise of student movements in the 1990s is part of the general reduced concern within social movements about universal interests that transcend class issues. Labor movements, which have taken center stage in social movements after the onset of industrialization, also changed their direction from struggles to safeguard general concerns of Korean society to workers' class interests. The narrowed focus of labor movements and the demise of student movements leave us with the question of who will pursue universal social interests in Korea. No society can long function if each social class cares only for its own interests. Some issues—such as environmental degradation—affect all classes and demand cooperative efforts of various social classes.

In the late 1980s a new force, addressing shared citizen needs, entered the Korean landscape: civil movements. The most representative illustration of ordinary citizens coming together as a civil movement in recent Korean history is the June Uprising of 1987. Hundreds of thousands of citizens, mostly middle class, staged a month of mass rallies demanding political democratization. The movement obtained substantial concessions from the ruling party. These conditions created a new social space, civil society—the social space in which matters of everyday life are discussed and practiced (Habermas 1989)—independent of the state-dominated political realm and driven to transform state structure and citizens' everyday lives.

The process of political democratization in Korea thus began with only minimal concessions of the dictatorial regime to the public. The enhanced legitimacy of the state originating from the democratization process since the late 1980s provided it with the moral authority by which it could effectively isolate and oppress radical social movements. Thanks to this enhanced political legitimacy, the state more fiercely oppressed radical social movements by students and industrial workers than past dictatorial regimes had. Political democratization alone had not been sufficient to fully redress social grievances. The state now tried to strip radical movements of any legitimacy by labeling them as reckless challengers to the duly established political system. The struggle for moral authority between the state and its challengers thus required a radical change in strategies of social movements.

The opening up of civil society allowed civil movements to flourish. In contrast to traditional popular movements, civil movements generally assume more moderate ideologies and strategies and pursue trans-class interests (H. Y. Cho 1995 and Yu 1995). They rarely question the legitimacy of the established order, whether political or economic, but rather monitor to see if it functions as intended. In Korea, two types of civil movement pursued that end. The first inherited the focus of popular movements of the 1980s and concentrates on politics and the economy. The second scrutinizes the quality of everyday life and most notably comprises environmental, feminist, and consumers' movements.

The Citizens' Coalition for Economic Justice (Kyŏngsillyŏn) and the People's Solidarity for Participatory Democracy (Ch'amyŏyŏndae)—with about twenty thousand and twelve thousand members, respectively—are the most representative of the first type. Both have 60–70 percent middle-class membership, though various population groups participate (D. Y. Cho 1999: 262). Reflecting their dominant constituency, they employ moderate protest strategies—such as public hearings, conferences, and workshops—that aim to quicken public interest in civil movements and their causes. This politicization of civil movements is distinctive in the history of popular movements. These organizations are creating new social-movement issues, such as supervision of the government budget, protection of individual privacy, and public access to government information.

The second type of civil movement is more specialized and less politicized as it seeks to improve the quality of citizens' everyday lives. Most successful among these are environmental movements. They have strong public appeal because of the environmental degradation that has accompanied rapid industrialization since the

1960s. The Korea Federation for Environmental Movements (Hwankyŏng undong yŏnhap) has become one of the most influential of the civil movement-organizations, with about eighty on staff and more than eighty-five thousand members. Feminist-movement organizations are also successfully mobilizing women in their effort to enhance women's status in Korea.

Social movements of both types have made great strides in creating new and diverse issues that draw ordinary citizens into civil movements directly related to their lives. However, serious problems that critically threaten their further development and influence require public attention. Most of all, low membership fees leave them financially vulnerable, making them inevitably rely upon governmental resources. Furthermore, in marked contrast to the large-scale demonstrations of traditional social movements, members' passive involvement in movement events and organizational downsizing diminish their effectiveness.

To address these issues, civil movements would do well to form a network among themselves. The effectiveness of such a strategy was well illustrated when the Citizens' Alliance for the General Election (Ch'ongsŏn yŏndae) drew together about 1,055 civil movement organizations to defeat corrupt candidates in the 2000 general elections: fifty-nine among eighty-six politicians they designated for rejection from the National Assembly were defeated. In addition to this impressive success, the alliance provided a model for civil movements: alliances among small-scale civil-movement organizations can have significant influence without forfeiting specialization among network members.

Civil movements must flourish if universal interests within Korean society are to be addressed. This is especially true because there is little hope that the student movement will be revitalized or that the labor movement will move beyond class interests. In this situation, tasks before civil movements are abundant—and critical to Korea's future. It remains unclear how effectively civil-movement organizations can handle new social changes, such as globalization and the advance of the information society. It is evident, however, that their responses to these macro structural transformations will significantly affect the future of Korean society.

Conclusion

Focusing on four types of movements—those of peasants, laborers, college students, and citizens—I have outlined the general trend of social movements in Korea, with special emphasis on the actors' motivations for social movements and their effect on Korean society. Before industrialization, peasants were most active in registering their grievances through various protests, first mounting rebellions against excessive taxation and then lodging formal disputes against landlords when colonial rule introduced the modern landlord system. Peasants organized the October Uprising in 1946, the last monumental social protest they made in Korea, to protest the threat to their subsistence represented by the American military government's agricultural policy. When the 1960s brought industrialization to Korea, the working class became the main actor in social movements, as industrialization displaced peasant movements from center stage in the class struggle. After occupying that position over the ensuing decades, labor movements led in the transformation of Korean society at some important junctures, avoiding exclusive focus on the economic interests of the working class. More recently, however, they changed their direction to fulfill class interests, such as increases in laborers' share in economic redistribution.

In contrast to these two class-based social movements, student movements have pursued universal social interests, transcending any specific class interests by focusing on such issues as political democratization and national reunification. They have long been divided in their perception about the main problem confronting Korean society and the strategy to solve it: some urged dissolution of state monopoly capitalism; others pursued liberation from foreign imperial forces, especially the United States. Though the conflict was resolved when student movements reorganized around a new center, the Federation of All College Student Associations in Korea, public support waned in the 1990s as a result of student radicalism. The demise of student movements is compensated for by the rise of another social movement caring for the universal interest of Korean society, civil movements. They try to gain public support by relying upon moderate strategies while focusing on improving citizens' everyday lives as well as traditional political and economic concerns shared by various popular movements in the past. It is unclear, however, how much they would prosper in new social circumstances, such as institutionalization of formal democracy and globalization, as they are still in the incipient stage with only about ten years of history.

The analysis of the general trend of social movements in this chapter reveals an important peculiarity: almost all social movements in Korea targeted the state, not the economic ruling class, except for tenant disputes in the colonial period. This is the case not only in social movements concerned with political issues, such as democratization of the political system and national reunification, but also in the class struggles of peasants and workers to improve their economic conditions. Before industrialization, peasants stood against the harsh taxation of the Chosŏn dynasty government and fiercely attacked the American military government to defend their rice from the forced collection. This tendency continued in labor movements that took on the ruling alliance between politically ambitious state elites and economically monopolistic capitalists. A class struggle between laborers and capitalists eventually evolved into a nonclass confrontation between the state and the working class.

The state has been targeted as the main enemy in social movements because the Korean state has maintained the ruling coalition with the economic ruling class, landlords in agrarian society and capitalists in industrial society. After establishing the coalition, the state actively controlled it for its own benefit and thus became an omnipresent and omnipotent entity by dominating all spheres of Korean society. Conversely, the populace, or *minjung,* have been continuously excluded from the ruling bloc and forced to concede their interests. This economic injustice, together with a lack of political legitimacy of the regime, encouraged the Korean people to protest against the ruling alliance. As a result, it is commonplace in Korean history to find a confrontation between a strong and oppressive state and a resistant society.

This direct confrontation between the state and protestors heightened the intensity and level of violence in social movements. Since the state monopolizes the legitimate means of physical violence, it naturally employs them when it faces prolonged strong protests from below. This is very different from an economic class relationship between the capitalist class and the working class, where economic means of exploitation and protest are applied. Once protestors have been confronted by the state's physical means of violence, they have escalated the level of their violence. The spiral escalation in the intensity of oppression and protests testifies that harsh oppression may reduce the occurrence of social protests, but only at the cost of enhanced levels of violence. Therefore, labor disputes in Korea have been more violent and radical, though less frequent, than in other East Asian developing countries.

The state in Korea still tries to be omnipresent and omnipotent, though it is not as dictatorial as before. The power of Korean society to resist state penetration, however, has significantly dwindled. Social movements in general do not enjoy the public support of the past. Any kind of social movements suffer from the waning of support, including civil movements that adopt more realistic and practical agendas and milder strategies. Though public indifference to social movements can be attributed to many factors, the the most important one is ironically the institutionalization of formal democracy in Korea. It considerably demobilized social movements by subsuming most agendas for social movements, which were not addressed by previous dictatorial regimes. The necessity for social movements, however, has not declined at all. The state has no intention to fully integrate lower classes into the ruling bloc, and real concession to them has never been made. In this situation, it is of the utmost importance to revitalize social movements to resist encroachment of state power and to nullify the state-controlled ruling bloc. This is a way to ensure the development of democratic society free from state dominance.

References

Asada, Kyoji. 1984. "Hang'il nongmin undong ŭi ilpanjŏk chŏnkaekwachŏng" (The elaboration of anti-Japanese peasant movements). *Hang'il nongmin undong yŏnku* (Studies on anti-Japanese peasant movements). Seoul: Tongnyok.

Cho, Dae-Yop. 1999. *Han'guk ŭi simin undong* (Civil movements in Korea). Seoul: Nanam.

Cho, Hee-Yon. 1995. "Minjung undong kwa 'Simin Sahoe,' 'Simin Undong'" (*Minjung* movements, "civil society" and "civil movements"). In Pal-Mu Yu and Ho-Ki Kim, eds., *Simin sahoe wa simin undong* (Civil society and civil movements). Seoul: Hanul.

Cho, Seung-Hyuk. 1984. *Han'guk kong'ŏphwa wa nodong undong* (Industrialization and the labor movement in Korea). Seoul: P'ulbit.

Choi, Jang-Jip. 1997. *Han'guk ŭi nodong undong kwa kukka* (The labor movement and the state in Korea). Seoul: Nanam.

Cumings, Bruce. 1981. *The Origins of the Korean War: Liberation and the Emergence of Separate Regimes, 1945–1947.* Princeton, N.J.: Princeton University Press.

Evans, P. B. 1979. *Dependent Development: The Alliance of Multinational, State, and Local Capital in Brazil.* Princeton, N.J.: Princeton University Press.

Government-General of Korea. Various years. *Chosen nochi nenpo* (Annual report on Korean agricultural lands). Keijo: Government-General of Korea.

Habermas, Jurgen. 1989. *The Structural Transformation of the Public Sphere.* Trans. Thomas Burger with assistance from Frederick Lawrence. Cambridge, Mass.: MIT Press.

Han, Woo-Keun. 1971. *Tonghakran kiin e kwanhan yŏnku* (A study on the causes of the Tonghak Rebellion). Seoul: Seoul National University Press.

Ilsongjŏng. 1988. *Haksaeng undong nonjaengsa* (History of debates on student movements). Seoul: Ilsongjŏng.

Kim, Dong-Chun. 1995. *Han'guk sahoe nodongja yŏnku* (A study of the workers of Korean society). Seoul: Yŏksa pip'yŏngsa.

Kim, Dong-No. 1994. "Peasants, State, and Landlords: National Crisis and the Transformation of Agrarian Society in Pre-Colonial Korea." Ph.D. dissertation, University of Chicago.

———. 1997. "Minran kwa nodong undong, kŭrigo kukka" (Peasant rebellions, labor movements, and the state). *Chŏnt'ong kwa hyundae* 2:112–134.

———. 1998. "Mikunchŏngki nongmin chojik kwa nongmin undong: Minjung ŭi sahoe seryŏkhwa wa kŭ Chajŏl" (Peasant organizations and peasant movements in the American military government period). *Sahoe wa yoksa* 54:121–163.

Koo, Hagen. 1993. "The State, *Minjung,* and the Working Class in South Korea." In Hagen Koo, ed., *State and Society in Contemporary Korea.* Ithaca, N.Y.: Cornell University Press.

———, and Eun-Mee Kim. 1992. "The Developmental State and Capital Accumulation in South Korea." In Richard P. Appelbaum and Jeffrey Henderson, eds., *States and Development in the Asian Pacific Rim.* London: Sage.

Kuk, Min-Ho. 1999. *Tong Asia ŭi kukka chudo san'ophwa wa yukyo* (State-led industrialization and Confucianism in East Asia). Kwangju: Chonnam University Press.

National History Compilation Committee. *Chosŏn wangjo sillok* (Veritable records of the Chosŏn dynasty).

Oh, Ji-Young. 1940. *Tonghaksa* (The history of Tonghak). Seoul: Yongch'ang sokwan.

Pae, Kyu-Han. 1999. *Haksaeng undong kwa taehaksaeng chach'ihwaltong* (Student movements and voluntary activities of college students). Seoul: Nanam.

Palais, James B. 1975. *Politics and Policy in Traditional Korea.* Cambridge: Harvard University Press.

Park, Hyon-Chae, and Cho Hee-Yon. 1989. *Han'guk sahoe kusŏgch'e nonchaeng* (Debates on social formation of Korea). Seoul: Chuksan.

Shim, Ji-Yon. 1991. *Taegu 10 wŏl hangjaeng yŏnku* (A study of the October uprising in Taegu). Seoul: Ch'unggye yŏnkuso.

Shin, Gi-Wook. 1996. *Peasant Protest and Social Change in Colonial Korea.* Seattle: University of Washington Press.

Yu, Pal-Mu. 1995. "Simin sahoe ŭi sŏngchang kwa simin undong" (The growth of civil society and civil movements). In Pal-Mu Yu and Ho-Ki Kim, eds., *Simin sahoe wa simin undong* (Civil society and civil movements). Seoul: Hanul.

TEN

The Making of Civil Society in Historical Perspective

HYUK-RAE KIM

This chapter explores the form of civil society peculiar to the Republic of Korea (hereafter Korea) and its genesis in historical perspective. For this, it analyzes academic discourses on the relationship between the state and civil society over three historical periods in modern Korea. The three distinct but intricately interrelated historical periods have characterized the relationship between the state and civil society and the development of civil society in particular. The first was from liberation to the end of the Park regime. Discourse on civil society during this period made no progress, as successive authoritarian governments practiced state corporatism and repressed civil society to achieve modernization through rapid economic growth. The second period lasted to the beginning of the 1987 Democratic Movement and abounded in academic discourse on the state and its critical role in economic development. Discussion of civil society as an alternative mechanism of governance emerged during this period. The third stage is the transitional period toward democracy, during which Korea is experiencing actual growth in civil society and interest-group politics. This chapter then evaluates the current state of civil society and proposes new visions in transition to democracy in Korea.

The concepts of state and civil society emerged as particular sets of institutional ensembles in specific historical circumstances and their meanings have varied over time and intellectual contexts. Both have grown out of the historical experience of state formation under European capitalism. The concept of civil society emerged in Europe at a time when those who controlled capitalist production sought access to political power. The search for political power constituted a space or relationship in which bourgeoisie and their allies negotiated a shared identity and political access. The notion of bourgeois civil society versus the state entered European political rhetoric colored by a particular historical setting of the West to describe confrontation between social forces from below and state power from above. Since then, civil society tends to refer to a realm separate from—often contrasting with or indeed counterbalancing-yet interdependent with state power.

Cultural, institutional, and historical differences in the nature of civil society between East and West largely derive from traditional differences between European concepts and those of the Confucian East. To understand the Confucian indigenous form of civil society peculiar to the East requires acknowledging that civil society has taken more than one historical path. Western patterns of civil society could not be perfectly replicated in the East, a very different culture and political environment. The effort to delineate the form of civil society distinct to the East might well complicate cross-national and temporal comparisons and raises the questions of whether the term is flexible enough to be broadly applied beyond its Western origin in place and time. Instead of adopting a universalistic approach or holding the case up to Western norms, it may prove more worthwhile to study the incipient form of civil society in its own historical context.

Social scientists have already proposed views on civil society in the Confucian East. Some seek parallels between historical events in East and West (Bratton 1989; Hall 1995), so to detect a Western type of civil society particularly in Korea (Chung 1995). Applying a Western standard, Chung (1995) argues that self, society, and world in Confucianism were so interwoven that no notion of the individual or of civil society as distinguished from the state was possible in traditional Korea. In contrast, others look for a Confucian form of civil society or for its anticipation in Confucian doctrine in East Asia (Chamberlain 1993; Cho 1997; Wakeman 1993). Cho (1997) claims that Confucianism, as a nonjurist, nonmercantile tradition, produced a politically (as opposed to economically) oriented civil society out of the self-differentiation of the literati in traditional Korea. Through local organizations such as private academies (sowon), community compacts (hyangyak), and mutual assistance associations (kye), local literati without office not only restrained the kingship but also prevented growth of a totalitarian state. In similar vein, scholars (Chamberlain 1993; Huang 1993; Rowe 1990, 1993; Wakeman 1993) devote attention to evidence of civil society in China prior to Western influence. They point out the premodern Chinese concept of the public sphere apparent in the multitude of voluntary activities of local elites outside or independent of the state.

This variety of definitions suggests the danger of generalizing from the Western model to Korea, given its unique history. A more flexible or encompassing understanding is apparently necessary if we are to speak of civil society with respect to various historical settings. This chapter proceeds with the broad understanding of civil society as an intermediary entity that stands between the private (society) and the public (state) and that has been derived from their mutual interaction in the historical process of modernization. This line of inquiry is consistent with recent analytical definitions of civil society that describe autonomous, voluntary private groups and associations in the nonstate sphere that work to empower citizens vis-à-vis a domineering state (Bratton 1989; Callahan 1998; Cohen and Arato 1992; Diamond 1994, 1999; Gellner 1994; Habermas 1989; Keane 1988: 14; H. R. Kim 2000b; S. Kim 1997, 1998, 2000; Steinberg 1997).

Since liberation from Japanese colonial rule in 1945, South Korea has focused on two major projects: economic development and political democratization. Apparent successes have led to its description as a "model country" of the East Asian miracle. Although at considerable social cost, the seven consecutive five-year economic planning projects implemented from the early 1960s to 1997 under authoritarian regimes did elevate Korea as representative of the East Asian capitalist model (H. R. Kim et al. 2000). State intervention in economic governance has been a crucial force in development, but it has impeded the growth of civil society. For the sake of rapid development, basic democratic rights were severely repressed. Successive authoritarian regimes until the 1987 Democratic Movement excluded labor and selectively co-opted capital interests to form a developmental coalition. But after 1987, activity in interest-group politics surged, and transition toward political democracy began.

In Korea's democratic transition from a state-dominated to a citizen-driven society, the state no longer is the sole guardian and provider of institutions that constitute the public domain. Instead, civil society and its prominent organizations, namely nongovernmental organizations (NGOs), have become salient political actors and emerged as institutional hybrids that undertake public functions through private initiatives (H. R. Kim 2000a, 2002, 2004). They actively endeavor to provide and ensure protection and advancement of such public goods as the environment, human rights, social security, women's issues, and grassroots development. They also serve as policy entrepreneurs, proposing and helping implement policies and forming organizations that protect and pursue public interests by monitoring government and business activities (Kim and McNeal 2005). Their activities now extend beyond nonprofit provision of goods and services to influencing the development of institutions of social governance. In a progressively decentralized and deregulated environment, they have flourished in scope and scale, and they continue to play important roles by campaigning for a variety of political and economic reforms in the ongoing transitional politics toward democracy in Korea.

The State and Civil Society in Historical Context

Since traditional Confucian Korea did not conceive of society as distinct from the state, the state did not dominate in all circumstances, even under bureaucratic monarchy (Cho 1997; H. R. Kim 2000b). Although Confucius did not speak specifically of civil society, he crucially affected its formulation and referred to its essence when he taught of the obligation of the educated to serve society through civil service. Traditional Korea abounded in self-governing, autonomous, voluntary groups such as private schools, community compacts, community bureaus, clan lineages and surname associations (*munjung*), and neighborhood associations. Local scholar-gentry elite voluntarily administrated community affairs independent of a centralized government. They handled many of the tasks the West normally relegates to the state, maintaining social order, building public works, dispensing welfare, and so forth. As Tu's (1993) phrase "Confucian habit of the heart" suggests, their activities not only satisfied their obligations to the state, but also helped elites become Confucian "superior men" through self-cultivation. They mediated between the state and community members, creating a sort of civil society.

The community compact, with its community bureau, provides a good example of these community-based groups. The compact served to promote community spirit and a sense of shared responsibility for community welfare in traditional Korea. Committed to local interests, this informal voluntary association was self-regulating and self-disciplined with a number of major objectives. Leaders of the literati without formal office were considered spiritual, not political, authorities (Cho 1997). They implemented community compacts that supported a structure of rules, moral injunctions, and mutual assistance for the benefit of the general community and its members. These local Confucian ethical directives had no direct effect on national policy, but they rendered direct magistrate control unnecessary. Relations between officials and the local elite regarding local public affairs were generally consensual rather than confrontational. The elite did not assert local rights against the state or seek formal limits on it, and the state found the elite useful in maintaining public order. In other words, the self-regulated, disciplined local gentry associations served state as well as local interests, establishing an equilibrium between the government's need for order and the local need for welfare.

Community-centered activity did not emerge simply as a way to compensate for lack of state involvement (Habermas 1989; S. J. Han 1997; H. R. Kim 2000b). Community elite acted in the interests of themselves and their locality, understanding virtually no distinction between them. The locality became part of the elite's self-identity and the subject of their concern. Intermediate between state and family, the locality provided the elite with a reason as well as a place to organize (Cho 1997; Rowe 1990). Local elites stood outside the state bureaucracy and were, in most practical respects, its equal in authority with regard to daily life and certainly not under its dominance. Through their activities, patterns of participation, particularly among the elite, came to be based on groups and localities, rather than on individuals and private property.

The seed of civil society sown in traditional Korea was not concerned with the institutions of capitalism, individualism, and property rights, but with the character and quality of community welfare as well as with the community-based locality, which had the character of the public sphere. In traditional Korea, the multitude of voluntary activities and local organizations was apparent in the public sphere outside and independent of the state. Through these activities and organizations, local literati without office consistently restrained the growth of a totalitarian state. Toward the end of the dynasty, the neo-Confucian tradition slowly became more open to new trends of pluralism that advocated Western concepts and the ideas. However, this embryonic and nascent form of civil society that emerged in traditional Korea was unfortunately suppressed and further severely repressed by the

Japanese colonial government from 1910 to 1945. The seed of civil society based on local institutions and organizations in traditional Korea was not grown any more during the Japanese colonial period.

State Corporatism and Civil Society under Siege

Starting with the 1960s, modernization was treated as a central issue in academic discourse (KSA 1990; KSA and KPSA 1992). The myth of modernization was part of an economy-oriented growth ideology that essentially ignored state and civil society questions. The April Revolution in 1960 had the potential to bring relations between the state and civil society to the fore. This epochal event might have led to exploration of the separation between them and its social ramifications, but it failed to do so because of the May 16 military coup. Although some debate concerning the middle class did occur, the coup dissuaded social scientists from examining civil society as a central issue. During this time, modernization was tacitly equated with both Westernization and development and was thought to justify authoritarian rule. The regime mistreated citizens under the slogan Together We Can Prosper. All sectors of society collaborated with the dictatorship, endorsing the ideology of rapid economic growth and what it entailed. The state and civil society were set aside from discussion; the focus remained on economic development.

The early 1970s brought a series of government-led economic initiatives focused on heavy and chemical industries. Rural reform, known as the New Village Movement, swept across the country. At the same time, labor movements became more frequent in the cities. Eventually, democratic reform moved front and center as the general population abandoned its formerly submissive position and mounted violent protests. Critical study of suppression by the military dictatorship and the lack of a civil society developed during the early 1970s. Scholars turned from research on rural society and the family to focus on study relevant to unification, participatory democracy, civil society, and critique of military dictatorship. Yong-Ha Shin (1973, 1974, 1975) did groundbreaking research on civil society. He investigated the enlightenment theory of civil society espoused by the Independence Club—a movement to establish and patriotically enlighten civil society—and explored the disintegration of the *yangban* status-based class. Shin contended that discussion of establishing a civil society was possible only after liberation from Japanese colonialism. Shin's research was pivotal in establishing the importance of academic discourse on civil society in Korea.

Academic discourses on civil society were further extended by considering its relationship to capitalism. The formation and maturation of civil society were linked to the expansion of wealth, urbanization, and social diversity, particularly to the growth of the urban middle class in association with state-led industrialization in the 1960s and 1970s (S. K. Kim 1992; Koo 1993; KSA and KPSA 1992; Moon and Kim 1996). Korean civil society drew part of its character from its relationship to the development of capitalism. State intervention in the process of industrialization politicized most decisions in economic and other areas. Such intervention gave rise to a capitalist class that suppressed civil society. Thus, the dependent character of Korean capitalist development undermined the ideological values essential to civil society by placing economic growth first. In addition, the political nature of Korean capitalist development created regional economic differences that worked against the interests and unity of civil society. Ironically, however, this same capitalist development eventually provided civil society with the means to resist ruling-class governance.

Throughout the 1970s, successive authoritarian regimes denied and restricted basic democratic rights in the name of rapid economic growth. They excluded labor and selectively co-opted capital interests to create a coalition for development (Koo 1993; Moon and Kim 1996). Although the roles of the state and market remain subject to debate, few dispute that state intervention was a determining force in economic development and impeded the development of civil society (Choi and Lim 1993; H. R. Kim 2000a; Lim and Choi 1997; Yu 1991, 1995). Not only did Korean dependent capitalist development involve an invincible state and throttle civil society; the environment was damaged, equitable distribution of development was neglected, and democratic development was postponed (Park and Cho 1989a, 1989b, 1991a, 1991b). The state accomplished its purposes by suppressing any bourgeoisie stirrings and granting the new ruling class broad autonomy in all areas of society. Thus the state established itself as the center of power by pegging ruling-class interests to its own. Radical labor movements intensified agitation against successive authoritarian regimes, but they were no match for state-centered authoritarianism and lacked organizational capacity and an established middle class to promote civil consciousness.

Korean capitalism has been guided by state corporatism rather than the social corporatism found in Europe, which recognizes the autonomy of social organizations, including labor (Choi 1993; Choi and Lim 1993; H. K. Kim 1993, 1995). It also differs from Latin American state corporatism, in which the state encourages some social groups while restraining others. In guiding capitalist development, Korean state corporatism has simply repressed civil society. In particular, the state purposefully barred labor unions from economic and capitalist policy decisions and strategically controlled market mechanisms to thwart labor's interests. Labor movements responded to this heavy-handedness by moving to the radical left.

The Democratic Movement and the Emergence of Civil Society

After the assassination of President Park Chung Hee in 1979, a Kwangju province disrupted the Seoul Spring of 1980 by rising against the state. Radical masses and citizens banded together on behalf of political, economic, and social democratization, calling for "restricted democratization to be abandoned." Fear ruled at the start of the 1980s, but a spectator role was no longer acceptable. Scholars cautiously advocated pluralism as a necessity for Korea (Choi 1993; S. Kim 1997, 1998; Lee 1982; H. J. Park 1995; K. Y. Shin 1991; Yu 1995). They argued that a civil society with increased autonomy could provide the flexibility needed to address social deficiencies and be a force for social change. Pressure-group advocacy and pluralism, rather than radical agitation, could be part of a future civil movement for reform.

With the appearance of new theoretical frameworks, social scientists heralded the 1980s as their Golden Age. Widespread opinion held that major social restructuring could solve problems resulting from industrialization, urbanization, and centralization of power. Extensive debates probed a wide range of concepts including bureaucratic authoritarianism, developmental state theory, dependency theory, world system perspective, and the necessary social organization for a Korean democratic state (Choi 1993; S. J. Han 1983; H. J. Lim 1987a, 1987b; Lim and Choi 1997; K. Y. Shin 1991, 1995). Both the state and the general public welcomed the debates, even though class disputes and middle-class reform issues had prompted them. In particular, discussion took up the political scientist Guillermo O'Donnell's thoughts on bureaucratic authoritarianism. Sang-Jin Han (1983, 1987) contended that the advantage of bureaucratic authoritarianism was its ability to maintain general social stability by achieving efficient and substantial industrialization. Its failure lay in thwarting democracy. He added, however, that although bureaucratic authoritarianism in the Fifth Republic in the 1980s had prevented democratization, general democratic political awareness had increased, enhancing the prospect of democracy. Hyun-Jin Lim (1987a, 1987b) invoked dependent development theory to dissect the relationship among the state, capital, and labor. His findings suggested that Korea's bureaucratic authoritarianism could not embrace democratization because the state served as an economic entrepreneur rather than as an agent for democratic reform. Also, it politically and socially excluded civil society. The state alone regulated whose interests would be represented and set policy during the Chun Doo Hwan regime in the 1980s, so citizen interest-group advocacy was moot. In sum, the regime mobilized the civil sector for economic growth and political stability, but politically disenfranchised it.

In the early 1980s, the military regime commanded all power and represented ruling-class interests. However, diverse civil-society sectors stirred and intensified labor protests against the state. Successive regimes nonetheless managed until 1987 to maintain a virtual monopoly on decision making and held full authority over public issues. Government intervention was the norm of state-centric governance and secured rapid industrialization and economic growth (Kim and McNeal 2005). Accordingly, social movements took mainly antigovernment and anticorporate positions. This profile changed radically after the June Uprising in 1987—an unprecedented "popular uprising," the turning point when Korea moved toward political democratization that would provide the organizational space for diverse civil movements and interest-group politics.

It is evident that while rapid economic development and state corporatist governance held the development of civil society at bay, their outcome came to advance it. As capitalism matured, rapid economic growth empowered industrial labor, whose forces had swollen as a result of the 1970s government-led heavy and chemical industrialization. Unprecedented economic growth also fostered a sizeable middle class. Both industrial labor and the middle class came to play significant roles in social-movement politics. Civil movements in the West were the province of the bourgeoisie, but in Korea industrial labor and the middle class were key. In resisting state dominance, they acquired strategies and organizational skills. After the 1987 Democratic Movement, these better-organized labor movements and citizen movements formed alliances, securing and enlarging the public forum for resisting monopolistic capital and state dominance. The types of social-interest groups burgeoned and came to occupy a realm separate from and independent of the state, from which they fought to expand citizens' rights and consolidate a pluralistic, autonomous social space similar to what Western democracies provide.

The Making of Civil Society in Transitional Politics

The 1987 Democratic Movement greatly advanced democratization and the autonomy of civil society. Traditional people's movement groups (*minjung undong tanch'e*) composed of blue-collar laborers, peasants, the urban poor, antiregime politicians, and students played an important role in the authoritarian breakdown and democratic transition. They became freed from the heavy-handedness of repressive regimes. People's groups (*minjung*) strengthened their leverage for fundamental reforms of society by forming such "front-oriented bodies" as the national teachers' union and feminist groups within their own organizations. However, coming into the 1990s, new civil-movement organizations called citizens' movement groups (*simin undong tanch'e*) comprising such middle-class citizens as white-collar workers, professionals, religious leaders, and intellectuals emerged to take up new areas of social need and focus on gradual institutional reforms. Representative NGOs—for example, the Citizen's Coalition for Economic Justice (CCEJ; Kyongje chongui silcho'on simin yonhap), the Korean Federation of Environmental Movements (KFEM; Han'guk hwan'gyong undong yonhap), and the People's Solidarity for Participatory Democracy (PSPD; Ch'amyo minju sahoe simin yondae)—became a major force in political processes and policy initiation and showed a new set of interests on the environment, women's issues, human rights, and economic justice (H. R. Kim 1997, 2000a, 2002, 2004; H. J. Park 1995). As traditional people's groups flourished and new social movements began to emerge, power dynamics within civil society differentiated and grew more complex.

Civil society in the early 1990s became a distinct social factor yet was embracing many issues and postures. During this critical juncture of separation within civil society, *minjung* continued to agitate against the state and often resorted to illegal and violent measures such as strikes and demonstrations. In May 1991 the accidental death of a college student at the hands of combat police during a student demonstration brought *minjung* to a critical juncture. The incident mobilized more than a million citizens nationwide in a demonstration that lasted nearly a month. Unlike the June Uprising in 1987, which involved unsophisticated, ad hoc mass participation, the 1991 demonstration featured organized mass participation. It demonstrated successful social-movement organization and mobilization, but it also revealed a gulf between the movement and the general public that propelled *minjung* into crisis.

Minjung organizational capacity had grown over time, but their focus had shifted away from the mainstream. Civil reformists with a revolutionary bent moved from the fringe of social movements into the center of *minjung*. In the process, the groups' theoretical and practical positions grew less tenable to the general public. Thus, activist leaders and scholars connected with *minjung* began to seek alternative theories and ideologies as well as means of organizing. The issues and tactics that new citizen movements (*simin undong*) in the late 1980s took up starkly contrasted with those of class-based, militant, and confrontational *minjung* movements of the past. Two visions of democracy competed for ascendancy. One derived from the people's *minjung* movements of the past. The other endorsed moderate and practical citizen movements focused on the procedural fundamentals of democracy. It was this gulf that created the *minjung* crisis.

Policy reforms implemented by the Roh Tae Woo government (1988–1992) in the wake of a hyper-repressive authoritarian regime were also responsible for the *minjung* crisis. Civilian repression declined substantially, in keeping with Roh's declaration of June 29, 1987. Roh proved quite open to political opposition, as his tolerance of independent mass media indicated. He also restored local political autonomy, suspended by the military regime in 1961, and lessened government control over university policies and activities. When the Kim Young Sam government (1993–1997) assumed power in 1993, Kim initiated a series of unprecedented reforms. The new government not only tolerated but encouraged moderate citizen movements, announcing initiatives similar to those citizens' groups suggested and augmenting their influence. Kim recruited from moderate citizen groups to fill several key public positions and even sought to normalize relationships with citizens' groups by publicly discussing proposals and policy and accommodating some demands. As a result, the Kim government won strong support from citizen groups.

In this environment, moderate citizen groups prevailed in the competition between visions of democracy. Class-based, confrontational strategies of the preexisting people's movement groups were abandoned in favor of nonviolent, lawful tactics and proposals of specific policy alternatives by new citizens' movement groups. The prodemocracy alliance of citizens' groups incorporated the triple solidarity of students, workers, and churches, and furthermore encompassed the middle class. The relationship between citizen-movement groups and the state became accordingly cooperative. Relations deteriorated, however, when Kim failed to adequately address several key issues raised in the politics of democratic transition.

Relations entered a new phase when Kim Dae Jung took office in 1998. Not only academics but also the popular press noted an explosion of citizen interest in securing democracy. Strong reader interest led newspaper dailies to detail the growing power of civil groups, which had broadened their range of issues and moderated their tactics and goals, eschewing radical and illegal activities. The government again sought to embrace citizen-movement leaders by co-opting them and appointing them to head or advise relevant organizations. As part of this tactic, the Second Nation-building Committee was organized in Kim Dae Jung's administration to advise him on means to promote participation by civilian groups in political decisions. The president also recruited several of his ministers from the movements to more effectively engage with them. In addition, the government and ruling party negotiated a bill on NGOs meant not only to assist them financially but also to provide other special benefits. NGOs could now compete for financial support by submitting project plans to a screening committee. The bill secured them free lease of buildings and offices, tax-exemption for donations, postage discounts, and more. These benefits strengthened and broadened the activities of civil groups. Such gradual developments between the state and citizen groups accelerated discourse on participatory democracy and the making of civil society in transition to democracy.

Dilemma and New Visions in the Making of Civil Society

Scholarly discourse on civil society in Korea during the 1990s shows broad areas of agreement. Most such writings agree that Korea's past featured state dominance over civil society, an absence of ideological moorings and civil consciousness or ethics, and pervasive regionalism and regional conflicts in politics (W. S. Han 1992; Jung 1995; S. K. Kim 1992; Y. I. Lim 1992; K. Y. Shin 1995; Yu and Kim 1995). The scholars concur that these factors fragmented the labor class and disrupted citizen groups. It is equally clear that several uniquely Korean experiences and circumstances enhanced the formation and maturation of civil society. The 1987 June Uprising promoted both the autonomy of civil society and subsequent labor movements in July and August, despite the continued presence of an authoritarian regime. The events were seen as steps in the process of citizen-movement self-realization and the enlargement of citizens' public space.

Scholars also generally recognize a distinct evolution of Korean democratization: strengthening of the authoritarian system, liberalizing of authoritarianism, reviving of civil society, and democratization (Choi and Lim 1993; Lim and Choi 1997). Korean democratization before the 1987 June Uprising was not initially taken up by capitalists or labor, but by people's groups. However, as democratization progressed in the late 1980s, middle-class citizens formed a massive resistance, but one vulnerable to collapse. In this process, the capitalist class most adamantly opposed democratization but gained the most from it. Ruling authoritarian elite and the capitalist class reaped the greatest gains, while middle-class citizens and labor were eventually defeated in the political realm. In addition, under the authoritarian regimes, political parties were unable to organize to represent the civil sector. In most cases, the majority party maintained its position only by playing lackey to the authoritarian regime. The majority party was constrained by limits the regime set while the opposition party continued to be oppressed. State intervention in politics thus deprived the party system of any autonomy. Consequently, the civil sector did not use political parties to represent its interests. It either sought to collaborate with the state or launched social movements meant to change the political system that so disempowered citizens. Movement politics connected to the intense conflict between state and civil society—not party politics—guided change in the political system.

For decades Korea has been moving from an authoritarian state to a democratic civil society. Transition initially involved intense confrontation between the repressive state and grassroots activists. Only after the 1987 Democratic Movement did democratization make significant gains. Since then, the sociopolitical environment has encouraged the rise of diverse interest groups. Active, broad middle-class support of the 1987 Democratic Movement was critical to its success. Middle-class citizens joined the struggle convinced that democracy required replacing indirect with direct elections and that economic development at the expense of political freedom was unacceptable. In the 1990s, the civil-society sector and its most prominent organizations, NGOs, pressed discreet issues through direct confrontation with the state, without detailed institutionalization and systematic coordination. Each interest group pursued its particular concerns, making the sector hyperactive and amorphous (H. R. Kim 2002, 2004; Kim, Moon, and Jung 1997). Conventional political institutions were thus marginalized. Moreover, in seeking to become a political presence, civil groups and NGOs campaigned against bureaucracy and collusion in the political arena. Ironically, it appears that their own weakness lay in lack of networking and cooperation among themselves. The absence of effective citizen networks impeded grassroots mobilization for collective action (H. R. Kim 2004). Overarching improvement of the government itself was of far less interest to citizens than activities in pursuit of public goods. Piecemeal victories led these groups to take on broad objectives without proper preparation or organizational strategies, thus distracting them from addressing more fundamental political issues.

This distraction with ill-defined ends became the dilemmas in the making of civil society, limiting the effectiveness of civil organizations and NGOs in Korea (H. R. Kim 2004). Accustomed to dealing with discrete social issues, NGOs and other civil organizations were unable to forge interrelationships or form networks. Thus they were incapable of engineering collaborative action across issues, regions, and social groups such as fundamental political reform required. The groups themselves sometimes suffered from internal competition and centralized organizational structure. They fell on their own sword in advocating the deinstitutionalization of civil society. As an emerging political force, civil society sought direct means through which to win participation in political decision making and broad political influence. Ironically, this advocacy of participatory democracy promoted retrenchment by conventional political actors and mitigated against consolidation of a representative political system with multiple parties (H. R. Kim 2004). It is thus evident that the most urgent tasks civil organizations face today are to stipulate their functions, rearrange their internal structures and intergroup networks, and move beyond discrete interests to advocating common social goods. Only by doing so can they be effective agents in transition to democracy and build up new visions in the making of civil society in Korea.

Conclusions

In Confucian traditional Korea, the premodern concept of civil society was apparent in the multitude of self-governing local organizations and voluntary activities of local elites outside and independent of the state. The seed of civil society sown in a traditional society was mainly concerned with the character and quality of the community-based locality, which often had the character of the public sphere. Toward the end of the dynasty, the neo-Confucian tradition became more open to the Western concepts and ideas. However, Japanese colonialism destroyed the indignous form of civil society peculiar to traditional Korea. Since liberation from Japanese colonial rule in 1945, Korea's state and civil society have endured a turbulent relationship.

Authoritarian regimes in the 1960s and 1970s severely retricted civil society. During those years, civil movements defied the military regimes to advocate democracy, and after the 1987 Democratic Movement, their efforts met with partial success. In the ensuing decentralized, deregulated environment, civil society and NGOs expanded in scope, scale, and general social impact. Citizen groups and NGOs have played an important role in democcatization by addressing general welfare and social issues neglected by the state. They have become policy initiators and social watchdogs. Even so, desire for a substantial democracy has grown unabated. Citizens want to participate significantly and responsibly in democratic transition. Historically, politics were the monopoly of politicians and political parties that believed citizen sovereignty inhered only in citizens' right to vote in periodic elections. In dismantling this undemocratic legacy in which legislation and enforcement were the exclusive prerogative of parties and politicians, civil groups and NGOs in recent years campaigned for political reform to provide an alternative governing paradigm that effectively incorporates civil society. Now in Korea, civil-society groups continue to play important roles by campaigning for a variety of political and economic reforms in the current and ongoing transitional politics toward democracy.

In theory, civil society is sometimes called the third or voluntary sector vis-à-vis the government and business sectors. Its effective mobilization requires shared values, dedication, and volunteer efforts. Third-sector constituents must emphasize cooperation over competition and horizontal relationships over vertical domination. The state, in contrast, can turn to regulation, legislation, or coercion and the business sector to trade, finance, and impersonal markets. In Korea many civil-movement groups, although in the third sector and claiming to represent the public welfare, were sometimes centralized and embroiled in hegemonic competition among themselves. Contrary to their espoused ethic of participatory democracy, civil groups developed a centralized structure, not unlike that of the state they attacked. Moreover, despite early gains, civil organizations were unable to overcome the chronic problem of regional party monopoly and to mobilize civic coalition. This inability brought to the fore the inability of the civil sector to move beyond specific public concerns to the all-embracing issue of democratic transition. In addition, the number of groups and agendas expanded too rapidly to allow meaningful analysis of the roles of citizens, civil organizations, and state in the search to consolidate democracy.

Future research needs to plumb the plurality of social life more thoroughly, without the theoretical fetters of Marxian-based economic determinism and class-oriented radicalism. To improve our theoretical paradigms and empirical analyses with respect to civil society requires examining uniquely Korean historical experience, unbiased by Western patterns. We must explore the implications that features distinct to Korean history have for civil society: centralized state dominance over civil society, bureaucratic/patriarchal authoritarianism based on Confucianism, deeply rooted cronyism and regionalism, North-South division, anticommunism, and so forth. We must also examine the gains sought from forming a civil society. This research involves addressing what a civil society is and whether Korea has a civil society. If so, when and how did it emerge and progress? Even though there is no doubt that civil-society groups and organizations play important roles in the current and ongoing transitional politics toward democracy in

Korea, we must work toward deeper theoretical studies and empirical analyses of civil society based on Korea's own historical context and experience.

References

Bratton, Michael. 1989. "Beyond the State: Civil Society and Associational Life in Africa." *World Politics* 41:407–30.

Callahan, William A. 1998. "Comparing the Discourse of Popular Politics in Korea and China: From Civil Society to Social Movements." *Korea Journal* 39:277–322.

Chamberlain, H. B. 1993. "On the Search for Civil Society in China." *Modern China* 19:199–215.

Cho, Hein. 1997. "The Historical Origin of Civil Society in Korea." *Korea Journal* 37:24–41.

Choi, Jang-Jip. 1993. *Han'guk minjujuǔi iron* (The theory of Korean democracy). Seoul: Hankilsa.

_____ and Hyun-Jin Lim. 1993. *Simin sahoe ǔi tochǒn* (Challenges of civil society: State, capital, and labor in the democratization of South Korea). Seoul: Nanam.

Chung, Chai-Sik. 1995. *A Korean Confucian Encounter with the Modern World: Yi Hang-no and the West.* Berkeley: Institute of East Asian Studies, University of California.

Cohen, Jean L., and Andrew Arato. 1992. *Civil Society and Political Theory.* Cambridge, Mass.: MIT Press.

Diamond, Larry. 1994. "Rethinking Civil Society: Towards Democratic Consolidation." *Journal of Democracy* 5 (1994): 3–17.

_____. 1999. *Developing Democracy: Toward Consolidation.* Baltimore: Johns Hopkins University Press.

Gellner, Ernest. 1994. *Conditions of Liberty: Civil Society and Its Rivals.* London: Hamish Hamilton.

Habermas, Jurgen. 1989. *The Structural Transformation of the Public Sphere: An Inquiry into a Category of Bourgeois Society.* Trans. Thomas Burger. Cambridge, Mass.: MIT Press.

Hall, John. 1995. *Civil Society: Theory, History, and Comparison.* Cambridge: Blackwell.

Han, Sang-Jin. 1983. "Kwanryochǒk kwonwijuǔi ha esǒ ǔi minjujuǔi chǒnmang" (The outlook for democracy under bureaucratic authoritarianism). In Korean Sociological Association, ed., *Han'guk saahoe ǒdiro kago itna?* (Where is Korean society headed?). Seoul: Institute of Contemporary Society.

———. 1987. *Minjung ŭi sahoe kwahakchŏk insik* (The social scientific recognition of the people). Seoul: Moonhak-kwa Chisung-sa.

———. 1997. "The Public Sphere and Democracy in Korea." *Korea Journal* 37:78–90.

Han, Wan-Sang. 1992. "Han'guk esŏ simin, kukka, kyekŭp: kwayŏn simin undongŭn kaeryang juŭichŏk sont'aek inka?" (Civil society, the state, and class in Korea: Is the civil movement necessary to reform?). In Korean Sociological Association and Korean Political Science Association, ed., *Han'guk ŭi kukkawa simin sahoe* (The state and civil society in Korea). Seoul: Hanul.

Huang, Philip C. C. 1993. "Public Sphere/Civil Society in China?" *Modern China* 19:216–40.

Jung, Chul-Hee. 1995. "Han'guk minjuhwa undongŭi sahoechŏk kiwŏn: misi dongwŏn maekrak kwa fŭreim hyŏngsŏng" (Social orientations of the Korean democratization movement: The formation of the micro-mobilization context and the frame). *Han'guk sahoehak* 29: 501–32.

Keane, John, ed. 1988. *Civil Society and the State.* London: Verso.

Kim, Ho-Ki. 1993. "Gŭramsichŏk simin sahoeronkwa pipanironŭi simin sahoeron" (Gramscian perspective on civil society and civil society theory in the critical theory: Critical exploration of the Korean-style application). *Kyŏngchewa sahoe* 38–58.

———. 1995. *Hyŭndae chabonjuŭi wa han'guk sahoe: kukka, simin sahoe, minjujuŭi* (Contemporary capitalism and Korean society: State, civil society, democracy). Seoul: Nanam.

Kim, Hyuk-Rae. 1997. "Korean NGOs: Global Trend and Prospect." *Global Economic Review* 26:93–115.

———. 2000a. "Contradiction and Continuity: The Independence Club and Korea's Transition to Modernity." In Yun-Shik Chang, ed., *Korea between Tradition and Modernity*, 184–91. Vancouver: Institute for Asian Research.

———. 2000b. "The State and Civil Society in Transition: The Role of NGOs in South Korea." *Pacific Review* 13:595–613.

———. 2002. "NGOs in Pursuit of 'the Public Good' in South Korea." In Sally Sargeson, ed., *Collective Goods, Collective Futures in Asia*, 57–74. London: Routledge.

———. 2004. "The Dilemma of the Making of Civil Society in Korean Political Reform." *Journal of Contemporary Asia* 34.1.:55–69.

_____, and David K. McNeal. 2005. "From State-centric to Nego-tiated Governance: NGOs as Policy Entrepreneurs in South Korea." In Robert P. Weller, ed., *Civil Life, Globalization, and Political Change in Asia: Organizing between Family and State,* 95–109. London: Routledge.

_____, et al. 2000. *Politics and Markets in the Wake of the Asian Crisis.* London: Routledge.

_____; Tae-Hoon Moon; and Young-Kuk Jung. 1997. "Han'guk ŭi iik kaldŭng yangt'ae wa chochŏng chedo" (The phase of the Korean interest conflict and its mediating system). In Young-Rae Kim, ed., *Iik chiptan chŏngch'i wa iik kaldŭng* (Interest-group politics and conflict of interest). Seoul: Hanul.

Kim, Sung-Kook. 1992. "Han'guk chabon juŭi palchŏnkwa simin sahoeŭi sŏngkyŏk" (The development of Korean capitalism and the characteristics of civil society). In Korean Sociological Association and Korean Political Science Association, ed., *Han'guk ŭi kukka wa simin sahoe* (The state and civil society of Korea). Seoul: Hanul.

Kim, Sunhyuk. 1997. "State and Civil Society in South Korea's Democratic Consolidation." *Asian Survey* 37:1135–44.

_____. 1998. "Civil Society and Democratization in South Korea." *Korea Journal* 38:214–36.

_____. 2000. *The Politics of Democratization in Korea: The Role of Civil Society.* Pittsburgh, Penn.: University of Pittsburgh Press.

Koo, Hagen. 1993. "Strong State and Contentious Society." In Hagen Koo, ed., *State and Society in Contemporary Korea.* Ithaca, N.Y.: Cornell University Press.

_____. 2001. *Korean Workers: The Culture and Politics of Class For-mation.* Ithaca, N.Y.: Cornell University Press.

Korean Sociological Association (KSA), ed. 1990. *Han'guk sahoe ŭi pipanchŏk insik* (Critical recognition of the Korean society). Seoul: Nanam.

_____ and Korean Political Studies Association (KPSA), eds. 1992. *Han'guk ŭi kukkawa simin sahoe* (The Korean state and civil society). Seoul: Hanul.

Lee, Hyo-Sun. 1982. "Sahoe undongkwa sahoe palchŏn" (Social movement and social development). *Han'guk sahoehak* 16: 29–38.

Lim, Hyun-Jin. 1987a. *Hyŭndae Han'guk kwa chongsok iron* (Con-temporary Korea and dependency theory). Seoul: Seoul National University Press.

———. 1987b. *Che 3saegye, chabonjuŭi, gŭrigo han'guk: iron kwa hyŏnsil* (Third World, capitalism, and Korea). Seoul: Bupmoonsa.

———, and Jang-Jip Choi. 1997. *Han'guk sahoe wa minju juŭi* (Korean society and democracy). Seoul: Nanam.

Lim, Young-Il. 1992. "Han'guk ŭi san'ŏp hwa wa kyekŭp chŏngch'i" (Industrialization and class politics of Korea). In KSA and KPSA, eds., *Han'guk ŭi kukka wa sinmin sahoe* (The Korean state and civil society). Seoul: Hanul.

Moon, Chung-In, and Yong-Cheol Kim. 1996. "A Circle of Paradox: Development, Politics and Democracy in South Korea." In Adrian Leftwich, ed., *Democracy and Development: Theory and Practice*. Cambridge: Polity Press.

Park, Hyun-Chae, and Hee-Yon Cho, eds. 1989a. *Han'guk sahoe kusŏngch'e nonchaeng I* (Debate over the components of Korean society 1). Seoul: Juksan.

———. 1989b. *Han'guk sahoe kusŏngch'e nonchaeng II* (Debate over the components of Korean society 2). Seoul: Juksan.

———. 1991a. *Han'guk sahoe kusŏngch'e nonchaeng III* (Debate over the components of Korean society 3). Seoul: Juksan.

———. 1991b. *Han'guk sahoe kusongch'e nonchaeng IV* (Debate over the components of Korean society 4). Seoul: Juksan.

Park, Hyung-Joon. 1995. "Sinsahoe undong kwa kyŏngsilryŏn undong" (The new social movement and the CCEJ movement). *Kyŏngchewa sahoe* 27:76–105.

Rowe, William T. 1990. "The Public Sphere in Modern China." *Modern China* 16:309–29.

———. 1993. "The Problem of 'Civil Society' in Late Imperial China." *Modern China* 19:139–57.

Shin, Kwang-Young. 1991. "Simin sahoewa sahoe undong" (Civil society and social movements). *Kyŏngchewa sahoe* 12:13–26.

———. 1995. "Simin sahoe kaenyŏmkwa simin sahoe hyŏngsŏng" (The concept and formation of civil society). In Pal-Moo Yu and Ho-Ki Kim, eds., *Simin sahoewa simin undong* (Civil society and civil movements). Seoul: Hanul.

Shin, Yong-Ha. 1973. *Tongnip hyŏphoe ŭi sahoe sasang yŏnku* (A study of social ideology of the Independence Club). Seoul: Institute for Korean Culture, Seoul National University.

———. 1974. *Tongnip hyŏphoe ŭi minchok undong yŏnku* (A study of the national movement of the Independence Club). Seoul: Institute for Korean Culture, Seoul National University.

————. 1975. *Tongnip hyŏphoe wa manminkongdonghoe: sahoe sasang p'yŏn* (The Independence Club and the convocation of ten thousand people). Seoul: Hanguk Ilbosa.

Steinberg, David I. 1997. "Civil Society and Human Rights in Korea: On Contemporary and Classical Orthodoxy and Ideology." *Korea Journal* 38:145–65.

Tu, Wei-Ming. 1993. *The Way, Learning, and Politics: Essays on the Confucian Intellectual.* New York: State University of New York Press.

Wakeman, Jr., Frederic. 1993. "The Civil Society and Public Sphere Debate." *Modern China* 19:108–38.

Yu, Pal-Moo. 1991. "Gŭramsi simin sahoeron ŭi ihae wa han'gukchŏk suyong ŭi munche" (The understanding of Gramscian civil society theory and the problems of Korean-style accommodation). *Kyŏngchewa sahoe* 12:37–57.

————. 1995. "Simin sahoe ŭi palchon kwa simin undong" (The development of civil society and civil movements). *Kyŏngchewa sahoe* 25: 104–21.

————, and Ho-ki Kim, eds. 1995. *Simin sahoe wa simin undong* (Civil society and civil movement). Seoul: Hanul.

ELEVEN

Division, War, and Reunification

BRUCE CUMINGS

Korea is still in the era of national division and opposing states, but for the first time since the country was divided in 1945 it is finally possible to imagine a unified Korea that has transcended more than fifty years of hot war and cold war. The dramatic steps toward peaceful coexistence that the governments of South Korea (Republic of Korea; ROK) and North Korea (Democratic People's Republic of Korea; DPRK) have taken since the turn of the new millennium can best be appreciated by looking first at the origins of division and war, and then at the path toward compromise that began in the mid-1990s. As an American, it has always seemed appropriate to me to begin with the purely American decision that first divided Korea, just as World War II was drawing to a close.

The Division of Korea

In the days just before Koreans heard the voice of Emperor Hirohito for the first time, broadcasting Japan's surrender and Korea's liberation on August 15, 1945, John J. McCloy of the State-War-Navy Coordinating Committee (SWNCC) directed two young colonels, Dean Rusk and Charles H. Bonesteel, to withdraw to an adjoining room and find a place to divide Korea. It was about midnight on August 10; the atomic bombs had been dropped, the Soviet Red Army had entered the Pacific War, and American planners were rushing to arrange the Japanese surrender throughout the region. Given thirty minutes to do so, Rusk and Bonesteel looked at a map and chose the thirty-eighth parallel because it "would place the capital city in the American zone"; although the line was "further north than could be realistically reached... in the event of Soviet disagreement," the Soviets made no objections, which "somewhat surprised" Rusk (U.S.

Dept. of State, *FRUS* 1945, 6:1039). A few days later, on August 15, General Douglas MacArthur issued General Order Number One for the Japanese surrender, including in it (and thus making public) the 38th-parallel decision. The Russians silently accepted this division into spheres of influence, while demanding a Russian occupation of the northern part of Hokkaido in Japan (which MacArthur refused).

American officials consulted no Koreans in coming to this decision, nor did they ask the opinions of their British or Chinese allies, both of whom were expected to take part in a planned "trusteeship" for Korea. Instead the decision was unilateral, and hasty. Still, it grew out of previous American planning. The United States had taken the initiative in big-power deliberations on Korea during the war, suggesting a multilateral trusteeship for postwar Korea to the British in March 1943 and to the Soviets at the end of the same year. President Franklin D. Roosevelt, worried about the disposition of enemy-held colonial territories and aware of colonial demands for independence, sought a gradualist, tutelary policy of preparing colonials (such as the Koreans) for self-government and independence. He knew that since Korea touched the Soviet border, the Russians would want to be involved in the fate of postwar Korea; he hoped to get Soviet commitment to a multilateral administration, to forestall unilateral actions, and to provide an entry for American interests in Korea.

The independence of Korea, which Koreans had fought for since 1910, would come only at an appropriate time, or "in due course"—a phrase famous to Koreans because it was used in the 1943 Declaration of the Cairo Conference (where Roosevelt had met with Winston Churchill and Joseph Stalin) and also by Prime Minister Hara Kei to justify Japan's "cultural policy" after the March First Independence Movement in 1919. The British and the French resisted Roosevelt's trusteeship idea because it threatened the integrity of their empires; so did the Korean people, who were humiliated by the prospect of yet more great-power "tutelage." Stalin made no commitments to this policy during the war, but he seemed to enjoy watching Roosevelt and Churchill wrangle over the future of empire in the postwar world.

Roosevelt rarely consulted the State Department, but planners in the department had been worrying about the implications for Pacific security of Soviet involvement in Korea since early 1942, within months of Pearl Harbor (U.S. Dept. of State, *FRUS* 1944, 5:1239–42; also idem, *Conferences*, 1945:358–59) and questioned whether a multipower trusteeship would give the United States enough influence in Korean affairs. They feared that the Soviets would bring in with them Korean guerrillas who had been fighting the Japanese in Manchuria, the numbers of which they exaggerated (to as many as thirty thousand). Because of their fears that a trusteeship might not work, various planners began to develop ideas for a full military occupation that would assure a predominant American voice in postwar Korean affairs. It might be a short occupation, or it might be one of "considerable duration"; the main point was that no other power should have a role in Korea such that "the proportionate strength of the U.S." would be reduced to "a point where its effectiveness would be weakened" (U.S. Dept. of State, *FRUS* 1944, 5:1239–42; also idem, *Conferences*, 358–359).

The decision simply to partition Korea at the 38th parallel was thus an outcome of this planning, but also a product of the exigencies of the moment and a thoughtless exercise of the prerogatives of the great power that had single-handedly won the Pacific War. In its careless extremity—dividing a nation that had been integral for at least a millennium—this decision also reflected the absence of President Roosevelt's experienced hand (he died in April 1945). His idea had always been to involve the Russians in a joint administration of Korea, to embrace them and their interests in a country that touched their borders, thereby to give them something while containing their ambitions. Division was a much cruder device, abjuring diplomacy or cooperation, and simply drawing a line in the dirt. Fifty years of violent conflict followed; indeed, from that thoughtless point of line drawing onward, no international diplomacy worked to solve any serious problem in Korea until the U.S.-DPRK nuclear agreement in October 1994 (an agreement that was based on post–cold war premises).

Still, the decision to divide Korea was premature, because it was a decision for cold war containment, and that policy did not appear until 1947. Until 1947 operative U.S. planning represented an internationalist phase in high U.S. diplomacy from 1943 onward, reflected in the trusteeship policy and Washington's desire to place a still-unified Korea under temporary multilateral administration, in cooperation with other great powers including the Soviets. The policy was first to occupy Korea and then see if a trusteeship might be worked out with the Russians, the British, and the Chinese. The United States gained Soviet adherence to a modified version of the trusteeship idea at the Foreign Ministers'

Conference in December 1945, an important agreement that eliminated irrelevant British and Chinese influence while suggesting
that the two powers might ultimately come to terms on how to
reunify Korea. Roosevelt, basing himself on the experience of
American colonialism in the Philippines, had argued that a Korean
trusteeship might last as long as forty or fifty years, but the
December 1945 agreement shortened the period of great-power
involvement in Korean affairs to no more than five years and
called for a unified provisional government of Korea to be set up.

Even by that early date, however, the agreement still came too
late, because the de facto policies of the two occupations had
identified the Soviets with Kim Il Sung and the people's committees that emerged throughout Korea, while the Americans backed
Syngman Rhee and opposed the committees and widespread
Korean demands for a thorough renovation of colonial legacies.
In other words Washington's internationalist policy was under-
mined not so much by the Soviets as by the determination of
Americans on the scene in Korea to begin an early version of the
cold war "containment" doctrine.

The American military command, along with such high-
ranking emissaries dispatched from Washington as John J.
McCloy, tended to interpret nearly all resistance to U.S. desires in
the South as radical and pro-Soviet. In particular the United
States saw the "People's Republic" that emerged in September
1945 in Seoul as part of a Soviet master plan to dominate all of
Korea. The radical activity that mushroomed after the Japanese
surrender, such as the ousting of landlords and attacks on Koreans
in the colonial police, was usually a matter of settling scores left
over from the colonial period or of demands by Koreans to run
their own affairs. But it immediately became wrapped up with
Soviet-American rivalry, and we can say that the cold war arrived
in Korea in the last months of 1945.

Once the American occupation chose to bolster the status quo
and resist a thorough reform of colonial legacies, it immediately
ran into monumental opposition from the mass of South Koreans.
Most of the first year of the occupation, 1945–1946, was given over
to suppression of many people's committees that had emerged in
the provinces. This suppression provoked a massive rebellion in
the fall of 1946 that spread over four provinces; after it was
suppressed, radical activists developed a significant guerrilla
movement in 1948 and 1949. They also touched off another major
uprising at the port of Yŏsu in October 1948. Much of this

disorder owed to the unresolved land problem, as conservative landed elements used their bureaucratic power to block redistribution of land to peasant tenants. The North Koreans of course sought to take advantage of this discontent, but unimpeachable internal evidence has shown that nearly all of the dissidents and guerrillas were southerners, upset about southern policies. Indeed, the strength of the left wing was in those provinces most removed from the 38th parallel—in the southwestern Chŏllas, which had historically been rebellious, and in the southeastern Kyŏngsang provinces, which had felt the greatest impact from Japanese imperialism.

"Several Hundred Conservatives": An Early Alliance

Within one week Americans in Seoul who had never met a Korean decided that they knew which Korean political leaders they liked: conservatives who included Kim Sŏng-Su and his brother Yŏn-Su, Song Chin-Woo, Cho Pyŏng-Ok, Yun Po-Sŏn, Chang T'aek-Sang, and many other Koreans who later became well-known. Soon dubbed the Korean Democratic Party (KDP; Han'guk minju-dang) at a meeting of party initiators on September 16 (with strong sponsorship by the Americans), this group was to be the "Liberal Democratic Party" of Korea, that is, a ruling conservative party such as later emerged in Japan. The KDP went on to structure the opposition from that time right down to the 1990s, when one of its stalwart members finally became president: Kim Young Sam (Chang T'aek-Sang, head of the Seoul Metropolitan Police and a close American ally, was Kim Young Sam's mentor). What these conservative figures would have become without this early American support, however, is another question.

The problem was that Korean society had no base for either a liberal or a democratic party as Americans understood it; it had a population the vast majority of whom were poor peasants and a tiny minority that held most of the wealth: landowners, who were the real base of the KDP. The elite of Korean society during the colonial period, nearly all of them were widely perceived to have fattened under colonial rule while everybody else suffered. The historical documentation could not be clearer: the United States intervened on behalf of this small if wealthy and prestigious group and helped to perpetuate their position and their privileges thereafter.

This decision also went directly against the occupation's instructions, whether those from the State Department that warned against involvement with any political group or those of the Joint Army-Navy Intelligence Study Number 75, which the Americans carried with them into Korea and which warned about the unequal land situation and the collaboration of landlords with the Japanese (Cumings 1981:129). General John R. Hodge, commander of the occupation, and his advisers liked such people because all the alternatives seemed worse, especially any political group thought to be left of center (as an American would define it). Much later General Hodge came to understand what Korean political conditions were really like, as opposed to the knee-jerk reactions of September 1945. In late 1947 he captured in his homespun way the essence of the American dilemma, as it fluctuated between the unhappy poles of supporting people whose one virtue was anticommunism and opposing native leftists while hoping for a liberal outcome for which Korean society had no base:

> We always have the danger of Fascism taking over when you try to fight Communism. It is a very difficult political situation that we run into. Germany was built up by Hitler to fight Communism, and it went to Nazism. Spain the same thing. On the other hand, when the Communists build up—when Communism builds up—democracy is crushed, and the nation goes Communist. Now, what is the answer on the thing? How in the dickens are you going to get political-in-the-middle-of-the-road out of the mess? Just bring[ing] it up for discussion. I don't know the answer. I wish I did. (U.S. National Archives, 1947)

There was no middle in Korea, thanks to the Japanese, and there would not be until the 1980s. The main problem for the conservatives was their lack of nationalist credentials. Therefore they wanted to bring back some of the exiled nationalists who had resisted the Japanese, while keeping the far more numerous exiled Communists at bay. They succeeded in convincing Hodge that Syngman Rhee in the United States and Kim Ku in China (still in the wartime capital of Chungking with Chiang Kai-Shek) should be brought back to head up the southern conservatives. With Rhee there was no problem, since he had befriended wartime intelligence people in Washington, and they were already trying to get him back to Seoul. The most important of these was M. Preston Goodfellow, who had been deputy director of the Office of Strategic Services (forerunner of the CIA) under William "Wild Bill" Donovan and had a background in Army intelligence; like

Donovan he was known for his interest and expertise in clandestine warfare. Goodfellow thought Rhee had more of "the American point of view" than other Korean leaders and arranged to deposit him back in Korea in October, with MacArthur's support (but over the objections of the State Department, which had long disliked Rhee). Goodfellow then arrived in Korea himself, seeking to set up a separate, anti-Communist southern government. Rhee flew into Korea on MacArthur's personal plane on October 16, 1945, and four days later General Hodge introduced him to the Korean public.

In October 1945, as it happened, the military commands in both North and South sponsored welcoming ceremonies for two returned exiles: Rhee was allowed to give a strongly anti-Communist speech with Hodge sitting at his side, and Soviet officers stood behind Kim Il Sung, introduced as a hero of the resistance to Japan on October 14, 1945. Did a Soviet "Goodfellow" deposit Kim back in P'yŏngyang? Apparently not. Original research in five languages (Wada 1992) has suggested that just before the Manchurian guerrillas returned to Korea, the top leaders such as Kim Il Sung, Kim Ch'aek, Ch'oe Hyŏn, Kim Il, and Ch'oe Yong-Gŏn agreed among themselves to promote Kim Il Sung as the maximum figure, for reasons that included his wider reputation and his personal force. By some indexes the others outranked him; Kim Ch'aek and Ch'oe Hyŏn were higher than Kim in the Chinese Communist hierarchy. In any case they did support Kim after he and his guerrilla group made its way back to Korea on September 19, and with an unstinting loyalty for the rest of their lives.[1] Along with other Manchurian guerrillas they became the core of the North Korean hierarchy.

Within a few months Kim Il Sung and Syngman Rhee were the dominant political figures in the two zones. Rhee was a septuagenarian who had lived in the United States for nearly four decades, had a Ph.D. from Princeton, and had taken an Austrian wife; a patriot well known for devoting his life to Korean independence, he was also a willful man of legendary obstinacy and strong anti-Communist beliefs. Kim Il Sung had begun armed resistance in the Sino-Korean border region shortly after Japan

---

[1] Kim and some sixty guerrillas in his band tried to return to Korea through Sinŭiju on the Chinese border, but bombing had blown the bridges, and so they left from Vladivostok on the Russian ship *Pugachev,* disembarking at Wonsan on September 19. Although a Soviet transport deposited these men in Korea, they returned independently of Soviet authorities. See Wada 1992:341–343.

established the puppet state of Manchukuo in 1932 and was fortunate enough to survive a rugged guerrilla war that had killed most of his comrades by 1945. Kim was thirty-three years old when he returned; he represented a younger generation of revolutionary nationalists filled with contempt for the failures of their fathers and determined to forge a Korea that could resist foreign domination—while at the same time opportunistically allying with Soviet forces. Although both leaders had the support of the respective superpower, neither was an easily malleable person, let alone a puppet. In setting up a government in postwar Korea, however, the Americans unquestionably acted first.

By the third week of November 1945, Hodge and his advisers had come up with a plan that would supplant the State Department's policy of trusteeship: a "Governing Commission" to be formed under Kim Ku at Hodge's direction that would quickly integrate with the military government and soon thereafter succeed it (with Hodge retaining veto power over its activities). The memorandum alluded to an ongoing plan to organize, train, and equip "Korean military and naval forces." As for the Russians, they would be "informed in advance" and encouraged to send people to join the commission, "but if Russian participation is not forthcoming plan should be carried out for Korea south of 38th parallel." The person who wrote this memo, William Langdon (another State Department adviser to Hodge) thought that a southern government thus constituted would be good for foreign interests: "The old native regime internally was feudal and corrupt but the record shows that it was the best disposed toward foreign interests of the three Far Eastern nations, protecting foreign lives and property and enterprises and respecting treaties and franchises. I am sure that we may count on at least as much from a native government evolved as above" (U.S. Dept. of State, *FRUS* 1945, 6:1129–33).

All this meant bypassing not just cooperation with the Russians in seeking a unitary independent Korea, but also trusteeship (as Langdon acknowledged). The trouble was, trusteeship was the existing American policy, urged upon the allies since 1943 and just then being discussed with the Russians at high levels. Kim Ku and some of his supporters in the KPG group returned to Korea on November 23, as an element of this planning.

Hodge was less than impressed with Kim Ku, however, since his first major act was to engineer the assassination of the head of the Korean Democratic Party, Song Chin-Woo, and his second act was to mobilize mass demonstrations against trusteeship when the results of the Foreign Minister's Conference were published in late December. His third was to attempt a coup d'etat as 1945 ended. The three acts were connected: when Hodge learned on December 29 that the United States had concluded an agreement on a modified trusteeship with the Russians, he called in various political leaders to prepare them for the news. Song Chin-Woo was one of them: in Hodge's words, he "went out and told his friends that he was ready to act sensibly and the next morning he was dead" (Cumings 1981:219). This assassination was the most important event since the liberation among the nonleftist groups, for it revealed that the political fault line was not right versus left, but patriot versus collaborator. Song Chin-Woo, like his lifelong friend Kim Sŏng-Su, was a wealthy man who had made many unfortunate compromises in the colonial period. On New Year's Eve Kim Ku issued a series of proclamations that amounted to a direct attempt to take over the government. This effort was easily repulsed, however, and on New Year's Day 1946 Hodge called Kim Ku on the carpet and gave him a "going over" that became the talk of the occupation; Hodge told Kim he would "kill him if he double-crossed me again," and Kim responded by threatening to commit suicide. Thereafter, "the coup d'etat fizzled" (Cumings 1981: 221).

General Hodge had contrived to violate established American policy at several levels, only to find his most cooperative politician dead and the secretary of state signed on to a deal with the Russians. But if he was wrong in 1945, he looked prescient in 1947. And so Hodge and his allies proceeded with the "positive action" necessary to create an anti-Communist South Korea. The establishment of official organizations for the south alone went on apace. The ROK was not proclaimed until August 15, 1948, but the southern political system was built in the first few months of the occupation and did not substantially change until the 1960s. In November and December 1945 Hodge and his advisers chose to act in four areas: first, to build up an army to defend the 38th parallel; second, to buttress the National Police as the primary political weapon for pacifying the South; third, to strengthen the alliance with rightist parties; and fourth, to suppress Koreans who didn't like such policies. An army that occupied Korea to disarm the Japanese was now intensively shaping a containment bulwark in South Korea.

South Korea's Left and Right Wings

The effective opposition to the developing southern system was almost wholly on the Left, mainly because Japanese policies had left Korea with such a tiny middle class. A mass popular resistance from 1945 to 1950 mingled raw peasant protest with organized labor union activity and, finally, armed guerrilla resistance. We can see this general picture in some of the first CIA reports on Korea. In one 1948 document, CIA analysts wrote that South Korean political life was "dominated by a rivalry between Rightists and the remnants of the Left Wing People's Committees," which the CIA termed a "grass-roots independence movement which found expression in the establishment of the People's Committees throughout Korea in August 1945," led by "Communists" who based their right to rule on the resistance to the Japanese. The leadership of the Right, on the other hand,

> is provided by that numerically small class which virtually monopolizes the native wealth and education of the country.... Since this class could not have acquired and maintained its favored position under Japanese rule without a certain minimum of "collaboration," it has experienced difficulty in finding acceptable candidates for political office and has been forced to support imported expatriate politicians such as Rhee Syngman and Kim Ku. These, while they have no pro-Japanese taint, are essentially demagogues bent on autocratic rule. (U.S. CIA 1948, 1949)

Thus, "the extreme Rightists control the overt political structure in the US zone," mainly through the agency of the National Police, which had been "ruthlessly brutal in suppressing disorder." The CIA went on to say,

> The enforced alliance of the police with the Right has been reflected in the cooperation of the police with Rightist youth groups for the purpose of completely suppressing Leftist activity. This alignment has had the effect of forcing the Left to operate as an underground organization since it could not effectively compete in a parliamentary sense even if it should so desire. Although membership in communist and left wing organizations was ostensibly legal under the American Occupation, "the police generally regarded the Communists as rebels and traitors who should be seized, imprisoned, and sometimes shot on the slightest provocation." (U.S. CIA, 1948, 1949)

Meanwhile, according to the CIA, the structure of the southern bureaucracy was "substantially the old Japanese machinery"; the Home Affairs Ministry exercised in southern Korea "a high degree of control over virtually all phases of the life of the people." With crucial support from the director of the KNP, Cho Pyŏng-Ok, whom many thought to be the most powerful Korean after Syngman Rhee, the Korean Democratic Party "built up its membership within the ranks of the police and local governments" (U.S. CIA 1948).

American officials publicly praised this regime as free or democratic while privately calling it a police state—over and over in internal memoranda. But they nonetheless misconstrued the reality. The south did have a police state, and it was an agent of a small class of landlords. But it was more than that, or it could not have survived even to June 1950. The landlord class held both obtuse reactionaries and vibrant capitalists. Korean capitalism may not have had articulate proponents, but it had impressive practitioners, of which the Kim Sŏng-Su group was the most formidable. This was hardly the visionary entrepreneur, however, looking for the main chance; the main chance had been the Japanese regime and the opportunities that close alliance with it brought to this, Korea's first *chaebol* (business conglomerate). Americans found this sort of capitalism hard to dignify or legitimate, as did Koreans, seeing little virtue in business that hewed close to the state. But it was a source of dynamism in the Korean economy, this state-led capitalism implanted by a Japanese "developmental" colonialism. It laid the foundations for the economic growth of the l960s. But it did not fit a textbook description of capitalism.

In 1947 a mass politics of the Right emerged in the South that both made it look like a classic police state and gave new strength to the system. These groups rested on a myriad of youth groups, an incipient corporatist organization of the working class, and a set of Korean political ideas that were a kind of homegrown fascism. The occupation, supported and funded by Korean National Youth (KNY), melded Chinese influences with Japanese methods of dealing with political recalcitrants. Its leader, Yi Pŏm-sŏk, was a fierce Korean nationalist (except where the Chinese Nationalists were concerned).

American policy, of course, never set out to create one of the worst police states in Asia. The Korean problem was what we would now call a "Third World" problem or a "North-South" problem, a conflict over how best to overcome the debilities of colonial rule and comparative backwardness. In the cold war milieu of the time, however, Americans always saw it as an East-West problem. The Soviets, we might say, pushed the North-

South angle as a way of besting the United States in the East-West conflict on the peninsula. That is, they stayed in the background and let Koreans run the government, they put anti-Japanese resistance leaders out front, and they supported radical reforms of the land system, labor conditions, and women's rights—all of which were pushed through by the end of 1946. Although very active behind the scenes, the Russians made it seem that Kim Il Sung was in charge—especially after they withdrew their troops from Korea in late 1948.

The critical background to the establishment of separate governments in Korea in 1948 was not in the realm of political parties, but in the social and political conflict between Left and Right throughout the peninsula. This conflict went on at the national level in 1945 and at the provincial and county levels in 1946, as local people's committees controlled county seats and fought with their antagonists. The suppression of the massive autumn harvest uprisings in 1946 (see Cumings 1981: 351–79) consolidated state control in the county seats, making the seizure of power by county people's committees unlikely thereafter. Villages continued to be isolated from central power, however, and leftists therefore migrated downward through the bureaucratic reaches of the system in search of space for organization.

The passions of liberation produced the two very different Koreas that are still with us today. The Democratic People's Republic of Korea was proclaimed on September 9, 1948, three weeks after the Republic of Korea was formed in Seoul; like the South, the North invited MacArthur to be present at this creation (he ignored the invitation). Kim Il Sung was named premier, a title he retained until 1972 (when under a new constitution he became president).

At the end of 1948 the Soviets withdrew their occupation forces from North Korea, a decision that contrasted strongly with Soviet policies in Eastern Europe, where in countries such as East Germany, Poland, and Czechoslovakia Soviet divisions remained until the fall of the Berlin Wall in 1989. But no Soviet troops were again stationed in Korea. At the same time, tens of thousands of Korean soldiers who had fought in the Chinese civil war filtered back to Korea. All through 1949 tough, crack troops with a Chinese, not a Soviet, experience returned to be integrated with the KPA. This enhanced Kim's power more than anything else, because he now had a blooded army that could fight. Like Syngman Rhee, his goal was the unification of his country. Unlike

Rhee, by 1950 he had assembled the wherewithal to reach that goal.

War and Division

The Korean War did not begin on June 25, 1950 (much special pleading and argument to the contrary). If it did not begin then, Kim Il Sung could not have "started" it then, either, but only at some earlier point. As we search backward for that point, we slowly grope toward the truth that civil wars do not start: they come. They originate in multiple causations, with blame enough to go around for everyone—and blame enough to include Americans who divided Korea and then reestablished the colonial government machinery and the Koreans who served it. How many Koreans might still be alive had that not happened? Blame enough to include a Soviet Union likewise unconcerned with Korea's ancient integrity and determined to "build socialism" whether Koreans wanted their kind of system or not. How many Koreans might still be alive had that not happened? And then as we peer inside Korea to inquire about Korean actions that might have avoided national division and fratricidal conflict, we get a long list indeed.

A Korean War was inconceivable before the division of Korea in August 1945. But because of that division, it has been conceivable ever since—right down to the present day. The first inklings of a North Korean invasion came not in 1950, but in the spring of 1946, when General Hodge told Washington that an attack might be imminent. The first evidence that powerful figures in both Koreas contemplated a war of reunification came in this same early period, a mere six months after the end of the Pacific War. However, neither the United States nor the Soviet Union would back military action to do away with the hated 38th parallel as long as their troops were likely to be drawn into it, so we can date the onset of this civil war becoming "hot" in Korea from early 1949, when Soviet troops were out and American troops were on their way out. That year was also the year of Chinese Communist victory, which had tremendous effect on both Koreas and on American and Soviet policy toward the peninsula. Of course, anyone familiar with Korean history would have expected that a China strong enough finally to throw off imperial subordination might have an impact on its near neighbor.

The war that came in June 1950 also followed upon guerrilla fighting in Korea's interior and on Cheju Island and upon nine months of battles along the 38th parallel in 1949. Border conflict lasted from early May until late December, taking hundreds of lives and embroiling thousands of troops. The veteran journalist A. T. Steele captured the flavor of this fighting in a remarkable account written in October 1949: "An unadmitted shooting war between the Governments of the U.S. and Russia is in effect today along the 38th parallel.... It is smoldering throughout the territory of the new Republic of Korea... only American money, weapons, and technical assistance enable [the Republic] to exist for more than a few hours." The ROK was "dedicated to liberty," Steele wrote, but it is "a tight little dictatorship run as a police state." Its jails overflowed with prisoners, thirty thousand according to his estimate; "torture of captured political antagonists is common-place," and "women and children are killed without compunc-tion" by both sides. Americans on the scene "are almost evangeli-cal in their fervor for Korean revival," but, Steele thought, "once the American props are withdrawn, South Korea will fall beneath the weight of Communist Asia" (*New York Herald-Tribune*, October 30, 1949).

The reason that war did not come in 1949 is at once simple, and essential to grasping the civil origins of the Korean conflict: some elements in the South wanted a war then, but the North did not—and neither did the United States or the Soviet Union. A year later this situation had changed. In particular, both sides sought a guarantee from their great-power backers, with Kim Il Sung making secret visits to Moscow and Beijing, and Syngman Rhee imploring Preston Goodfellow and other American friends for help.

After the 1949 border fighting died down, both Syngman Rhee and Kim Il Sung sought backing from their big-power guarantors for a major assault on the other side. Rhee did this primarily through his "kitchen cabinet" of American advisers, especially Preston Goodfellow, and Kim did it through at least two secret visits to Moscow and others to Beijing in early 1950. Both expected that the summer of 1950 would open as did the summer of 1949, and both wanted to settle the hash of the other side once and for all. Kim was apparently the more successful, getting new equipment from Moscow and Stalin's apparent acquiescence to his plans, and direct support from Mao in Beijing. A January 1950 document shows Stalin appearing to be more interested than at any previous point in Kim Il Sung's plans for South Korea, without a hint of what Stalin's own strategic thinking might be (Stalin's telegram 1950). Rhee, however, got a clear message from Goodfellow that he would get American support only if South Korea were attacked without provocation.

When full-scale conventional war came in June 1950, the official American position was that the Soviets and the North Koreans stealthily prepared an attack that was completely unprovoked, one that constituted an all-out invasion. On June 26, Kim Il Sung, on the contrary, accused the South of making "a general attack" across the parallel. Rhee had long sought to touch off a fratricidal civil war, he said, having "incessantly provoked clashes" at the front line; in preparing a "northern expedition" he had "even gone so far as to collude with our sworn enemy, Japanese militarism" (Kim 1950). Some of these charges were true, but the charge of making a general attack across the parallel is false: the North attacked, and all along the parallel by 6 A.M. at the latest.

The evidence that scholars now have (there is much more to come from unopened archives) is compatible both with an unprovoked North Korean invasion (one prefigured in North Korean and Soviet planning as we have seen) and with an interpretation linking the summer of 1949 to June 1950: that the North waited until it had the majority of its crack soldiers back from China and the support or acquiescence of Stalin and Mao, and then positioned its troops to take advantage of the first Southern provocation in June 1950 or simply to attack and claim a direct provocation (since there had been so many in 1949). Kim Il Sung thus bears the grave responsibility of raising the civil conflict in Korea to the level of general war, with intended and unintended consequences that no one could have predicted. To say that the war was the culmination of previous struggles and that Rhee wanted to do the same thing is true but does not gainsay Kim's responsibility for the consequences that followed. But it was still Korea that Kim invaded, not Japan or Borneo.

Whatever happened on or before June 25, it was immediately clear that this was not aggression across generally accepted international lines; Koreans had invaded Korea. Nor was this the point at which the civil conflict began; it began with the national division. Therefore the question pregnant with ideological dynamite —Who started the Korean War?—is the wrong question. It is not a civil war question; it only holds the viscera in its grasp for the generations immediately afflicted by fratricidal conflict. No

Americans care anymore that the Southern army first fired on Fort Sumter; they do still care about slavery and secession. No one wants to know who started the Vietnam War. Some day Koreans in North and South will reconcile as Americans eventually did, with the wisdom that civil wars have no single authors. It took Americans about a century to do this; it is therefore not surprising that Korean reconciliation is still pending after fifty years.

When this war finally ended on July 27, 1953, the North had been devastated by three years of bombing attacks that hardly left a modern building standing. Both Koreas had watched as a virtual holocaust ravaged their country, and turned the vibrant expectations of 1945 into a nightmare. The point to remember is that, as a British diplomat once said, "every country has a right to have its War of the Roses." The true tragedy was not the war itself, for a civil conflict purely among Koreans might have resolved the extraordinary tensions generated by colonialism, national division, and foreign intervention. The tragedy was that the war solved nothing: only the status quo ante was restored, only an armistice held the peace.

Reconciliation and Reunification

In the new millennium the Korean Peninsula is only beginning to emerge from two time warps. The cold war was more frigid there than anywhere in the world, and it has not ended: the peninsula is a museum of that world-ranging conflict. Added to that anachronism is a Second World War deep freeze: the Northeast Asian region remains locked in a 1940s settlement that easily outlived the end of American-Soviet rivalry, the best evidence of which is the hundred thousand American troops that continue to occupy Japan and South Korea. For these internal and external reasons, Korea cannot establish its own definitions of reality (and thus risks being misunderstood and misconstrued in the West, particularly in the United States), and the denouement to Korea's fractured modern history and its ultimate place in the world remain unresolved. The two Koreas still face each other across a heavily fortified demilitarized zone, shaped by an errant decision in 1945 to divide their country and by the civil war that followed. Both Koreas continue to be deeply deformed by the necessity to maintain an unrelenting struggle that might well have been solved with some abrupt and radical surgery in 1945. The Korean War itself solved nothing except to make another war an impossible route to reunification, but it did solidify armed bulwarks of containment, a "division system" (in Paik Nak-Ch'ŏng's words) that the United States, the ROK, and the DPRK remain committed to, even in the post–cold war world of the 1990s and in spite of much recent progress in North-South relations (see Cumings 2002).

It is odd to think that changes that went nowhere in Korea were promulgated at the same time as vast changes in the world, namely the fall of the Berlin Wall, whereas changes that did go somewhere began only when the ROK had its first genuine political transition since 1945, when Kim Dae Jung was elected in the midst of a massive financial crisis at the end of 1997. This suggests that the real impetus for change must come from within Korea—and is coming from within.

Hopes of reconciliation in Korea had been raised by the two Koreas before, only to be dashed. In July 1972 they published several principles for reunification that grew out of secret talks between Kim Il Sung and Yi Hu-Rak, the director of the South's central intelligence agency. Under Roh Tae Woo the Seoul government developed a "Nordpolitik" policy on the German model of "Ostpolitik," seeking to open talks and trade with P'yŏngyang. In the fall of 1990 for the first time prime ministerial talks were held. Roh's Nordpolitik appeared to achieve its greatest success on December 13, 1991, when the prime ministers of the ROK and the DPRK signed the Agreement on Reconciliation, Nonaggression, Cooperation, and Exchange at Seoul. Its twenty-five articles called for mutual recognition of the respective political systems, an end to mutual vilification and confrontation, "concerted efforts" to turn the Korean War armistice into a durable peace; guarantees of nonaggression, economic cooperation, and exchange in many fields; and free travel through both halves of the country for the estimated ten million Koreans from families separated by the war. Unfortunately, the presumably "epochal" principles from the 1972 and 1991 meetings were as fleeting as the proposed summits. This experience naturally led many observers to think that Kim Dae Jung's "sunshine policy," enunciated first at his inauguration in February 1998, would also lead nowhere. Instead President Kim proceeded to sponsor changes unlike any since the war ended in 1953.

This time things were different, for several reasons. The main reason is that several years of diplomacy had prepared the ground for success, through dramatic changes in South Korean and American policy, through a steady Chinese policy of trying to bring

North Korea into diplomacy, and through compromises in recent years by the North that belie its obstinate, nasty image. A three-year crisis over the North's nuclear program nearly led to war in June 1994, but energetic diplomacy got the North's nuclear reactor frozen with the October Framework Agreement in 1994—and it is still frozen. In 1997 the North agreed to "four-power talks" (the United States, China, both Koreas) to replace the continuing technical state of war, while quietly dropping its previous refusal to deal with a South that never signed the armistice. Those talks are still ongoing; they are very important because their stated goal is to bring a final end to the Korean conflict through a peace settlement. A hullabaloo in 1998–1999 over a huge underground installation said to harbor nuclear facilities ended with the North yielding to unprecedented American inspections of this site and other security facilities.

At the end of August in 1998 the North launched a rocket that entered the stratosphere above Japan, in a failed attempt to put a satellite in orbit—thus to herald the fiftieth anniversary of the DPRK on September 9, 1998. This event was widely (and easily) misconstrued as a massive new threat of long-range missiles from the North, and so another "North Korean crisis" occupied the media for many months. No doubt the North also enjoyed fostering this fearsome image, because its missiles, like its nuclear reactor, have been useful bargaining chips with the United States over the past decade. But that provocative missile launching was followed by a major agreement with Washington in September 1999 to halt missile tests in return for a slow and partial lifting of the fifty-year-old American economic embargo on the North. When the Clinton administration finally lifted parts of the embargo in mid-June of 2000, the North again reaffirmed its commitment to a moratorium on missile tests.

The turn of the new millennium seemed also to herald a major turning point in North Korean foreign policy. After January 2000 P'yŏngyang went on a diplomatic offensive, opening relations with Italy, Australia, the Philippines, and Canada and holding discussions about doing the same with Germany, France, England, and of course Washington.

Still, it was Kim Dae Jung who led the process of reconciliation. President Kim did more to change policy toward the North than any previous South Korean or American president, in spite of Seoul's facing a far greater immediate threat than anyone else. At his inauguration in February 1998 he pledged to "actively pursue reconciliation and cooperation" with North Korea and declared his support for P'yŏngyang's attempts at better relations with Washington and Tokyo (in total contrast with his predecessors, who hated any hint of such rapprochement).

Kim Dae Jung was also the first head of state publicly to call for an end to the fifty-year-old U.S. embargo against the North, which he did during a visit to Washington in June 1998. Kim also shipped food and other forms of aid to the North without demanding concessions and refused to allow himself to be provoked by North Korean hard-liners—thus ending the tit-for-tat practice of each side never moving an inch farther than the other side, a process that for decades had assured that there could be no progress in North-South relations. Kim encouraged many South Korean businesses to invest in the North, and especially massive investment by the Hyundai founder and native of northern Korea Chung Ju-Yong, who has been in the forefront of North-South economic relations for years.

But it was of course the June 2000 summit that dramatized this many-sided diplomacy, while also marking the emergence of Kim Jong Il as a statesman (he had met few foreigners or heads of state before, leaving that to the titular president, Kim Yong-Nam). No northern leader had ever shaken hands with a southern president, but Kim Jong Il welcomed Kim Dae Jung at the airport and showed him a Confucian's utmost respect, walking slowly behind his elder counterpart with a body language so culturally appropriate that even South Korea's right wing decided that he couldn't be a complete barbarian. He proceeded to discourse with Kim (and everyone else) with apparent ease of command and much diplomatic aplomb.

Kim Dae Jung's patient and persistent sunshine policy grew out of his long-term study of the North-South problem and his lived experience as a leader whose adult lifetime spans the entire existence of the national division and both Korean states. This is a man who suffered for decades at the hands of Korea's dictators and learned the hard way the virtues of dialogue, reconciliation, peace, and the necessary magnanimity to strive in those directions. I would stress in particular this magnanimity, which grows out of his deeply felt Catholic religious beliefs and which has meant a refusal to respond to provocations by North Korean hard-liners in his first year in office—provocations that no doubt were a test of his will. President Kim wants to leave office as the man who ended the Korean War, which is the necessary prelude to an eventual reconciliation and reunification. He has a good chance of success, because of elements that may not be so obvious in the Korean situation.

Two critical preconditions are at the bottom of all the recent progress: first, North Korea did not collapse after the Berlin Wall fell; second, war no longer was an option for anyone. And there is one critical future (or post?) condition for continuing success, and that is the long-term presence of American troops in Korea.

I never thought that North Korea would collapse, and one of the few virtues of getting older (really one of the only ones when I think about it) is that I can cite several points beginning in 1990 when I wrote that it would not collapse. I wasn't sure North Korea wouldn't collapse, of course; life, otherwise known as history, teaches us when we are wrong, and I have often been wrong. I simply felt that if I was wrong about this, I should go into another line of work, because it would mean that my understanding of and my scholarship about North Korea would have also been wrong. North Korea has not simply been just a Communist state, let alone a "puppet" of Moscow or Beijing, but also a revolutionary nationalist state, and a postcolonial and anti-imperial state: and to be quite specific, it is also a state constituted as an anti-Japanese entity.

In any event by 1998 when Kim Dae Jung was inaugurated, one had to assume that North Korea was going to be around for some time to come, and so he pledged himself to peaceful coexistence and to refrain from trying to provoke a North Korean collapse or to "absorb" the North, on the German model of unification. These are the critically important assumptions in all of Kim Dae Jung's sunshine policy, and explain why North Korea finally decided upon a new, many-sided diplomacy. It had not collapsed and disappeared, and now the South pledged itself to live amicably with the North for at least another generation, without expecting a quick unification.

There was another deeply serious element in the noncollapse of North Korea, however, because P'yŏngyang's collapse was to hope for the next Korean War. Perhaps the most dramatic statement came in March 1996, on the heels of CIA director John Deutsch's testimony in Congress that it was not a question of whether North Korea would collapse, but only a question of when. Within forty-eight hours Vice-Marshal Kim Kwang-Jin declared, "The point now is not whether a war will break out in the Korean peninsula...but when it will be unleashed."

But what really put war out of the question was the near-war of June 1994. At that time war came much closer than most people realized, and the costs would have been catastrophic: millions of Koreans dead, the peninsula devastated, and upwards of 100,000 American body bags and $100 million to $1 billion in expenditures—in an election year. Fortunately war was avoided (no one wanted it), and so a diplomatic path began to unfold.

In spite of a hotbed of noisy opposition in the U.S. Congress and a continuing American media commotion about the North Korean threat, middle-level State Department officials patiently negotiated one agreement after another with P'yŏngyang, in a long series of talks on various problems that had troubled relations since 1991. The six-month-long review of Korea policy they began in the fall of 1998 markedly changed the direction of U.S. policy and culminated in the Perry mission to P'yŏngyang in June 1998. Ambassador William Perry issued a public version of this policy review in October 1999, the essence of which is a policy of engagement also predicated on the coexistence of two Koreas for another considerable period of time, a progressive lifting of the American embargo against the North, and a deepening of diplomatic relations. In the year 2000 we saw the quick and successful fruition of this strategy. Chinese diplomacy also played a major role in bringing the United States and North Korea into diplomatic negotiation, and in the recent past, Japan also began to help a great deal by giving full backing to Kim Dae Jung and to the Clinton administration.

The Third Condition: Maintenance of U.S. Troops

Kim Dae Jung said he wanted U.S. troops to remain in the ROK for the foreseeable future; that is not surprising. During the Clinton administration, Secretary of Defense William Cohen said he wanted U.S. troops to remain even after unification—also not surprising. But it is quite surprising that the North may agree. Why?

In recent years North Korea has quietly reconsidered its strategic orientation: long determined to get the United States out of Korea, P'yŏngyang now appears to want the United States to stay involved, to deal with changed international circumstances since the collapse of the Soviet Union, to help the country through its current, difficult transition, to keep the South from swallowing it, and to deal with a China and a Japan that are both strong at the same time, for the first time in modern history.

More than two years ago, North Korea expert Selig Harrison interviewed a North Korean general who told him that though the North may call publicly for the withdrawal of American troops, in reality American troops should stay in Korea to help deal with a strong Japan and also to protect itself against absorption by the South (Harrison 1997). During the June 2000 summit, Kim Jong Il said essentially the same thing directly to Kim Dae Jung. This dramatic shift in North Korea's posture is the key toward understanding how the ongoing diplomacy might finally dissolve the extraordinary tensions that have inhabited Korea for half a century. It explains why Kim Dae Jung has said he wanted to end the Korean War before leaving office, but that Korean reunification must still be twenty or thirty years in the future; above all it explains why P'yŏngyang does not fear the consequences of the ongoing reconciliation.

The United States spends as much as $20 to $30 billion a year to maintain its Korea commitment, including the increasing irritant of a Marine division in Okinawa and troops of various services at many other bases in Japan, and it does so long after the purpose of this commitment—to contain Soviet and Chinese communism—has evaporated. This was and is a containment policy, but with a dual face: contain the enemy and the ally. In Korea, this has meant a civil war deterrent structure, necessitating outright command of the southern forces. The end of the cold war has made little difference in these arrangements, to the surprise of many; but it is not surprising if we know the origins of this strategy.

This enormous commitment is just one aspect of the American strategic position in East Asia and the Pacific: Japan also remains within the postwar settlement hammered out in 1947–1953 and shows no signs of getting out of it, Okinawan protests to the contrary. In recent years the Pentagon has also been on guard against any challenge for control of Pacific security, a posture that has led many Chinese to see a growing American encirclement of China. The "Nye Doctrine" of 1995 projected two more decades of the same strategy, and Defense Secretary Cohen said that American forces would stay in the region indefinitely and would remain in Korea even after unification.

In this light a pacified Korean Peninsula in which the two states coexist, if not a unified Korea, fits the logic of American strategy in Asia for the first time since—well, since Dean Rusk first drew a line at the 38th parallel fifty-five years ago. But it still remains for Koreans to figure out how the ultimate reunification will come about.

References

Cumings, Bruce. 1981. *The Origins of the Korean War.* Princeton, N.J.: Princeton University Press.
_____. *Parallax Visions.* Durham, N.C.: Duke University Press.
Harrison, Selig. 1997. "Promoting a Soft Landing in Korea." *Foreign Policy,* no. 106 (Spring).
Haruki, Wada. 1992. *Kin Nichisei to Manshu konichi senso* (Kim Il Sung and the anti-Japanese war in Manchuria). Tokyo: Heibonsha.
New York Herald-Tribune. 1949.
Kim, Il Sung. 1950. "Appeal to All the Korean People." June 26. Translated broadcast transcript in U.S. National Archives, RG 242, SA2005, item 2/67.
"Stalin's telegram to Russian ambassador to P'youngyang Shtykov on January 30th." 1995. *Cold War International History Project Bulletin,* no. 5 (Spring 1995): 9.
United States. Central Intelligence Agency. 1948. "The Current Situation in Korea." February 28. ORE 32-48. National Records Center archives.
_____. 1949. "Communist Capabilities in Korea." March 18. ORE 15-48. National Records Center archives.
United States. Department of State. 1944 and 1945. *Foreign Relations of the United States (FRUS).* Washington, D.C.: Government Printing Office, 1955. Documents in National Records Center archives.
_____. 1945. *The Conferences of Malta and Yalta.* Washington, D.C.: Government Printing Office, 1955. Documents in National Records Center archives.
United States. National Archives. 1947. Hodge meeting with visiting Congressional delegation. October 4. USFIK 11071 file, box 62/96.

Index

111–112, 119, 126–127, 207,
211, 213, 217
state–business alliance 17, 30, 179,
181
status symbols 53–54
status system 36–37, 39, 183
stratification system 36–37, 40, 60
student movements 191, 193–197,
199–200
subcontracting 98, 101
sunshine policy 3, 126, 197, 242,
244–245
sword-won alliance 123

Taiwan 57, 112, 114–115
tenancy disputes 184
Thailand 80, 127
Thailand crisis 80
Theory H 22, 24
Theory P 23–24
Three Min Principles 194
Tonghak peasant war 181–84
Tongnip Sinmun 137

unification policy 28
union activism 59
United States 54, 70
United States Agency for International Development (USAID)
111
universalism 17
urbanization 10, 12, 145, 147, 158,
170, 174, 176, 211–212
US-DPRK Nuclear Agreement 228

Veblen, Thorsten 65
vertical integration 82, 95, 98, 101
Victims Relief Act 151
Vietnam War 121, 241

Weber, Max 27–28, 47, 69, 115
white industries 86
white-collar workers 6, 45–46, 51,
53, 56, 58–59, 214
women's movements 132, 138,
142, 150
women's rights 137, 143, 151, 237

worker-student alliance 187, 194
working class 7, 42, 46, 57, 60
World Bank 111
World War II 37, 163, 184, 226,
241

yang 133
yangban 7, 37–41, 47, 50, 54–55,
132–133, 135–137, 179–180,
210
yangbanization 8, 55
Yi dynasty 37, 39, 116, 131–134,
136–138, 144, 176
yin 133
Yongnam 18, 20, 22–24, 26–27, 31
yongojooui 68
yŏnjul 8–9, 17–18, 26–27, 30–32
Yushin constitution 122, 124

zaibatsu 89

Contributors

Kye-Choon Ahn is professor of sociology at Yonsei University. He received his Ph.D. in sociology from the University of Chicago in 1973. He served as president of the Population Association of Korea (1988–90) and the Korean Sociological Association (1995). His major publications include *Understanding Modern Sociology* (1988), *Professionalism in Korean Society* (1994), and *Fifty Years of Sociology and Social Change in Korea* (1998) (in Korean). His current interest lies in the area of population aging, and he is now working on population structure and population changes in Korea. He is a member of the American Sociological Association, Population Association of America, and International Union for the Scientific Study of Population.

Bruce Cumings is Norman and Edna Freehling Professor of History at the University of Chicago. He received his Ph.D. from Columbia University in 1975 and subsequently taught at Swarthmore College (1975–77), the University of Washington (1977–86), and Northwestern University (1994–97). He is the author of the two-volume study *The Origins of the Korean War* (1981, 1990) and of *War and Television* (1992), *Korea's Place in the Sun: A Modern History* (1997), and *Parallax Visions: Making Sense of American East Asian Relations* (1999), and is the editor of the modern volume of the *Cambridge History of Korea*. He is a frequent contributor to *The Nation, Current History,* and the *Bulletin of Atomic Scientists.* He was elected to the American Academy of Arts and Sciences in 1999 and is the recipient of fellowships from NEH, the MacArthur Foundation, and the Center for Advanced Study at Stanford. He was also the principal historical consultant for the Thames Television/PBS six-hour documentary *Korea: The Unknown War.*

Karl J. Fields is professor and chair of the Department of Politics and Government, former director of Asian Studies, and associate professor of politics and government at the University of

Puget Sound in Tacoma, Washington. He received his Ph.D. in political science from the University of California, Berkeley, in 1990. He has published on various topics of East Asian political economy, including government-business relations, economic reform, and regional integration. His first book, *Enterprise and the State in Korea and Taiwan* (1995), examined the role of government and big business in the economic miracles of Taiwan and South Korea. His current book project analyzes the business empires owned and operated by Taiwan's Nationalist Party.

Dong-No Kim is associate professor of sociology at Yonsei University. He received his Ph.D. in sociology from the University of Chicago in 1994. His main publications include "Theoretical Foundation of Marx's Historical Sociology: The Historical Specificity of Capitalism and Its Transcendence by Human Praxis" (*Critical Sociology* 21, 1995), "The Transformation of Familism in Modern Korean Society: From Cooperation to Competition" (*International Sociology* 5, 1990), "Low Efficiency of Social System and the IMF Economic Crisis" (*Sahoe paljon yonku* 5, 1999), and "Modernity and Exploitation in the Colonial Period: Creation and Criticism" (*Changjak kwa bipyong* 99, 1998). His current research interests lie in colonial modernity in Korea, comparative studies on peasant movements, and the power dynamic between the state and society.

Hyuk-Rae Kim is professor of Korean Studies and director of the Institute for Modern Korean Studies at the Graduate School of International Studies, Yonsei University. He received his Ph.D. in sociology from the University of Washington in 1992. His main research interests lie in economic/social governance, civil society, and NGOs. He has recently published articles in major international journals as well as chapters from Ashgate (2003), Edward Elgar (2001), and Routledge (2002, 2005). His recent publications include the coedited volumes *Mad Technology: How East Asian Companies Are Defending Their Technological Advantages* (2005), *Korean Studies Forum* (2002), and *Politics and Markets in the Wake of the Asian Crisis* (2000). He edited two special issies of *Korea Observer: Civil Society and Consolidating Democracy* (2004) and *Globalization and Socio-Cultural Changes* (2006). He is currently working on manuscripts concerning economic sociology and negotiated social governance.

Seung-Kyung Kim is associate professor in the Department of Women's Studies and director of the Asian American Studies

Program at the University of Maryland at College Park. Her research interests include gender and the politics of labor, international division of labor, and gender and transnational immigration. She is the author of *Class Struggle or Family Struggle?: Lives of Women factory Workers in South Korea* (1997), and her articles have been published in various anthologies and refereed journals such as *Feminist Studies, Women's Studies Quarterly, Asian Journal of Women's Studies,* and *Anthropology Today.* The coeditor of *Feminist Theory Reader: Local and Global perspectives* (2002), she is currently working on the women's movement in contemporary South Korea.

Wang-Bae Kim is associate professor of sociology at Yonsei University. He received his Ph.D. in sociology from Yonsei University in 1992. He was visiting professor at the University of Chicago from 1997 to 1999. His main research focuses on the issues of social class, labor, inequality, and urban space. His recent publications include *Tosi, kongkan saenghwal sekye* (Urban space and life work; 2000) and *Sanŏpsahoe ŭi nodonggwa kyegŭpŭi chaesaengsan* (Reproduction of labor and class in industrial society; 2001). He is currently working on a project examining the newly emerging urban petit bourgeoisie after the economic crisis in 1997.

Yong-Hak Kim is professor of sociology at Yonsei University. He received his Ph.D. in sociology from the University of Chicago in 1986. He has served as an associate editor and consultant editor of the *American Journal of Sociology* and *Rationality and Society* for many years. He has written numerous books regarding social structure and action in social theories, the methodological issues of comparative sociology, and labor unions in Korea. His research interests lie in the areas of social networks and organizations.

Hagen Koo is professor of sociology at the University of Hawai'i at Manoa. His recent works include *State and Society in Contemporary Korea* (ed., 1993) and *Korean Workers: The Culture and Politics of Class Formation* (2001).

Bok Song is professor of sociology at Yonsei University. He received his Ph.D. in political science from Seoul National University in 1980. His major publications include *Organization and Power* (1990), *Conflict Structure in Korean Society* (1997), and *What's Oriental Value?* (in Korean; 1999).

INSTITUTE OF EAST ASIAN STUDIES PUBLICATIONS SERIES

CHINA RESEARCH MONOGRAPHS (CRM)

40. Frederic Wakeman, Jr., and Wen-hsin Yeh, eds. *Shanghai Sojourners*, 1992
Sp. Kaidi Zhan. *The Strategies of Politeness in the Chinese Language*, 1992
42. Barry C. Keenan. *Imperial China's Last Classical Academies: Social Change in the Lower Yangzi, 1864–1911*, 1994
43. Ole Bruun. *Business and Bureaucracy in a Chinese City: An Ethnography of Private Business Households in Contemporary China*, 1993
44. Wei Li. *The Chinese Staff System: A Mechanism for Bureaucratic Control and Integration*, 1994
45. Ye Wa and Joseph W. Esherick. *Chinese Archives: An Introductory Guide*, 1996
46. Melissa Brown, ed. *Negotiating Ethnicities in China and Taiwan*, 1996
47. David Zweig and Chen Changgui. *China's Brain Drain to the United States: Views of Overseas Chinese Students and Scholars in the 1990s*, 1995
48. Elizabeth J. Perry, ed. *Putting Class in Its Place: Worker Identities in East Asia*, 1996
Sp. Phyllis L. Thompson, ed. *Dear Alice: Letters Home from American Teachers Learning to Live in China*, 1998
49. Wen-hsin Yeh, ed. *Landscape, Culture, and Power in Chinese Society*, 1998
50. Gail Hershatter, Emily Honig, Susan Mann, and Lisa Rofel, comps. and eds. *Guide to Women's Studies in China*, 1999
51. Wen-hsin Yeh, ed. *Modern Chinese Literary and Cultural Studies: Theoretical Issues*, 2000
52. Marilyn A. Levine and Chen San-ching, eds. *The Guomindang in Europe: A Sourcebook of Documents*, 2000
53. David N. Keightley. *The Ancestral Landscape: Time, Space, and Community in Late Shang China*, 2000
54. Peter M. Worthing. *Occupation and Revolution: China and the Vietnamese August Revolution of 1945*, 2001.
55. Guo Qitao. *Exorcism and Money: The Symbolic World of the Five-Fury Spirits in Late Imperial China*, 2003
56. Robert J. Antony. *Like Froth Floating on the Sea: The World of Pirates and Seafarers in Late Imperial South China*, 2003
57. Joshua A. Fogel, ed. *The Role of Japan in Liang Qichao's Introduction of Modern Western Civilization to China*, 2004
58. Xin Liu, ed. *New Reflections on Anthropological Studies of (greater) China*, 2004
59. Virginia Harper Ho. *Labor Dispute Resolution in China*, 2003.
60. Jon Eugene von Kowallis. *The Subtle Revolution: Poets of the "Old Schools" during Late Qing and Early Republican China*, 2006
61. Joseph W. Esherick, Wen-hsin Yeh, and Madeleine Zelin, eds. *Empire, Nation, and Beyond: Chinese History in Late Imperial and Modern Times—a Festschrift in Honor of Frederic Wakeman*, 2006

KOREA RESEARCH MONOGRAPHS (KRM)

13. Vipan Chandra. *Imperialism, Resistance, and Reform in Late Nineteenth-Century Korea: Enlightenment and the Independence Club*, 1988
14. Seok Choong Song. *Explorations in Korean Syntax and Semantics*, 1988
15. Robert A. Scalapino and Dalchoong Kim, eds. *Asian Communism: Continuity and Transition*, 1988
16. Chong-Sik Lee and Se-Hee Yoo, eds. *North Korea in Transition*, 1991
17. Nicholas Eberstadt and Judith Banister. *The Population of North Korea*, 1992
18. Hong Yung Lee and Chung Chongwook, eds. *Korean Options in a Changing International Order*, 1993
19. Tae Hwan Ok and Hong Yung Lee, eds. *Prospects for Change in North Korea*, 1994
20. Chai-sik Chung. *A Korean Confucian Encounter with the Modern World: Yi Hang-no and the West*, 1995
21. Myung Hun Kang. *The Korean Business Conglomerate: Chaebol Then and Now*, 1996
25. Jeong-Hyun Shin. *The Trap of History: Understanding Korean Short Stories*, 1998
26. Hyung Il Pai and Timothy R. Tangherlini, eds. *Nationalism and the Construction of Korean Identity*, 1999